MACHIAVELLI ON INTERNATIONAL RELATIONS

Machiavelli on International Relations

MARCO CESA

OXFORD

UNIVERSITY PRESS

OXFORD
UNIVERSITY PRESS

Great Clarendon Street, Oxford, OX2 6DP,
United Kingdom

Oxford University Press is a department of the University of Oxford.
It furthers the University's objective of excellence in research, scholarship,
and education by publishing worldwide. Oxford is a registered trade mark of
Oxford University Press in the UK and in certain other countries

Published in the United States of America by Oxford University Press
198 Madison Avenue, New York, NY 10016, United States of America

British Library Cataloguing in Publication Data
Data available

Library of Congress Cataloging in Publication Data
Data available

ISBN 978-0-19-967369-8

Printed in Great Britain by
CPI Group (UK) Ltd, Croydon, CR0 4YY

To the memory of Kenneth N. Waltz

Contents

Part III. Domestic Orders, Disorders, and Foreign Affairs

Excerpts Included in the Anthology

PRINCE

DISCOURSES ON THE FIRST TEN BOOKS OF LIVY

Book I

Book II

Book V

Book VI

Book VII

Book VIII

LEGATIONS

Other Works:

Private Letters:

Note on Sources

The excerpts from *The Prince*, the *Discourses on the First Ten Books of Livy*, the *Florentine Histories*, the *Legations*, the *Report on the Affairs of Germany* and *An Account of the Affairs of France* are from *The Historical, Political, and Diplomatic Writings of Niccolò Machiavelli*, translated by C. E. Detmold, Boston: J. R. Osgood and Co., 1882, 4 volumes.

The excerpts from the *Art of War* are from *The Works of the Famous Nicolas Machiavel, Citizen and Secretary of Florence*, translated by H. Neville, London: Starkey, 1675.

The excerpt from the *Life of Castruccio Castracani of Lucca* is from *The Prince*, translated by W. K. Marriot, London: Aldine House, 1908.

The excerpts from the following letters are from *The Prince and Other Works*, translated by A. Gilbert, Chicago: Packard, 1941: Letter to Giovanni Ridolfi, 12 June 1506; Letter to Giovan Battista Soderini, 13–21 September 1506; Letter to Francesco Vettori, 29 April 1513; Letter to Francesco Vettori, 26 August 1513; Letter to Francesco Vettori, 10 December 1514.

All translations have been checked against the text provided by the Edizione Nazionale delle Opere di Niccolò Machiavelli (Roma: Salerno, 2001–) and revised accordingly, both in substance and style. The same definitive edition has been an invaluable source for the footnotes. Since Machiavelli's private correspondence has not appeared yet in the Edizione Nazionale, I have availed myself of *Lettere*, a cura di F. Gaeta, Torino: UTET, 1984 and *Lettere a Francesco Vettori e a Francesco Guicciardini*, a cura di G. Inglese, Milano: Rizzoli, 1989.

The translations of the following works are mine: *Speech Concerning Pisa*; *Provisions for Retaking Pisa*; *Words to Be Spoken on the Law for Appropriating Money*; Letter to Francesco Vettori, 20 June 1513; Letter to Francesco Vettori, 10 August 1513; Letter to Francesco Vettori, 16 April 1514.

As for the key-term *virtù*, as a general rule I have rendered it into English according to the sense of the context. However, I have left it untranslated when it is combined with 'fortune' and whenever its meaning is so rich that any attempt to convert it into a foreign language would either dilute its connotations or lead to exceedingly long sentences.

All references to works contained in the anthology are indicated only by their excerpt number. If two or more works are grouped under the same heading, the title of the work, book (when appropriate), and chapter are added to the excerpt number. References consisting only of work title, book, and chapter indicate that such materials are not included in the anthology.

Chronology of Machiavelli's Times and Life

1469		Born in Florence on 3 May.
1492	August: Alexander VI is elected pope.	
1494	September: Charles VIII, King of France, descends into Italy, claiming rights on the Kingdom of Naples.	
	November: in the attempt to come to terms with the king, who is entering Tuscany, Piero de' Medici surrenders the main fortresses, including that of Pisa. The Florentines overthrow the Medici government and re-establish their republican institutions.	
1495	February: Charles VIII takes Naples.	
	March: the Italian states (Venice, Milan, Naples, the Pope) and Emperor Maximilian I create the League of Venice to fight France.	
	July: the French are defeated at Fornovo and leave Italy.	
1498	April: Louis XII succeeds to Charles VIII as King of France.	June: appointed Secretary to the Second Chancery.
		July: appointed Secretary to the Ten of War.
		July: Mission to Caterina Sforza Riario, lady of Forlì.
1499	September: Louis XII takes Milan; the Milanese territories are divided among his allies, i.e. the Swiss and the Venetians.	
	December: Duke Valentino, with the support of Louis XII and Pope Alexander VI, begins his conquest of the Romagna.	
1500	November: Treaty of Granada, signed by Louis XII and Ferdinand II, King of Aragon, for the partition of the Kingdom of Naples between France and Spain.	July–January 1501: 1st Mission to the King of France.
1501	April: Duke Valentino completes his conquest of the Romagna and becomes a powerful and threatening neighbour for Florence.	
	September: the French take Naples.	
1502	June: fomented by Duke Valentino, Arezzo and the Valdichiana rebel against Florentine rule. War breaks out between France and Spain over the Kingdom of Naples.	June–July: 1st Mission to Duke Valentino.
	August: Florence takes Arezzo back thanks to the support of Louis XII.	
	September: Piero Soderini is elected Gonfalonier of the Florentine republic for life.	October–January 1503: 2nd Mission to Duke Valentino.

Year		
1503	October: Julius II is elected pope; rapid decline of Duke Valentino.	October–December: 1st Mission to the Court of Rome.
1504	December: in the war over the Kingdom of Naples, the French are defeated at the Garigliano river and leave Southern Italy.	January–March: 2nd Mission to the King of France.
1506	March: armistice between France and Spain. The former keeps Milan, the latter is assigned Naples.	August–October: 2nd Mission to the Court of Rome.
1507		January: appointed Secretary to the Nine of the Militia. December–June 1508: Mission to the Emperor.
1508	December: Pope Julius II promotes the League of Cambrai against the Venetians, who have consolidated their mainland position at the expense of the Church, the Emperor, and Milan. Besides himself, the alliance includes France, Spain, and the Emperor.	
1509	May–June: the Venetians, severely defeated by the French at Agnadello, lose next to all their mainland dominions. June: deprived of Venetian support, Pisa surrenders to Florence's fifteen-year effort. July–November: Venetian counter-offensive, leading to the recovery of several territories.	November–December: Mission to Mantua on business with the Emperor. June–October: 3rd Mission to the King of France.
1510		
1511	August: Julius II promotes a general anti-French alliance—the Holy League—that includes, besides himself, Venice, Spain, and the Swiss. England will join later.	September–October: 4th Mission to the Court of France.
1512	October: opening of the Council of Pisa, promoted by Louis XII against Julius II. April: French victory at Ravenna. June: the Swiss drive the French out of Milan and Italy. Milan becomes a Swiss protectorate. August: deprived of French support and under Spanish military pressure, the Florentines depose Soderini. September: the Medici are reinstated as rulers of Florence.	November: dismissed from his positions.

Year		
1513	March: Leo X succeeds Julius II;	February: arrested under the charge of participation in an anti-Medici plot. March: liberated; retires to his property in Sant'Andrea in Percussina. Writes most of the *Prince*.
	Treaty of Blois: Venice and France agree on sharing Lombardy. April: truce between France and Spain. League of Malines, consisting of the Emperor and the King of England (joined later by the Pope and the King of Spain), to keep France out of Italy and the Low Countries. June: the Swiss defeat the French at Novara and drive them out of Italy.	
1515	January: Francis I succeeds to Louis XII as King of France. September: the French–Venetian alliance defeats the Swiss at Marignano and forces them to leave Milan.	1515–16: Begins to write the *Discourses*.
1516	January: Charles of Habsburg succeeds to Ferdinand II as King of Spain.	
1519	June: Charles of Habsburg succeeds Maximilian I as Emperor Charles V.	1519–20: writes the *Art of War* (published in 1521). 1520–25: writes the *Florentine Histories*.
1521	June: outbreak of the war between Charles V and Francis I.	
1523	November: Clement VII is elected pope.	
1525	February: Francis I is defeated at Pavia and made prisoner by Charles V.	
1526	March: Francis I, having accepted the terms imposed by Charles V, is set free. He denounces the agreement shortly afterwards. May: the anti-Habsburg League of Cognac is established. Members include France, the Pope, Venice, Milan, and Florence. November: an army of Lutheran lansquenets descends into Italy.	July–December: Missions to Francesco Guicciardini at the Camp of the League of Cognac.
1527	May: the lansquenets sack Rome; the Medici are driven out of Florence.	February–April: Mission to Francesco Guicciardini at the Camp of the League of Cognac. Dies in Florence on 21 June.

Emperors, Kings, and Popes
in Machiavelli's Time

EMPERORS

Frederick III, 1453–1493
Maximilian I, 1493–1519
Charles V*, 1519–1556

KINGS OF FRANCE

Louis XI, 1461–1483
Charles VIII, 1483–1498
Louis XII, 1498–1515
Francis I, 1515–1547

SPAIN

Isabella I, Queen of Castile, 1474–1504
Ferdinand II, King of Aragon, 1479–1516
Charles I*, King of Spain, 1516–1556

POPES

Sixtus IV (Francesco della Rovere), 1471–1484
Innocent VIII (Giovanni Battista Cybo), 1484–1492
Alexander VI (Rodrigo Borgia), 1492–1503
Pius III (Francesco Todeschini Piccolomini), 1503
Julius II (Giuliano della Rovere), 1503–1513
Leo X (Giovanni de' Medici), 1513–1521
Adrian VI (Adriaan Florenszoon Boeyens), 1522–1523
Clement VII (Giulio de' Medici), 1523–1534

---

* Emperor Charles V and King Charles I of Spain were, of course, the same person.

Map 1: Italian States, circa 1500

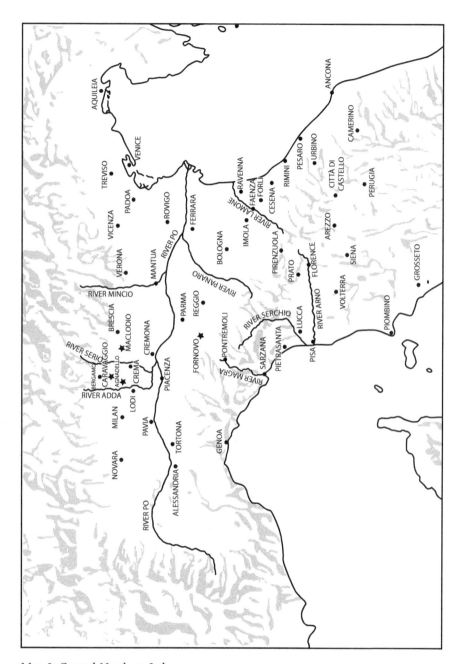

Map 2: Central-Northern Italy

Introduction

1. MACHIAVELLI THE INTERNATIONAL THEORIST

While other 'classics' of international theory—such as Thucydides, Hugo Grotius, Thomas Hobbes, Jean-Jacques Rousseau, and Immanuel Kant—have been the subject of a number of studies, Niccolò Machiavelli has, by and large, been neglected by contemporary students of international relations. A few, well-known maxims are usually singled out as representative of his entire thought; once such a lip service has been paid, one moves on. Alternatively, those who are willing to dig a little deeper read the *Prince* and a few chapters from the *Discourses on the First Ten Books of Livy* at best. Yet, the *Art of War*, the *Florentine Histories*, the *Legations*, various minor political writings, and the private letters contain a number of additional insights and offer penetrating analyses that cannot possibly be ignored.[1]

Such a state of affairs is somewhat paradoxical because the importance of international affairs in Machiavelli's thought cannot be denied. A substantial part of his writings as Secretary to the Second Chancery and to the Ten of War of the Florentine republic, from 1498 to 1512 (that is, the dispatches that he wrote during his diplomatic missions and several political writings) deals with foreign affairs and military issues;[2] the pervasiveness of external threats permeates the *Prince*;[3] the second book of the *Discourses* is explicitly concerned with the rise of Rome as a great power, and a number of fundamental

---

[1] To my knowledge, only a dozen articles and book chapters, in the English language, deal with Machiavelli from the point of view of political science and international relations theory: see Alker (1992), Berridge (2001), Boucher (1998, 90–113 and 125–44), Doyle (1997, 93–110), Fischer (1995), Forde (1992, 1995), Mindle (1985), Regent (2011), Sobek (2005), Sullivan (1973), Walker (1993, 34–49), Waltz (1959, 210–23), and Wight (2005, 3–28). Many of those works take into consideration only parts of Machiavelli's production. Admittedly, the international dimension of Machiavelli's thought is also emphasized by scholars who specialize in political philosophy, history of political thought, political theory, and other disciplines as well, e.g. de Grazia (1989, 164–73), Hörnqvist (2004), Hulliung (1983), Mc Canles (1984), and Pocock (2003). Extremely useful, finally, two works in French: Renaudet (1956, 243–72) and Descendre (2008).

[2] A concise account of those years can be found in Black (2010).

[3] Chabod (1965a, 20), Von Albertini (1995, 51), and Descendre (2008, 18).

ideas about international affairs are scattered around the other two books as well; the *Art of War*, needless to say, is entirely devoted to military themes; in the *Florentine Histories*, the chapters on external issues are more than twice as many as those on Florence's domestic politics;[4] and even the private letters, above all those addressed to Francesco Vettori between 1513 and 1514, frequently discuss the most pressing international problems of the day.[5] In addition, from a semantic perspective, it has been suggested that in Machiavelli's vocabulary the term *stato* (state) refers to a political unit in its competitive relations with other political units, just like the term *cose di stato* (matters of state) refers to foreign policy and security affairs[6]—which gives a further twist to the relevance that he assigns to international affairs. In one word, Machiavelli has constantly the external milieu in mind.

What is more, such a milieu is conceptualized as something fundamentally different from the domestic environment. Granted, both contexts are inherently conflictual: Machiavelli believes in social peace no more than he believes in international peace.[7] But the outside world is always more unstable and more dangerous. As early as 1503, in *Words to Be Spoken on the Law for Appropriating Money*, Machiavelli draws a sharp line between domestic affairs and international affairs: 'among private individuals, laws, contracts, and agreements make them keep faith, but among sovereigns only force does'.[8] From the outset, then, the two fields are presented in different terms: at home, relations among citizens are regulated by the law, but abroad, relations among states are regulated by force. This crucial insight runs throughout Machiavelli's major writings; it is no exaggeration to claim that it accounts for most of his views on international politics. That international affairs and domestic affairs constitute two separate, albeit related, realms is clearly suggested also by the well-known binomial 'laws and armies'—first put forward in 1506: a state that intends to preserve itself and grow needs laws and armies in order 'to be able to check on its subjects and to defend itself against its enemies'.[9] That is, the binomial 'laws and armies' is related to the binomial 'domestic affairs and external affairs': different contexts require different means.

By the same token, 'although deceit is detestable in all other things, in the conduct of war it is laudable and honourable'.[10] Machiavelli is aware, of course, that deceit can lead to success. Yet, although deceit is always permitted, it is not 'honourable': it can result in acquisition and gain, but not in glory.

---

[4] Cf. Lynch (2012, 2).

[5] Najemy (1993) is a comprehensive work on the Machiavelli–Vettori correspondence.

[6] Descendre (2008).

[7] On the important role that Machiavelli assigns to class conflict as 'the cement of a commonwealth', see Skinner (1978, 180–2).

[8] 2.1.1. On this fundamental work, see Marchand (1975, 60–6).

[9] *First Provision for Infantry*, 6 December 1506 (my translation).

[10] *Discourses on the First Ten Books of Livy* (henceforth, *Discourses*) III, 40.

The only case in which the rules of the game contemplate a reciprocal lack of trust—thereby making deceit 'honourable'—is war. 'Ambition' too receives a different treatment depending on the context. At home, 'ambition' usually has a negative connotation, as it is often associated with the pursuit of individual goals at the expense of the common good; laws and institutions keep it in check. But abroad, things change. Not only is external ambition free of constraints, but, in the form of expansion, it becomes almost a necessity. In addition, it is functional to the achievement of some collective good; as such, it contributes to the consolidation and the prosperity of the state.[11]

Domestic conflict can cripple any state, to be sure: the case of Florence, throughout its history, is emblematic, to Machiavelli. Yet, under certain conditions domestic conflict is a source of energy and vigour: republican Rome built its greatness upon the controlled antagonism of two groups: the optimates and the people kept each other in check thanks to political institutions (the senate and the tribunates) by means of which the power of one group was counterbalanced by the power of the other group, a consensus on the fundamentals (which prevented conflict from escalating into open violence), and shared habits and customs. The two groups kept competing with each other down to the fall of the republic, but always finding a point of equilibrium in some collective goal—at the advantage of the state as a whole.[12] Domestic conflict is by no means inevitable, however. If a republic is organized in an oligarchic—as opposed to popular—fashion, it will be weaker vis-à-vis the external world, but peaceful inside. Abroad, again, the picture looks quite different. To begin with, conflict is taken for granted: Machiavelli writes about a 'natural hatred between neighbouring princes and republics'.[13] True, an international balance of power, just like a domestic balance of power, can result in some temporary stability among states as well. But the world outside can never be reconciled under the same common good. In fact, there is no notion at all of some universal good, in Machiavelli; states grow and expand at the expense of each other, and the triumph of Rome coincides with the destruction of all the other states. Thus, the use of violence is the rule, and not the exception—hence, the need to always be well armed. Finally, there are no institutions at all, among states,[14] and deceit, albeit not 'honourable', is widely practised. After all, is it not true that 'the actions of all men, and especially those of princes, where there is no court to which to appeal, are judged by the result'?[15] Needless to say, there is no tribunal, among states. The

---

[11] Cf. Price (1982) and Machiavelli's poem *On Ambition*.
[12] Cf. Matteucci (1972).   [13] *Discourses* III, 12.
[14] Fischer (1995, 270-1) suggests at least one exception, i.e. the Emperor, who acts as a mediator among the German free cities, thereby contributing to peace (*Discourses* II, 19, cf. 4.1.4). But, as Machiavelli notices twice (and Fischer himself acknowledges), this is truly a very special case. In addition, the Emperor is not simply a mediator: the cities know well that he would take advantage of their troubles and subjugate them if only he had the chance.
[15] 1.2.1 (*Prince* XVIII).

way in which Machiavelli deals with treaties and pledges is probably the best illustration of all this. That promises among sovereigns are hardly kept is taken as a matter of course: 'it could easily be shown how many treaties of peace, and how many engagements, have been made null and void by the faithlessness of princes'.[16] Promises are broken for a number of reasons: when their observance would be contrary to one's interest;[17] when they have been extorted by force;[18] when power is asymmetric—and the stronger party must be expected to defect;[19] when the conditions that induced one to pledge one's faith no longer exist;[20] when the temptation to seize a promising opportunity is simply too great to be resisted.[21] It is only force (and necessity), in conclusion, that makes states keep their promises. In *Words to Be Spoken on the Law for Appropriating Money*, as we have seen, Machiavelli contrasts the domestic setting with the external setting. But the insight about the role of force among states finds an even earlier expression in a dispatch sent to Florence during his second mission to Duke Valentino, in November 1502: 'alliances between princes are maintained only by arms, inasmuch as the power of arms alone [can] enforce their observance'.[22] Twenty years later, in the *Florentine Histories*, he makes exactly the same point: 'force and necessity, and not written treaty obligations, cause princes to observe their faith'.[23]

Finally, even those who read Machiavelli from angles that are diverse from each other agree that external affairs are different from internal affairs. In his interpretation of Machiavelli's thought as a conscious effort to regulate the inevitable recourse to force, Sheldon S. Wolin argues that such an 'economy of

[16] 1.2.1 (*Prince* XVIII); similarly, 'Today no attention is paid to faith and obligations' (1.1.3).

[17] Cf. 1.2.1 (*Prince* XVIII).

[18] 'Promises touching public affairs, and which have been made under constraint, will always be disregarded when that constraint no longer exists' (2.1.3).

[19] 'And even if there was a treaty according to which the King of France should come down or should hand Milan over to ... others, I do not see how he, being more powerful, could comply with the agreement, unless he is a fool, nor do I see how the King of Spain could trust such a promise' (2.2.3).

[20] 'Not only do princes pay no attention to pledges which they have been forced to give, when that force has ceased to exist, but they frequently disregard equally all other promises as well, when the motives that induced them no longer prevail' (2.2.3).

[21] 'And although it was not the intention of the Romans to break the treaty and convention they had made with the Capuans, yet the facility of subjugating them seemed so great to the soldiers that it suggested the thought of taking the country and the independence from the Capuans' (3.4.4).

[22] 4.4.4. Although Machiavelli talks about alliances between 'princes', the subject matter here is an alliance between the Duke and the Florentine republic.

[23] 2.2.5 (*Florentine Histories* VIII, 22). Based upon the importance of religion, republican reliability and moral virtues, and the counterproductive consequences that may result from violating the *jus gentium*, Berridge (2001, 548) comes to different conclusions. To him, 'good faith was still in Machiavelli's account a common reflex in interstate dealings'. He then qualifies his own argument: good faith plays an important role 'unless too severely tested'. This is precisely the point: in Machiavelli's external world, survival is *always* at stake, as we will argue later.

violence' finds a more congenial environment at the domestic level; outside, the use of force can hardly be lessened in a significant way.[24] Maurizio Viroli, while stressing the elements of continuity between Machiavelli and the Roman tradition of civic philosophy, acknowledges that politics as 'justice and reason' fades away when states are threatened by external enemies.[25] To J. G. A. Pocock, the external environment of the prince is purely strategic, structured as it is on the relation of forces with the other princes; but at the domestic level, sheer 'strategy' is not enough: the interaction of *virtù* with fortune becomes paramount, and the game involves not only strategic rules but psychological and moral issues as well. As for republics, foreign policy and the domestic institutional setting are deeply interconnected, for sure: the problem is precisely how a republic can exercise control over its external environment, provided that justice may rule at home, but certainly not abroad.[26]

To sum up, not only is Machiavelli always very interested in international politics, but he also looks at it as a field of its own—related to, but separate from, domestic politics. Does he have a 'theory' about it? Machiavelli's thought has been interpreted—both in its substance and in its form—in a number of different ways over the last century or so. An objective thinker, almost a 'scientist',[27] at least in the *Prince*.[28] On the contrary: somebody always aware of the tragic dimension of political life.[29] A humanist;[30] a humanist republican;[31] a humanist republican rhetorician;[32] an imperialist republican rhetorician;[33] an imperialist republican ideologue;[34] a politician;[35] a political analyst.[36] Accordingly, we read, on the one hand, that he intended to discover universal laws,[37] and to codify the principles followed by the ancients;[38] and on the other hand that he aimed not so much at explaining facts but at convincing his readers.[39] Not to mention the unsolved debate on his method: to some, he adopted an inductive procedure,[40] to some a deductive procedure;[41] to some he availed himself of both—deduction in the *Prince*, induction in the *Discourses*,[42] to some neither.[43]

Friedrich Meinecke was rightly struck by what he called the 'mixture of pessimism and idealism, of mechanistic and vitalistic elements' that compose Machiavelli's views on *virtù*.[44] And Federico Chabod's overall judgement on the *Prince* captures the various dimensions of Machiavelli's thought in a synthetic way that is probably still unsurpassed: 'the worlds of logic, imagination and

---

[24] Wolin (1960, 220–4).   [25] Viroli (1998, 48–9).
[26] Pocock (2003, 166 and 213, on principalities and republics, respectively).
[27] Ercole (1926) and Holschki (1945).   [28] Renaudet (1956).
[29] Croce (1943, 251–3) and Sasso (1993).   [30] Gilbert (1965).   [31] Pocock (2003).
[32] Viroli (1998).   [33] Hörnqvist (2004).   [34] Hulliung (1983).
[35] Bausi (2005).   [36] Butterfield (1962).   [37] Holschki (1945).
[38] Gilbert (1965).   [39] Hulliung (1983), Viroli (1998), Hörnqvist (2004).
[40] Holschki (1945), Chabod (1993).   [41] Butterfield (1962), Martelli (1971).
[42] Gilbert (1965).   [43] Sasso (1993).   [44] Meinecke (1962, 33).

emotion . . . are blended into a single organism, so compact that if you detach the smallest element the whole will crumble in your hand'.[45] Reason—cold analysis based on the configuration of interests and the distribution of power; fantasy—the well-known images of Fortune as a river and as a woman, the creative way in which Machiavelli redefined and rearranged traditional notions; and passion—the exhortation at the end of the *Prince*, the invectives against the indolent Italian princes, the calls for action—are indeed the basic ingredients of Machiavelli's political thought as a whole. When it comes to international affairs, however, the rationalist component prevails. One is often left with the impression that, to him, what happens among states is almost taken for granted, simply the logical result of a concatenation of events, of variables that can be calculated in advance, and that the room for individual action is quite narrow. This is perhaps the decisive evidence of some deep difference between the domestic and the external realms, and the ultimate justification for the claim that what he says about international affairs deserves attention in its own terms.

In dealing with the central problem of human action, and of success and failure of human action, Machiavelli focuses on the relations between Fortune and *virtù*, and oscillates between rationalism, fatalism, and activism.[46] *Virtù*, in this context, is an extraordinary will and determination, a superior energy, an exceptional ability, thanks to which human beings try to face Fortune. The latter can be simply the course of events, i.e. something to be explained in rational terms, or alternatively a mysterious, blind force that cannot be resisted.[47] Fortune, in addition, provides the opportunity that *virtù* must exploit. Machiavelli writes memorable pages on all this. He rationally sees the limits of *virtù*: without the opportunity, *virtù* is impotent;[48] in addition, despite their *virtù*, human beings can find themselves in a given historical situation about which there is nothing they can do. At the same time, he cannot come to terms with this conclusion, for what he is concerned with here is not so much an abstract 'philosophical' system but a way of living and acting: human beings must never give up; on the contrary, they must react and do their best under any circumstance, for they can never know in advance what Fortune has in mind. Success and failure, finally, are explained along

---

[45] Chabod (1965a, 23–4).

[46] The literature on this fundamental issue in Machiavelli's thought is extremely rich, and it often addresses another important theme that cannot be taken into account here, i.e. the moral problem. For insightful discussions, see Meinecke (1962, 25–48), Gilbert (1965, 178–80, 192–9), and Skinner (1978, 128–38, 182–6; 1981, 31–60). On the specific issue of *virtù*, Whitfield (1947, 92–105) remains one of the best works; there is a thorough analysis in Price (1973); Wood (1967) puts forward an interpretation of *virtù* almost exclusively in military terms, strongly criticized by Hannaford (1972).

[47] See 1.3.3.

[48] In *Prince* VI, in discussing the great achievements of Moses, Cyrus, Romulus, and Theseus, Machiavelli comments: 'without such opportunity their *virtù* would have been wasted, whilst without that *virtù* the opportunities would have been in vain'.

similar lines, as they depend on the coincidence or the mismatch, respectively, between circumstances and individual predispositions. Human beings act following their natural inclinations: some are cautious, some are impetuous. Thus, if a cautious man is called to act at a time when audacity would be needed, he fails; likewise, if an impetuous man is forced into action under circumstances that would require caution, he comes to ruin. It would be nice if human beings could adapt their attitudes according to the times. But human nature cannot be changed.[49]

Now, in discussing all this, Machiavelli has individuals in mind. The examples he makes are Scipio, Hannibal, and Julius II. Granted, states are made of individuals. In some cases they even coincide with individuals and their personalities: Duke Valentino *is* his own state; Julius II's recklessness is the main driving force behind the recovery of many papal territories that have been lost; Maximilian's puzzling personality accounts for many of his policies. More frequently, though, states are collective, impersonal actors: the Venetians, the Swiss, the Florentines. Although Machiavelli mentions Louis XII quite often, it is clear that the French king's personal traits are less important than Maximilian's in accounting for foreign policy, because France is a centralized state, with a solid administrative structure.[50] Maximilian's inconclusiveness, in turn, is not simply the reflection of his own nature but also of the fragmented institutional arrangement of the empire.[51] And, independently of their personalities, all the popes have always shared, for centuries, the same strategic goal, namely not to permit any power to become the master of Italy.[52] *Virtù* can also be the quality of an entire people—or of its ruling élite, to be sure. In this case, it manifests itself in some organizational form, like political institutions and, above all, the army. That is, although collective *virtù* refers to a spiritual dimension that keeps together the members of a community, it is coupled with tangible, material components—and it is the latter that often play a decisive role among states: the relation of forces is paramount, it is easily calculable, and analysis is then guided by reason alone.

It has been noted that Machiavelli is often inconsistent. This is accounted for in terms of his intellectual goals—he was less interested in explaining facts, or in building a coherent abstract framework, than in persuading the reader with a convincing argument[53]—or is taken as further evidence that he constantly revised his major works, above all the *Discourses*, dealing with the most pressing Florentine and Italian issues of the day, and without paying too much attention to what he himself had written earlier.[54] Nobody could expect total coherence in such a huge and varied production that covers the span of some thirty years. Interestingly enough, though, most of his inconsistencies are related to domestic affairs. In other words, Machiavelli may express different

---

[49] Cf. 1.3.2.   [50] Cf. 3.1.1.   [51] Cf. 3.1.2.   [52] Cf. 2.2.1.
[53] Gilbert (1965, 166–7).   [54] Bausi (2005, 175–7, 212–13).

views on what liberty is about, on the nature of the Spartan, French, and Venetian constitution, on monarchy, on the role of Fortune in human affairs—but his ideas about how states interact and the reasons that explain their actions remain remarkably consistent throughout his writings and life.

In what continues to be one of the most suggestive interpretative essays, Mario Martelli argues that Machiavelli—both as a political writer and as a man of letters—always structures his thoughts around some pre-existing 'rules' that make 'facts' intelligible. 'Facts' are recognized for what they are precisely because they illustrate some 'rule', and are looked at in a stylized form, after extrapolating them from their historical context, in order to confirm those 'rules'. Such 'rules', in turn, constitute the *corpus* of his doctrine.[55] Although Machiavelli was certainly not a systematic thinker, he developed quite early on a set of definitive views on politics that he never changed. This seems to be the case above all for international politics, whose main manifestations and outcomes are the subject of consistent assessments. If by 'theory' we mean a rigorous intellectual construction in which every single item (or 'rule') is assigned a precise place and role within a coherent whole, then Machiavelli has no theory of international politics. But if we settle for a less ambitious standard of what a theory is about and we focus on trends and regularities that are to be explained in rational terms, things change. The pages that follow will try to substantiate this claim.

2. AMBITION AND FEAR

Human nature—it is well known—is assumed to be constant in Machiavelli's thought. Since human beings are, generally speaking, always selfish, not only can their behaviour be explained rationally, but it can also be anticipated. The notion of a constant human nature, in turn, is subsumed under the larger principle of the immutability of things, which is put forward a number of times.[56] It is all this that makes the knowledge of history useful in a practical sense, insofar as one can draw from the past lessons of political behaviour that are based on the imitation of the political and military conduct of the great ancient peoples.

Two psychological traits are particularly important for political behaviour, namely ambition and fear. The former drives human beings to wish for glory

---

[55] Martelli (1971).

[56] The idea of an immutable human nature is first mentioned in a 1502 writing, *On the Mode of Dealing with the Rebellious Peoples of Valdichiana*. Cf. also 1.2.3 and 1.3.1 (all the three excerpts). Machiavelli's unflattering views on human beings can be found in 1.2.1 (all the three excerpts), and in *Discourses* I, 3 and 9.

and riches,[57] and more generally to entertain immoderate desires.[58] In political terms, men are not content with what they possess and want to exercise command over others.[59] After all, the desire to conquer is 'most natural and common'.[60] The importance of ambition, then, should not be underestimated. However, fear is said to prevail *always*—including over ambition.[61] And Francesco Vettori, in one of his late letters to Machiavelli, writes 'I heard you say a number of times that fear is the greatest master that can be found'.[62] Similar unconditional statements on fear alone are not frequent in Machiavelli's work. More often, ambition and fear are placed on equal footing, as the former feeds the latter: 'the natural hatred between neighbouring princes and republics' arises from 'ambition to dominate and concern for one's own state';[63] war results from the 'desire to subjugate' and 'the fear to be subjugated';[64] 'some men desire to have more, some others fear to lose what they have, and enmities and war are the consequences'.[65] Shall we blame it on ambition, then? Not quite, for we also read that 'men do not believe themselves sure of what they possess except by acquiring still more':[66] here, fear is no longer the understandable reaction to somebody's ambition, but ambition—or the desire to have more—is presented as an outgrowth of fear. If we focus on the context structured around A's aggressive designs that provoke, in turn, B's concern, the dynamic is elementary. But if we leave A's intentions out of the picture for a second, we are told that B is still afraid of losing something, and that such a fear drives him to desire more of what he already has. The point is rather important, and we will come back to it. For now, let us take into consideration what seems to be a plausible variant of the relationship between ambition and fear. In his account of how the Florentines decided to launch a war of aggression on Lucca in 1429, Machiavelli notices that men are 'more influenced by the hope of gain than by the fear of loss; for the latter, unless very near, is not felt; and the former, being still remote, is believed in'.[67] That is, fear predominates when the danger is imminent, which seems to suggest a sort of sequential order between ambition and fear: it is only

---

[57] In *On Ambition*, Machiavelli argues that glory and riches are the two goals at which human beings aim under the impulse of two Furies—Ambition and Avarice. Glory and riches are also mentioned in 1.3.3 and in *Discourses* I, 37.

[58] Cf. 1.2.2 (*Discourses* I, 37); 1.3.1. (*Discourses* II, 'Introduction'); and 3.4.4.

[59] Cf. 3.2.1.   [60] 4.3.4.

[61] 'The Florentines were thus agitated by two different feelings; the one the desire to possess Lucca, and the other the fear of war with the Duke of Milan. Fear, however, prevailed, as is always the case' (2.2.4).

[62] Letter of 5 August 1526 (my translation).   [63] *Discourses* III, 12.

[64] Cf. 3.2.2. This is the external counterpart of a very similar domestic dynamic: 'in every state there will be found two different dispositions, which result from this—that the people wish not to be ruled and oppressed by the nobles, whilst the nobles wish to rule and oppress the people' (*Prince* IX).

[65] 1.2.2 (*Discourses* I, 37).   [66] 1.2.2 (*Discourses* I, 5).

[67] 4.3.2 (*Florentine Histories* IV, 18).

after fear has faded away—or, more generally, it is only in the absence of fear—
that ambition can enter the stage. This is stated quite clearly in the very title of
Discourses I, 46: men 'first seek to secure themselves against attack, then they
attack others', which seems to echo 'when men are no longer obliged to fight
from necessity, they fight from ambition'.[68] The key-term, here, is 'necessity'—
yet another important word in Machiavelli's vocabulary. Although necessity
shapes much of his thought, it is above all in international affairs that its
weight can be felt.

Necessity is a 'causal pressure',[69] a 'factor determining actions, but outside
man's control'.[70] As such, it constrains human choice. At the same time, it is
closely connected to *virtù*, especially collective *virtù*. While it is true that 'men
act either from necessity or from choice', '*virtù* is greater where there is not
much room for choice'.[71] As a matter of fact, 'men act right only upon
necessity; but from the moment that they have many options and are free to
choose, then they never fail to carry confusion and disorder everywhere'.[72]
Machiavelli explicitly acknowledges that it is thanks to necessity that human
beings have achieved their most remarkable results.[73] For example, the ancient
military commanders were aware of the '*virtù* of such a necessity': as battle
approached, they saw to it that their troops found themselves exposed to the
necessity of fighting and that the enemy did not. Thus, they often opened the
way for the enemy to retreat, and closed it to their own soldiers.[74] In a nutshell,
necessity pushes men to do things that they would not have done had they not
been pressed so hard. At first sight, one might believe that necessity is at play
under extreme circumstances only, most notably some impending danger. But
the role of necessity is broader than this: in predicting that the Swiss, who are
now keeping Lombardy under control, will soon desire to extend their influence beyond that area, Machiavelli argues that 'things go on little by little, and
men are often forced by necessity to do what they did not intend to do'.[75]
Thus, even expansion is explained in terms of necessity.[76] The anticipated
'ambition' of the Swiss is not simply the result of choice but stems from a set of
circumstances that will predispose them to do something that they are not
currently contemplating—that is, from necessity. As we will see, what has been

---

[68] 1.2.2 (*Discourses* I, 37).   [69] Meinecke (1962, 37).
[70] Gilbert (1965, 193).   [71] 3.2.1.   [72] *Discourses* I, 3.
[73] 'We have already pointed out the advantage of necessity in human actions, and to what
glorious achievements it has given rise. Some moral philosophers have even maintained that
without it neither the hand nor the tongue of man, the two noblest instruments of his glory,
would have served his purpose perfectly, nor carried human achievements to the heights which
they have attained' (*Discourses* III, 12).
[74] *Discourses* III, 12.
[75] 4.1.3. Similarly, 'desperation often finds solutions that choice has not been able to find'
(Letter to Francesco Vettori, 16 April 1527, my translation).
[76] The *locus classicus* is 3.2.2, as will be discussed below.

called Machiavelli's 'theory of necessary conquest'[77] has a strong defensive connotation.

The typical—and most compelling—form taken by necessity is security. The latter plays a central role that is widely recognized, for it is in its name that Machiavelli justifies behaviour that violates conventional morality:[78] 'a man who always wishes to profess goodness *will inevitably come to ruin* amongst so many who are evil';[79] when the *life and liberty* of the country are at stake, all means are acceptable.[80] These are not simply justifications and recommendations based on Machiavelli's personal views, but reflect a compelling logic: *because* security is at stake, a certain behaviour is the rational response. In his classical work, Felix Gilbert argues that to Machiavelli politics is 'choice and decision', for the final outcome reflects man's response to the challenges—and the opportunities—produced by necessity. Machiavelli sees things in constant flux, and never adopts a static perspective. For this reason, human beings have often the chance to intervene and force fortune's hand, even in the most desperate situation.[81] Yet, as Harvey Mansfield put it, well understood necessity replaces deliberate choice.[82] None of this can suggest in advance what behaviour will be eventually adopted, of course: on the one hand, the margins of oscillation are too wide, and on the other necessity has to be 'well understood'—something that, men being what they are, cannot be taken for granted. Be that as it may, the only safe prediction that can be made from how Machiavelli frames the problem is that those who ignore the imperatives of security will pay a cost. Again, there is no need to conceive of security only in terms of some immediate threat: 'prudence' consists precisely of anticipating a danger before it materializes and acting accordingly—not by accident, the wise prince will see troubles from afar (*discosto*).[83] In this sense, then, fear is indeed the 'greatest master'.

International affairs are the realm in which these dynamics can be fully appreciated. Fear often shapes the attitude towards the external world of all the states about which Machiavelli writes, or better still it is frequently used as the main lens through which their decisions and actions are interpreted. In a way, this is hardly surprising: the Italian states, since the first descent of the French in 1494, have been leading a very precarious life. As a result of French, Swiss, and Spanish involvement, government has been changed in Naples, Florence, and Milan; all of them, as well as the popes and the Venetians, in addition, are now facing the implications of their dependence on, and weakness vis-à-vis,

---

[77] Sasso (1993, 526–7).

[78] Cf., for example, Mansfield (1996, *passim*), Mindle (1985, 222), Skinner (1978, 132–3) and Sasso (1993, 466–8).

[79] 1.2.1 (*Prince* XV); emphasis added.   [80] 2.1.3 (*Discourses* III, 41).

[81] Gilbert (1965, 192–200).   [82] Mansfield (1996, 277).   [83] *Prince* III.

the foreign powers.[84] But even previous ages, when Italian political life was self-contained, are similarly characterized by the prominent role of fear. Accordingly, we are told that the policy of the popes was always inspired by the goal of preventing the unification of Italy under a single power, that Venice was born out of fear and ended up terrorizing all the other states, that Florence, Naples, and Milan, at various times in the fifteenth century, were kept from pursuing 'ambitious' goals by some impending or potential threat.[85] What is more, even the policies of the two great powers of the day, Spain and France, reflect the constraints of fear. The case of France is particularly instructive, for she is indeed the most formidable power of the time. And yet Machiavelli's assessment of her strategic position in 1511 is entirely conducted in terms of security: 'France fears', 'the French would not be much afraid', 'the Swiss are much feared by the French'—these are the words of which he avails himself.[86]

Both republics and principalities have to cope with the uncertainties that permeate the world outside. This sense of endless instability, deep precariousness, and constant risk is constitutive of Machiavelli's conceptual world.[87] From the early writings onwards, the international milieu is presented as a context characterized by a merciless struggle for life; only those who can avail themselves of violent means can hope to survive. In *Words to Be Spoken on the Law for Appropriating Money* (written in 1503, it is worth repeating), we are told that all states against which we cannot defend ourselves (that is, independently of their current intentions) are to be considered enemies; that friends will be friends only as long as we are strong enough to make them respect us; that pacts and treaties will be guaranteed only by expediency and force. In one word, insecurity is a fact, plain for all to see. The inevitable consequence is the need to secure oneself. *Virtù*, then, is needed to face Fortune—the latter being not simply some generic way in which human things go, but the threats emanating from such an unstable milieu. This is why Machiavelli invokes *virtù*—not a mere humanistic reflex. Yet, as we know, depending on the circumstances, *virtù* may not be enough. Hence, the search for security must contemplate all the possible means, including those that violate traditional moral standards. This objective insecurity—and not the evil human nature—is why Machiavelli justifies the adoption of his heterodox measures.[88] To make matters even worse, all decisions cannot but be uncertain

---

[84] For a historical analysis of international affairs in Italy during Machiavelli's lifetime, see Aubert (2003).

[85] See the excerpts in 2.2.   [86] Cf. 2.2.2. On Spain, see 2.2.3.

[87] Cf. Sasso (1993, 105).

[88] Cf. Sasso (1993, 123–35, 442–4, 454–9) and Renaudet (1956, 243–5). For a different opinion tracing Machiavelli's most controversial recommendations back to human nature, see Skinner (1978, 137).

because the good is always accompanied by some evil,[89] nor can one avoid one difficulty without coming into another.[90] But the only alternative is the risk of losing control of events, of being overwhelmed by the enemies.

The binomial 'ambition and fear' corresponds to the binomial 'glory and security'. Just as ambition is subordinated to—and not eliminated by—fear, glory and greatness are what can be hoped for only once security has been achieved.[91] Thus, it is hard to accept the views of those who insist on Machiavelli's supposed exaltation of the 'predatory nature' of republics, whose main aim, greatness, is to be gained through 'violent expansion' within the framework of a 'heroic ethic', of some 'heroic and violent values', and who conclude that his 'hopes for republican greatness override all considerations of necessity'.[92] To begin with, Machiavelli is neither a bellicist nor a militarist.[93] His armed forces—ostensibly the main instruments of all that grandiose violence—are at the service of security, as will be shown shortly; similarly, not a single one of the twenty-seven 'general rules' in the final pages of the *Art of War* mentions glory or greatness; Castruccio, on his deathbed, regrets to have pursued glory at the expense of security;[94] deceit, as we have seen, does not produce glory (except in war), but is contemplated nonetheless because any another conduct might be too dangerous; and even expansion—arguably the most tangible manifestation of greatness—is first of all a prerequisite to live safely. As a diplomat of a weak state, Machiavelli had a first-hand knowledge of the harsh realities of international politics; it is hardly credible that, having seen what he must have seen, he could indulge in dreams of imperial greatness, of glory for its own sake, only because he had a fervid fantasy or was imbued with humanistic models and ideas. Greatness and glory are certainly components of his political world, but their role should not be blown out of proportion: expansion is, first, necessary; then, it is beautiful as well.

Many underline the centrality of force in Machiavelli's thought.[95] Men do their best only if they are predisposed to behave by institutions and laws

---

[89] Cf. *Discourses* III, 37.   [90] Cf. 3.2.2 and 4.4.1.

[91] Skinner (1981, 29–30) and Viroli (1998, 91, 96–7).

[92] Hulliung (1983, 219–29). Regent (2011) ignores the 'heroic and violent' components but makes a similar point: greatness is all that matters. For a detailed analysis of 'glory', see Price (1977).

[93] Cf. de Grazia (1989, 170) and Rousseau (1970, 21).   [94] Cf. 2.1.2.

[95] 'The dominating idea in these two works [the *Prince* and the *Discourses*] is an appeal to recognize the crucial importance of force in politics' (Gilbert 1965, 154); 'Machiavelli places an exceptionally strong emphasis on the role of sheer force in the conduct of government' (Skinner 1978, 130). Norsa (1936), Von Albertini (1995, 49), and Wolin (1960) express similar views. Machiavelli himself makes it very clear: 'There is no sort of proportion between one who is well armed and one who is not so; nor is it reasonable that he who is armed should voluntarily obey the unarmed, or that a prince who is without a military force should remain secure amongst his armed subjects' (*Prince* XIV).

backed by force;[96] material power usually prevails over spiritual power.[97] But, once more, it is in external affairs that force, in its military dimension, plays a paramount role—hardly a surprise, in light of all that we have argued so far. The fundamental ideas expressed in *Words to Be Spoken on the Law for Appropriating Money* are that the state is 'force', that it must rely on a solid military organization, that armed forces are decisive, and that if the latter are lacking neither prudence nor wisdom nor diplomatic adroitness can be enough.[98] These themes emerge over and over again in Machiavelli's later works: without armed forces, states cannot be preserved;[99] if you are not powerful, you cannot be secure;[100] if you are unarmed, you are in the hands of Fortune.[101] How could it be otherwise? If the external world is dangerous, populated as it is by enemies and friends who can be worse than enemies, if one's weakness can be an irresistible temptation for the other's strength, then republics and principalities alike are always vulnerable, and their very survival depends on their ability to defend themselves, i.e. on their military capabilities.[102] Military force prevails over cunning and deceit: the latter are necessary as long as one is too weak to engage in open action, but once one has grown powerful enough, then force alone suffices.[103] Military force prevails over wealth, or, 'iron' prevails over 'gold'; that is, as long as you can rely on sufficient military strength, money is of secondary value. Rich states do not always win the war, for 'gold alone will not procure good soldiers, but good soldiers will always procure gold'.[104] Adequate military forces allow you to fight a 'short and sharp' war: a quick and decisive clash in which your enemy will not have the time to avail himself of his money.[105] Finally, military force prevails over domestic institutions, at least in one important sense: the survival of the state depends less on the quality of its constitution than on the quality of its army.

As we have seen, the binomial 'laws and armies' denotes the coexistence of two different realms, the domestic one and the external one. In some cases, 'laws and armies' are treated on equal footing: the greatness of Rome was based upon both,[106] all cities must rely on both,[107] both are the constitutive ingredients of any form of government,[108] each performs different and relevant functions.[109] Yet, 'good armies' are more often considered a sort of precondition for 'good laws', in all Machiavelli's major writings: in the *Prince*, we read that 'there can be no good laws where there are not good armies, and

---

[96] Cf. 3.2.1 and *Discourses* I, 3. See also Skinner (1981, 64–7).

[97] 'All prophets who came with arms in hand were successful, whilst those who were not armed come to ruin' (*Prince* VI).

[98] Cf. Chabod (1993, 339).   [99] Cf. 2.1.1 and 2.3.3 (*Art of War*, 'Introduction').

[100] Cf. 3.2.1.   [101] Cf. *Discourses* III, 31.

[102] Gilbert (1986, 26–7), Sasso (1993, 189–93), Renaudet (1956, 243–4).   [103] Cf. 3.4.3.

[104] *Discourses* II, 10. Cf. also *Art of War* VII.   [105] Cf. Rousseau (1970, 25–7).

[106] Cf. 4.3.1.   [107] Cf. 2.1.1.

[108] Cf. *Rationale for Infantry*, 1506.   [109] Cf. *First Provision for Infantry*, cit.

the laws will be apt to be good where the armies are so';[110] in the *Discourses*, we are told that 'where good armies prevail there also will good institutions prevail',[111] and that without a good military organization 'there can neither be good laws or anything else good';[112] and in the *Art of War* Machiavelli goes to some length to elucidate the connection between the two: all the human institutions that are created at home would be in vain if they were not adequately defended by the military against the external enemies. In fact, 'such defence, if well arranged, maintains those institutions, even if the latter are not well arranged'.[113] In other words, social and political institutions are not sound if they are not coupled with solid military institutions. Not only are the latter needed to cope with external threats but also to promote, among the citizens, such military virtues as loyalty, abnegation, courage, determination that have a civic counterpart: just as a good citizen is a good soldier, a good soldier is a good citizen.[114] This is why if military organizations are good, the other institutions will be good as well: laws that are created for the defence of the homeland cannot contain any tyrannical or servile element: 'a republic that has armies of her own is less easily subjected to servitude by one of her own citizens'.[115] And even if somebody were to avail himself of the military organization to make himself a tyrant, this would be more preferable than being subjugated by a foreign power.[116]

---

[110] 2.3.1 (*Prince* XII).   [111] *Discourses* I, 4.

[112] 2.3.1 (*Discourses* III, 31).   [113] 2.3.3 (*Art of War*, 'Introduction').

[114] Cf. Pocock (2003, 199–203). In a similar vein, Fachard (1996).

[115] 2.3.1 (*Prince* XII). Cf. Renaudet (1956, 256).

[116] 'Even if a tyrant came up, it would be a lesser evil to be at his discretion than to be at the discretion of some foreigner' (*Discourse on the Mounted Militia*, 1510, my translation). Machiavelli was the author of the military reform introducing a national militia in Florence in 1506. His deepest scepticism about the reliability of both mercenaries (on whom Florence depended for all practical purposes) and allies (above all France) had convinced him that only a national military force could have provided the republic with some security as well as some freedom of action. The issue was quite controversial, because of its political implications. Although everybody acknowledged the financial and military advantages of the reform, many—above all the upper class—feared that the militia would be turned by ambitious individuals into an instrument of personal power, thus leading to the end of republican liberties. In order to dissipate those fears, recruitment had to be confined to the countryside. This, in turn, raised another problem: since the inhabitants of the countryside did not enjoy the full rights of citizenship, how could they possibly be expected to fight and die for their city rulers? Would not they take up those very arms against their masters, instead? This inherent contradiction led to a set of complicated technical remedies, and the net result was that the effectiveness of the militia was always very modest. The literature has often underlined those structural problems of Machiavelli's reform (Chabod 1993, 336–8; Sasso 1993, 199–213). Other scholars, however, have placed more emphasis on Machiavelli's basic insight, i.e. the need to restore some intimate connection between the civilian and the military fields, between patriotism and military training, in the last analysis between political and military institutions (Gilbert 1986, Mallett 1990). In fact, Machiavelli did try to substantiate the link between 'good laws and good armies': his reform was designed to weaken the judicial and political control exerted by the old Florentine oligarchy upon the countryside thanks to a fairer justice and the concession of exemptions. This would lead to a greater social equity and would strengthen the farmer-soldier's loyalty towards the Florentine institutions (Guidi 2009, 381–6).

We have thus come full circle. We have moved from the distinction between the internal and the external realms, and we now conclude that not only are the two spheres different, but also that the world outside prevails over the world inside. Such a primacy is expressed, first of all, in a peremptory statement: 'so long as external affairs are quiet, internal affairs will be quiet too'.[117] But it can also be derived from a series of observations. To begin with, it is the external milieu that interferes with the 'Polybian cycle' governing the transformation of domestic political regimes.[118] The latter would indeed tend to endlessly move from one form to another following purely internal dynamics, except that at some point such a cycle is interrupted—and is interrupted from the outside: 'It may well happen that a republic lacking strength and good counsel in its difficulties becomes subject after a while to some neighbouring state that is better organized than itself'.[119] Even more importantly, the two basic modes that the external environment can assume, i.e. peace or war, have direct implications for domestic affairs. A prolonged state of peace has negative repercussions insofar as it ends up producing 'idleness' among the citizens (that is, a generalized ineptitude for any useful action, a widespread fecklessness resulting in inertia), if not outright problems, such as dissensions and disunion.[120] In short, a benign external milieu is actually dangerous, paradoxical as it may sound, because it can prevent the state from being ready for war when war comes. Hence, the importance of cultivating military practices even in peacetime.[121] Conversely, if the external world is hostile, this has positive consequences inside: an impending threat keeps the city united,[122] suggests the adoption of institutional innovations in order to cope with it,[123] keeps military organizations alive—with all the good implications that this entails.[124] More generally, if the very existence of the state depends on its ability to wage war, then the two constitutive decisions that are made when a new city is founded, i.e. the selection of the site and the constitutional arrangement, must reflect this basic external imperative. In both cases, as we will see below, Machiavelli puts forward two alternatives; in both cases, one of them would be preferable, in sheer domestic terms; and in both cases, the other is eventually recommended for external reasons: the outside world and the fear that it generates create a potent incentive to be

---

[117] *Prince* XIX.

[118] In Book VI of his *Histories*, Polybius developed the theory of *anacyclosis*, according to which six forms of government transform into each other following a fixed sequence; when the series is completed, the cycle starts over again.

[119] *Discourses* I, 2. Cf. Mansfield (1996, 273–4).

[120] The point is made a number of times: cf. 3.2.2 and 3.2.3 (*Discourses* II, 25), but also *Discourses* III, 16 and *Florentine Histories* V, 1 and VII, 28.

[121] Cf. 2.3.1 (*Discourses* III, 31), *Discourses* I, 12 and III, 16.

[122] Cf. 3.2.3 (*Florentine Histories* II, 26); 4.1.4 (*Discourses* II, 19); and 4.2.1 (*Discourses* I, 33).

[123] Cf. the introduction of dictators in Rome, 4.2.1 (*Discourses* I, 33).

[124] Cf. 2.3.2.

territorially endowed and domestically organized in such a way as to facilitate defensive and expansionist policies.[125]

3. STRATEGIC INTERACTION

Although the differences between principalities and republics are very deep at the domestic level, the need that all states feel to exert some control over the external milieu leads them to adopt similar policies in their interactions, independently of their institutional arrangement. Admittedly, there is some variety in the basic external posture of principalities and republics; but such a variety is a matter of degree rather than substance. That both forms of government are equally sensitive to security considerations can easily be extrapolated from the general argument; that they are also equally sensitive to 'ambition' is stated explicitly.[126] Both principalities and republics, in addition, react similarly to some of the incentives and disincentives that result from the relation of forces: they both avail themselves of deceit when they are not so strong as to rely on sheer force only,[127] and they both take advantage of a third party's weakness.[128] Within this homogeneous framework, republics do display certain features of their own. It should be noted, however, that the real cleavage is not so much between principalities and republics in general, but between *types* of principality and republic.[129] Hereditary principalities are inherently more solid and secure, as they are based upon a system of government that is deeply institutionalized. As such, it takes a formidable enemy to overrun them, and even if they are lost, they can be recovered.[130] On the contrary, new and 'mixed' principalities—i.e. those that result from an individual who seizes power or from the annexation of a new province by some

---

[125] Cf. 3.2.1 and 3.2.2.

[126] 'There are two different kinds of war. The one springs from the ambition of princes or republics that seek to extend their empire; such were the wars of Alexander the Great, and those of the Romans, and those which two hostile powers carry on against each other' (*Discourses* II, 8).

[127] Cf. 3.4.3.   [128] Cf. 3.4.4.   [129] Cf. Doyle (1997, 95–6).

[130] 'It is enough merely that the prince does not transcend the order of things established by his predecessors, and then to accommodate himself to events as they occur. So that if such a prince has but ordinary sagacity, he will always maintain himself in his state, unless some extraordinary and superior force should deprive him of it. And even in such a case he will recover it, whenever the occupant meets with any reverses. We have in Italy, for instance, the Duke of Ferrara, who could not have resisted the assaults of the Venetians in 1484, nor those of Pope Julius II in 1510, but for the fact that his family had for a great length of time held the sovereignty of that dominion. For the natural prince has less cause and less necessity for irritating his subjects, whence it is reasonable that he should be more beloved. And unless extraordinary vices should cause him to be hated, he will naturally have the affection of his people' (*Prince* II).

hereditary principality, respectively—are exposed to all the dangers that derive from the new conquest.[131] Those are the ones on which Machiavelli focuses in the *Prince*. It is among republics, however, that the most significant differences can be found, depending on the extent of popular participation. Here the basic partition is between aristocratic republics, such as Sparta and Venice, in which the people are not involved in government, and popular republics, such as Rome, in which the people are included in the decision-making process.[132] Now, although all republics tend to be slow in their deliberations[133]—and such a slowness can create serious problems in the conduct of foreign policy—when the people have a say in public affairs we can notice some additional consequences. To begin with, the people show a certain tendency to adopt reckless decisions;[134] at the same time, they seem more reluctant than princes to break treaties for some immediate advantage.[135] More importantly, popular participation makes sure that the 'common good' will be pursued, and this gives rise to a profound attachment of the people to their free institutions.[136] As a result, republics can be subdued only with the greatest effort,[137] and once taken they are extremely difficult to keep. In fact, 'whoever becomes master of a city that has been accustomed to liberty, and does not destroy it, must himself expect to be destroyed by it'.[138] Finally, popular participation means, among other things, an army made of citizens, and this is, as we have seen, the best instrument for defensive and offensive purposes. Protection against external enemies is essential for the preservation of internal liberty, and expansion itself may be necessary for the defence of that liberty.[139] The same expansion, in turn, leads to more dominion and more wealth, from which the republic as a whole will benefit. In conclusion, popular republics are especially inclined to pursue expansionist policies, are very well equipped to do so,[140] and are harsh masters of the countries that they subjugate.[141] Such an aggressive attitude applies even to relations with other republics: the 'natural hatreds' among neighbouring states are particularly pronounced *between* republics.[142] In fact,

---

[131] 'This is the inevitable consequence of another natural and ordinary necessity, which ever obliges a new prince to vex his people with the maintenance of an armed force, and by an infinite number of other wrongs that follow in the train of new conquests. Thus the new prince finds that he has for enemies all those whom he has injured by seizing that principality; and at the same time he cannot preserve as friends even those who have aided him in obtaining possession, because he cannot satisfy their expectations, nor can he employ strong measures against them, being under obligations to them. For however strong a prince may be in troops, yet will he always have need of the good will of the inhabitants, if he wishes to enter into firm possession of a new country' (*Prince* III).

[132] Cf. *Discourses* I, 5–6 (and 3.2.2).   [133] Cf. 3.4.2.

[134] Cf. 3.4.1.   [135] Cf. 3.4.6.   [136] Cf. 3.4.7.   [137] Cf. 3.4.7.

[138] *Prince* V. Cf. also 4.4.2.   [139] Cf. Skinner (1981, 73–7).

[140] Cf. 3.2.2, 3.4.7, 5.3, and *Discourses* I, 58. On the connection between liberty at home and expansionism abroad, see Herodotus V, 78 and Thucydides I, 17.

[141] 'The hardest of all servitudes is to be subject to a republic' (3.4.7). See also *Discourses* II, 6.

[142] Cf. *Discourses* III, 19. As Gilbert (1969) notices, unlike some of his contemporaries, Machiavelli never mentions 'republicanism' as a common element binding Venice and Florence. On the contrary, the two republics are the bitterest enemies.

the 'militarization of citizenship' that lies at heart of Machiavelli's republican theory implies that the more republics develop their civic *virtù*, the more they will be at war with each other in order to defend their free institutions against all possible threats.[143]

Yet, the simple fact that popular republics are better prepared for war and more likely to succeed in it than other forms of government does not mean that the general trends of international politics are fundamentally altered by constitutional differences. All states are moved by 'ambition' and above all 'fear'; all states are sensitive, in the first place, to the relation of forces. And state action cannot be explained in terms of individual preferences or inclinations only, but must be traced back to a wider relational system shaped by the distribution of power and the configuration of interests: 'When one sets out to judge if anybody is going to do a thing, it is necessary first to see if he wishes to do it, then what assistance he may have, and what hindrance in doing it'.[144] Machiavelli's states, great powers and small powers alike, principalities as well as republics, are always predisposed by their situational context to act in a predictable way. The relational system suggests alignments, almost by position, and creates the preconditions for alliances: in 1450, Duke Sforza knows that Florence will soon have to cope with the combined hostility of Venice and Naples, and that for this reason she will be his most loyal ally; accordingly, he aptly exploits Florence's propensity to cooperate with him.[145] The relational system transforms generic fears into specific threats: in the upcoming confrontation between France and the Pope, in 1510, Florence has to face a twofold risk, that is, its French ally may be defeated or it may come to terms with the Pope, to Florence's detriment;[146] in the Italian diplomatic constellation of 1513–14, the Pope will be anyway at the mercy of whoever will emerge as a victorious power.[147] The relational system produces opportunities: in 1437, the defeat of the Milanese forces operating in Tuscany frees Florence's hands and predisposes the city to attack Lucca;[148] after taking Milan in 1512, the Swiss have realized that nobody can resist the fury of their armies; thus, they are now likely to overrun Lombardy and possibly all of Italy, no matter what their original intentions might have been.[149] Finally, the relational system generates constraints: if one does not expand, this is because the others do not let him;[150] in 1506–07, France and Venice cannot oppose Maximilian's descent into Italy, although they would like to: they don't trust each other and are prevented from using force by the unsupportive attitude of the

---

[143] Cf. Pocock (2003, 213). [144] 4.1.1.
[145] Cf. 5.1 (*Florentine Histories* VI, 25). [146] Cf. 5.2 (Dispatch of 3 August 1510).
[147] Cf. 2.1.4 and 5.3. [148] Cf. 4.2.2 (*Florentine Histories* V, 10).
[149] Cf. 4.1.3 (Letter to Francesco Vettori, 10 August 1513) and 5.3.
[150] Cf. 4.1.3 (Letter to Francesco Vettori, 26 August 1513), 4.1.4, and *Discourses* III, 12.

other powers.¹⁵¹ It is then up to the ruler's political ability (or lack of it) to react to such incentives and disincentives in an appropriate manner: Louis XII makes no fewer than six mistakes in his Italian policies, thus wasting the most favourable opportunity;¹⁵² Ferdinand II, on the contrary, with a single stroke—the 1513 truce with France—pulls himself out of a difficult situation, hinders his enemy's plans and passes the buck on to his allies.¹⁵³

More generally, in Machiavelli's external world one's constraints are the other's opportunities,¹⁵⁴ one's weakness will be taken advantage of by the other's strength,¹⁵⁵ one's 'ambition' feeds the other's 'fear'. All this is taken as a matter of course by all: facing Florence's aggression, the Lucchese comment: 'if we could, we would do the same to them, or even worse'.¹⁵⁶ And everybody knows that 'out of the very same troubles some succumb, some flourish; but it is the most feeble who must always succumb'.¹⁵⁷ Once more, then, the outside world is permeated with risk and uncertainty; once more, exerting control over the other states becomes the precondition for stabilizing such a dangerous milieu. But is stability possible at all? Machiavelli sharply denies it. Human affairs are, by nature, in a state of 'perpetual movement'.¹⁵⁸ When they have reached their top, they 'of necessity' come down, and when they have touched their bottom, they must come up again.¹⁵⁹ The dynamism of such a notion entails that no situation lasts forever, that nothing remains the same. This is why, in passing, Fortune favours the bold, i.e. those who, with a sudden and decisive action, can bring about her help.¹⁶⁰ Yet this very dynamism adds precariousness to precariousness, uncertainty to uncertainty. Its implications for international politics are quite important: no settlement can be stable, no arrangement can be safe, and even if you are secure today, tomorrow you may no longer be. Machiavelli's views on expansion, alliances, the balance of power, and peace reflect all this.

What is the ideal site, and what is the best constitutional arrangement, for a new city? A sterile region would seem, at first sight, the right choice. Here, the people would be compelled to be industrious; as such, they would be less

---

¹⁵¹ Cf. 4.1.1. By the same token, it is unlikely that France and Spain will reach an agreement because this would entail, for the former, either the alienation or the outright hostility of England (cf. 5.3).

¹⁵² Cf. 4.3.4.   ¹⁵³ Cf. 1.1.3.   ¹⁵⁴ Cf. 2.2.5.   ¹⁵⁵ Cf. 3.4.4.   ¹⁵⁶ 4.2.3.

¹⁵⁷ Third Mission to Siena, Dispatch of 17 July 1505.

¹⁵⁸ 'There is nothing permanent and stable in human affairs' (*Florentine Histories* III, 5); 'as all human things are in a perpetual movement, and can never remain still, they inevitably either rise or decline' (3.2.2); 'human affairs being in a state of perpetual movement, always either ascending or declining' (1.3.1, *Discourses* II, 'Introduction').

¹⁵⁹ 'As nature does not permit mundane affairs to remain in a definitive state, when they have attained their highest state of perfection, as they cannot rise further, they of necessity decline. And similarly, when they have descended, and by their disorders have reached the lowest level, they must of necessity rise again, inasmuch as they cannot go lower' (*Florentine Histories* V, 1).

¹⁶⁰ Cf. Gilbert (1965, 194).

exposed to idleness and more united. The selection of an 'ungrateful soil' would thus be 'more useful and wise'. Yet, the external threat posed by those who 'desire to exercise command over others' promptly leads Machiavelli to opt for a fertile region instead: this will naturally provide the new state with large means 'to repel all who might attack it and to crush all who might oppose the development of its power'.[161] A similar logic presides over the choice of the constitution. As we have seen, Machiavelli contemplates two basic models of republics; one is represented by aristocratic Sparta and Venice, the other by popular Rome.[162] The former two were highly successful in preventing the quarrels between the people and the senate that afflicted the latter: Sparta never extended citizenship to foreigners, Venice never availed herself of the lower classes for her armies. Rome, instead, did the opposite; thus the people grew in number, power, and, as a result, in restlessness. Yet the very cause of Rome's domestic troubles—popular participation—constituted the source of her external strength, that is, her large armies. Vice versa, while Sparta and Venice led a tranquil domestic life, they were inherently feeble abroad; as such, as soon as they tried to expand significantly, they came to ruin. Now, since a republic can be attacked by those who either fear her power or are tempted by her weakness, the founders of a new city should ideally make it not so strong as to make others afraid of it and locate it in some unassailable place, while simultaneously giving up—and even forbidding by law—all expansion. 'If things could be kept in such a balance'—Machiavelli comments at this point—'this would be the best life for the citizens, and would insure to any state real tranquillity.'[163] Yet, in this case too the dangerous nature of the outside world immediately surfaces again: 'But as all human things are in a perpetual movement, and can never remain still, they inevitably either rise or decline, and necessity induces you to many acts to which reason does not induce you; so that, if a republic has been organized in such a way as to be apt to maintain herself without expanding and yet necessity forced her to do so, her foundations would give way and she would quickly be brought to ruin.'[164] In other words, expansion is no longer an option that can be freely exercised but becomes a matter of necessity. The same point is made even more forcefully: 'it is impossible for a republic to remain in the quiet enjoyment of her liberty and its limited territory; for even if she does not molest others, others will molest her, and from being thus molested will spring the desire and necessity of conquests'.[165] There is an element of sheer power-drive (the 'desire' or, ambition, to conquer),[166] just as the pursuit of 'glory' certainly plays a role (the Roman way 'leads to more glory').[167] Yet, the general argument has a predominantly defensive profile: the choice is between molest and being molested

---

[161] 3.2.1. Sound domestic institutions will then avoid the dangers of idleness.
[162] Cf. *Discourses* I, 5–6 (and 3.2.2).   [163] 3.2.2.   [164] 3.2.2.
[165] 4.1.4.   [166] Cf. Meinecke (1962, 42).   [167] 3.2.2.

or, between expand and perish.[168] The chances of survival of a state that is internally organized to live peacefully are not the same as those of a state that is organized to wage war. Machiavelli's endorsement of the Roman constitution thus reflects his appreciation for an institutional arrangement that proved so successful in coping with the external imperatives of defence and expansion thanks to the inclusion of the people in the political process.[169]

Again, although republics organized like Rome are better designed to survive, all states have to cope with the same external pressures. Filippo Maria Visconti, the Duke of Milan, is moved exactly by similar considerations in 1438: 'Filippo resolved to take the Romagna from the Pope; judging that, once he held that country, the Pope would not be able to molest him, and the Florentines, seeing the fire so near, would either not move from fear of him, or if they would, they could not readily attack him'.[170] Nor should this come as a surprise. As things are in a 'perpetual movement', refusing to expand means to relinquish the possibility of controlling the external milieu, to accept being exposed to the blows of Fortune.[171] And this is true for principalities and republics alike.

If being strong enough to deter attack, but not so strong as to instil fear, would be ideal on paper but dangerous in practice, how powerful should one be then? How far should expansion go? The answer is implied in the very nature of the problem. The extreme dynamism of Machiavelli's world prevents one from pausing or, even worse, stopping. If human things 'inevitably either rise or decline', one is constantly pushed ahead, for if one believes himself to be secure and settles today, tomorrow one may have to face some new threat that has in the meantime risen. Machiavelli's analysis of the forms of expansion makes this quite clear.[172] Expansion can be pursued in three ways, he writes: through a confederation of republics on equal footing—the Etruscans, in the past, the Swiss now; hegemonic alliances—the Roman method; finally, the sheer subjugation of the conquered peoples—which is what the Athenians and the Spartans did. The last policy is promptly dismissed as 'useless': in order to rely on mere violence, one has to be exceedingly powerful, in terms of allies and population; if one is not, one cannot afford it. The Roman method is considered the best: by availing themselves of alliances whose leadership was firmly in their hands, the Romans were always on the move, and added conquest to conquest. Their associates were kept in a subordinate position that did not entail a manifest and immediate loss of freedom. Yet, little by little, they 'ended up devoting their efforts and blood to their own subjugation', because when they suddenly found themselves 'surrounded by Roman sub-

---

[168] The point is stressed by many: Ercole (1926, 272–88), Gilbert (1965, 178), Mansfield (1996, 57–78), and Sasso (1967, 257–8), to name just a few.
[169] Gilbert (1965, 178), Sasso (1967, 266).   [170] 4.2.2 (*Florentine Histories* V, 17).
[171] Cf. Pocock (2003, 198–9).   [172] 4.4.2.

jects, and at the same time pressured by a powerful city like Rome', it was too late: 'from allies they became subjects too'.[173] Finally, the method based on confederations among equals is the next best: one is not easily dragged into war, and conquests are preserved without much difficulty. Its main shortcoming, though, is that 'it does not admit of extensive conquests'. The decision-making power is diffused across the various members of the confederation and the benefits of expansion are to be divided among them; this makes expansion more complicated and less attractive, respectively. In addition, confederations display a natural limit in size, and do not extend beyond a dozen members. In other words, their process of growth—both internal and external—is finite, and bound to come to an early end. Aristocratic constitutions at home and confederations abroad thus suffer from the same problem: they both inherently give up expansion from the very beginning, and this is dangerous.[174]

Independently of the specific goal of expansion, alliances perform a broader role that is quite consistent with our general argument. If the outside world is characterized by uncertainty and instability, one way of making it less uncertain and less unstable is to secure the conformity of other states by tying their hands and making their behaviour predictable as well as functional for our goals. Alliances are above all a means to this end. When Machiavelli—as a diplomat and as a political writer—discusses alliances, his focus is less on the goals in common that the partners ostensibly share than on the implications of their relationship for their respective freedom of action. In other words, Machiavelli's alliances are not simply a joint effort against a common enemy; prior to this, and often more important than this, the stake is the reciprocal control of one ally over the other. As such, the distribution of power decisively affects not only the relations between rivals but the relations between allies as well. The analysis of the events leading to the 1420 alliance between Florence and Milan clearly shows the ambivalent nature of that treaty: the Duke of Milan needs it in order to act as he pleases with regard to Genoa; Florence wants it in order to restrain him.[175] In 1437, the Venetians avail themselves of the treaty obligations that Florence has assumed with them to disrupt her expansionist plans.[176] A quick look at Florence's relations with France reveals that Louis XII never hesitates to exert full pressure upon his ally to get what he wants. In 1500, due to her military weakness and dependence, Florence is explicitly threatened into submission to French desires. What is at stake, on this occasion, is a large sum of money that the King claims. If Florence complies, she will retain the King's good graces and he will keep

---

[173] Cf. the bitter words pronounced by Annius Setinus, a Latin praetor: 'Now we can bear servitude under the specious name of a treaty among equals' (3.4.3). According to Pocock (2003, 216), this is why 'the hardest of all servitudes is to be subject to a republic' (cf. fn. 141). On the 'Roman method' see also *Discourses* II, 3, 19, and 23.

[174] Cf. Pocock (2003, 215).   [175] 4.4.5 (*Florentine Histories* IV, 3).

[176] 2.2.4 (*Florentine Histories* V, 13).

her enemies from injuring her; but if she does not, he will consider that she is no friend of his, will recompense himself anyway, while no third party's support will be enough to help her.[177] And in 1510, as tension between Louis XII and Julius II is mounting, the French try with all means—including the promise of some territorial gain—to entrap their reluctant ally. In one of the dispatches sent to Florence during that troubled legation, Machiavelli writes: 'these people here irretrievably want to involve you in this war'.[178]

Machiavelli's conception of alliances is best appreciated in his assessment of neutrality. The latter is one of those compromises that he frequently condemns for the false sense of security they so easily instil.[179] Unsafe for the weak, and of little benefit to the strong, either way neutrality implies giving up the opportunity to stabilize the external environment via an alliance. The immediate target, again, is the ally himself, and the context in which the decision is made is shaped by the relation of forces and the fear that this either does or does not provoke. If two states that are more powerful than you are fighting against each other, you have reason to fear the conqueror. In this case, neutrality is dangerous, for you will be prey to the victor, nor will the vanquished be willing to help you. If, on the other hand, you choose sides and your ally wins, although you are still at his discretion, at least he will be obliged to you; should he lose, you can still rely on him for the time being and possibly for the future as well. But if the two states at war are less powerful than you so that you need not be afraid of the conqueror, avoiding neutrality is all the more advantageous: 'you bring about the defeat of one with the help of another who should save him, if he were prudent; for if he wins, he remains at your discretion, and it is impossible for him not to win if you aid him'.[180] In a nutshell, the main question, between allies, is who remains at the discretion of whom.[181] There are of course alliances—above all defensive alliances—that

---

[177] Cf. 4.4.3.

[178] Cf. 5.2 (Dispatch of 13 August 1510). On the various occasions in which Florence might have reduced her dependence on France but failed to do so, see Bertelli (1972).

[179] Cf. 4.4.1, 5.3, and Letter to Francesco Vettori, 20 December 1514. Machiavelli's negative view of neutrality echoes the opinion of important figures of classical antiquity, including Livy (IX, 3, 12 and XXXII, 21, 34) and Tacitus (*Germania* XXXVI).

[180] 4.4.1.

[181] For this reason, one should abstain from entering an offensive alliance with a partner that is stronger than oneself—unless constrained by 'necessity'. The point is made as early as 1502, during Machiavelli's first mission to Duke Valentino (cf. 4.4.4). While the Venetians could have avoided their 1499 alliance with France against Milan which eventually led to their disastrous defeat of 1509, in 1510–12 the Florentines should have taken sides in the coming war between France on the one hand, and Spain and the Pope on the other (cf. 4.4.4). A few years later, Pope Leo X finds himself in the same situation: 'whoever the victorious side may be, it seems to me that the Church will have to remain at the discretion of others. Therefore I judge it better for her to be at the discretion of those who will be most reasonable, and whom she has known before, rather than at the discretion of those whose intention she cannot know because she is not well acquainted with them' (5.3; see also Letter to Francesco Vettori, 20 December 1514). Francesco Sforza too has to deal with a similar predicament: cf. 5.1 (*Florentine Histories* VI, 12). The

reflect a substantial degree of cooperation against a common threat. Nevertheless, in this case too the allies always keep an eye on each other. In 1427, Florence and Venice succeed in containing Filippo Maria Visconti, Duke of Milan; yet, as soon as the Duke is defeated, the Florentines are only too happy to make peace with him because they have grown 'suspicious of the Venetians, for it seemed to them that they had spent enough to make others powerful'.[182] Similarly, in 1452, Florence, Milan, and France form an alliance to counter the Venetian–Neapolitan league, with good results; as the French suddenly disengage, in 1454, the Florentines do not regret it, 'for having recovered their own castles they no longer feared the King of Naples, and on the other hand they did not wish that the Duke [of Milan] should recover anything more than his places in Lombardy'.[183]

Machiavelli has little faith in the effectiveness of coalitions against a great power: the Roman experience, coupled with the events of his lifetime and his general views on alliances, logically point at this conclusion. To begin with, if a growing power adopts the Roman method of expansion, its neighbours will not realize how dangerous it can become until it is too late, as we have seen. At this point, even if they try to crush it, they are not likely to succeed; in fact, their attack may well be counterproductive, as it will end up making their enemy more united, bolder, and even stronger.[184] When the rising power has consolidated its regional position so that its neighbours are now too afraid to move against it, it can afford the luxury of choosing which of them will be its next target, while keeping the others quiet.[185] As for the states that are far away, they are confident in their own strength and are too distant to be seriously concerned; not only will they not contain the rising power, but they will even help it, with offers of friendship and alliance. In fact, this is seen as a general rule: 'as one is apt to do with a growing power', Machiavelli writes in commenting on the friendly Carthaginian policy with regard to Rome at the beginning of her rise.[186] Further, success breeds success: as soon as a great power comes up unchallenged, all the minor powers will rush to place themselves under its protection. The small Italian principalities offered their friendship to Louis XII after his seizure of Lombardy in 1499,[187] and now they

---

stronger partner, for his part, can always do as he pleases. If he no longer needs the cooperation of his weaker ally, he will drop him. Here is the general rule: in 1341, 'the Venetians, *according to the fashion of all who ally themselves with others less powerful*, after having won Treviso and Vicenza, made terms with Mastino [II della Scala], regardless of the Florentines' (*Florentine Histories* II, 33, emphasis added).

[182] 4.4.5 (*Florentine Histories* IV, 15).   [183] 5.1 (*Florentine Histories* V, 31).

[184] Cf. 4.2.1 (*Discourses* I, 33).   [185] Cf. 4.3.1.

[186] Not only the Carthaginians: the Gauls, Philip of Macedon, and Antiochus made the same mistake: 'each one of these believed that, whilst the Romans were occupied with the other, they would be overcome, and that then it would be time enough either by peace or war to secure themselves against the Romans' (4.3.1).

[187] Cf. 4.3.4.

will do the same to the Swiss.[188] Such a selfish, albeit myopic, attitude shared by all states explains also why large coalitions, provided they are formed, can hardly be successful against a great power. If the latter is strong enough to withstand the first assault, it can always exploit the differences that will inevitably arise among the confederates: this is what the Venetians did in 1484 and the French in 1513.[189] Not to mention the case in which the allies themselves do not seem able to agree on the next step after prevailing on the battlefield.[190]

One might doubt that Machiavelli entertains the very idea of balance of power. In the doctrine, if not the theory, of the balance of power that will soon be developed in modern Europe, alliances will be seen as one of the typical means to achieve an approximately even distribution of power among states. But in Machiavelli's thought, alliances perform by and large other functions, nor do they seem effective anti-hegemonic measures. In addition, the Italian state system from the Peace of Lodi (1454) to Charles VIII's invasion (1494) will soon be hailed by Machiavelli's contemporaries (one name suffices: Francesco Guicciardini[191]) as a golden age in which Italy was free and at peace thanks to the political equilibrium among its major powers. But Machiavelli expresses unflattering views about those decades that, to him, were characterized neither by peace nor by war, but by baseness,[192] and during which all the Italian princes did was 'to observe each other', 'to secure themselves against one another' by marriages and alliances.[193] Yet, neither the general role he assigns to alliances nor his reproof of the Italian political equilibrium is enough to argue that Machiavelli has no notion of balance of power. That states tend to 'secure themselves against one another' is a universal law, in his world. What he dislikes about the fifteenth-century Italian state system is the means by which that policy was conducted, that is marriages and alliances, as opposed to military preparedness and strength: the result was a balance of impotence, not a balance of power, and the consequences of all this became plain for all to see as soon as the foreign powers got

---

[188] Cf. 4.1.3 (Letter to Francesco Vettori, 10 August 1513) and 5.3.

[189] Cf. 4.4.6 (*Florentine Histories* VIII, 26) and 5.3, respectively. On France, cf. also 4.2.1 (*Discourses* III, 11).

[190] For example, Louis XII and Maximilian I after the Battle of Agnadello (cf. 4.4.7).

[191] See his *History of Italy* I, 1.

[192] 'If then the strength and ability of these new states did not insure them any long-continued periods of peace, yet were they neither exposed to great dangers from the asperities of war. For that cannot be called peace when principalities often assail each other; nor can that be called war where men do not kill each other, and the cities are not sacked, nor the principalities ruined. Their wars had so declined in vigour that they were begun without fear, conducted without danger, and terminated without damage; so that that energy which in other countries is apt to become extinguished by long-continued periods of peace, was lost in the Italian provinces through baseness, as will clearly appear from what we shall write of the period from 1434 to 1504' (*Florentine Histories* V, 1).

[193] *Florentine Histories* VII, 23. Cf. Chabod (1965b, 59–60) and De Caprariis (1986).

involved in Italian affairs.[194] Power, in addition, is a state attribute, and it does not easily add up in alliance politics, as each state reserves itself the right to move about as it can and pleases. But that power must be met with power is nevertheless quite clear in Machiavelli's thought. The game is thus entirely left in the hands of the major actors. The latter may or may not be tied to each other via alliances—what truly matters is their capabilities and their relational system. To begin with, 'necessity' may recommend expansion, as we know. Machiavelli's 'theory of necessary conquest' contemplates that if one's rivals are growing more powerful—and therefore more threatening—in territorial or other terms, one may well be forced to engage in expansion in order to counterbalance their growth.[195] Such a dynamic perspective that sees balancing as an open-ended process is then coupled with a more static view. Machiavelli's analysis of actual or potential peace settlements is always based upon the distribution of power and the configuration of interests, in an almost mechanistic view of international politics. During the spring and the summer of 1513, Machiavelli and Francesco Vettori entertain a lively correspondence in which, among other things, they discuss the current international situation, including the prospects of peace.[196] To Machiavelli, the best arrangement would contemplate a four-power agreement which would result in a twofold interlocking system, one between the four signatories and the three powers that would be left out, the other between the four signatories themselves. France, Spain, Venice, and the Pope could easily arrive at a deal at the expense of England, the Swiss, and the Emperor. Under those terms, the four powers would achieve their goals while the three dissatisfied powers, being unable to harm their rivals, would be prevented from pursuing a revisionist policy. In addition, the Swiss and the Emperor 'would be left as a thorn in the side of the King of France, and he, in order to defend himself, would always have to be ready for war against them, which would make all the others secure from him, and each of them would keep an eye on the other'.[197] Louis XII made many mistakes in his Italian campaigns. Among them, he contributed to the weakening of Venice, with which he had previously partitioned Lombardy. What he did not realize was that as long as the Venetian republic was strong she would not have permitted others to try and take Lombardy—in other words, she would have been functional to the defence of the French portion of that province as well.[198] To sum up, Machiavelli does not have a 'theory' about an even distribution of power in the international system; at the same time, the arrangements that look stable to him are structured around opposing forces that elide each other in their mutual antagonism.

---

[194] Cf. Chabod (1965b, 59–60) and Machiavelli's invective against the Italian princes in 2.3.3 (*Art of War* VII).
[195] Cf. Sullivan (1973).   [196] Cf. 2.1.4 and 4.1.2.   [197] 2.1.4.   [198] Cf. 4.3.4.

Such settlements, needless to say, are extremely frail. Is it not true that human affairs 'can never remain still'? Sooner or later, the stronger, the bolder, the more fortunate will always end up breaking the equilibrium to their own advantage. Precariousness, then, keeps ruling; uncertainty never fades away. No matter how hard states try to stabilize the outside world, their efforts are in vain. Is there any solution? We have seen above that refusing expansion is tantamount to giving up the opportunity to exert some control over the external environment. But how far should expansion go? In the abstract, the process is unlimited: Rome conquered the entire world. Rome is an exception, however. In practice, Machiavelli sets pragmatic limits: one should never expand unless one can afford it, that is, unless one can rely on an adequate domestic institutional arrangement and appropriate military means. Athens, Sparta, Florence herself, and above all Venice, all are blamed for having conquered more than they could keep.[199] But let us assume, for the sake of the argument, that expansion can indeed go on forever, that is, until the whole world is subjugated. After all, the Romans made it. Would, then, unlimited successful conquest lead to absolute security?

We have seen how 'necessity' shapes human decisions, in Machiavelli's thought, and how such 'necessity' often entails some fear, especially among states. Fear, then, is a fundamental moving force behind state action, including expansion. Domestic and military institutions are organized accordingly: civic *virtù* and military *virtù* reinforce each other. When many states interact, one will always have a good reason to be afraid of somebody, and such a fear will exert its beneficial pressures: in classical antiquity, Europe was 'full of republics and principalities, which from the fear one had of the other, were forced to keep alive their military organizations, and honour those who greatly prevailed in them'.[200] Thus, competition in a dangerous environment enhances human qualities and develops organizational skills. It follows that if competition comes to an end, its propulsive force will be gone too. 'For after the Romans had subjugated Africa and Asia, and had reduced nearly all Greece to their obedience, they felt assured of their liberty, and saw no enemies that could cause them any fear. This security and the weakness of their enemies caused the Roman people [...] to bestow the consulate [...] on those who best knew how to entertain the people, and not on those who best knew how to conquer their enemies. After that [... on those who] had most wealth and power, so that the really meritorious became wholly excluded from that

---

[199] On Sparta and Athens, cf. 4.4.2 and *Discourses* II, 3; on Sparta and Venice, cf. 3.2.2; on Florence and Venice, cf. 4.1.4; on Venice, cf. *Discourses* III, 31. As Sasso (1967, 279) points out, however, the ruin of those cities is not simply the result of unwise decisions. In light of what is argued in 3.2.2 and 4.1.4, even if they had abstained from a deliberate imperialist effort at some point they would have found themselves involved in some 'necessary' expansion anyway.
[200] 2.3.2.

dignity.'[201] That is, fear leads to expansion, and unlimited victorious expansion leads to the end of fear. At this point the only great power left actually rules over its external environment. Yet the moment of triumph coincides with the beginning of the decline: as soon as external pressures are released, internal decay is set off, and everything—political institutions, social habits, armed forces—will be affected. This is hardly surprising, in light of the primacy of the outside world over the inside world. Finally, since human affairs are in a 'state of perpetual movement', one's decline will be coupled with somebody else's rise, and a new cycle is ready to begin.

REFERENCES

Alker, H. R. (1992), 'The Humanistic Moment in International Studies: Reflections on Machiavelli and Las Casas', *International Studies Quarterly*, 36, 4:347–72.

Aubert, A. (2003). *La crisi degli antichi stati italiani (1492–1521)*. Firenze: Le Lettere.

Bausi, F. (2005). *Machiavelli*. Roma: Salerno.

Berridge, G. R. (2001), 'Machiavelli: Human Nature, Good Faith, and Diplomacy', *Review of International Studies*, 27, 4:539–56.

Bertelli, S. (1972), 'Machiavelli e la politica estera fiorentina', in M. P. Gilmore (ed.), *Studies on Machiavelli*. Firenze: Sansoni, 29–72.

Black, R. (2010), 'Machiavelli in the Chancery', in J. M. Najemy (ed.), *The Cambridge Companion to Machiavelli*. Cambridge: Cambridge University Press, 31–47.

Boucher, D. (1998). *Political Theories of International Relations: From Thucydides to the Present*. Oxford: Oxford University Press.

Butterfield, H. (1962, originally 1940). *The Statecraft of Machiavelli*. New York: Collier.

Chabod, F. (1965a, originally 1924), 'An Introduction to *The Prince*', in *Machiavelli and the Renaissance*. Trans. D. Moore. New York: Harper & Row, 1–29.

Chabod, F. (1965b, originally 1925), '*The Prince*: Myth and Reality', in *Machiavelli and the Renaissance*. Trans. D. Moore. New York: Harper & Row, 30–125.

Chabod, F. (1993, originally 1953), 'Il segretario fiorentino', in *Scritti su Machiavelli*. Torino: Einaudi, 241–368.

Croce, B. (1943, originally 1924), 'Per la storia della filosofia della politica', in *Etica e politica*. Bari: Laterza, 250–73.

De Caprariis, V. (1986, originally 1949), 'Il problema dell'equilibrio nel pensiero di Machiavelli', in *Scritti*. Messina: P & M, vol. I, 147–57.

Descendre, R. (2008), '*Le cose di stato*: sémantique de l'état et relations internationales chez Machiavel', *Il pensiero politico*, 41, 1:3–18.

---

[201] *Discourses* I, 18. See also *Discourses* III, 16. Machiavelli is not the first to mention the disappearance of external threats as a cause of Rome's 'corruption': among his classical forerunners, Polybius (*Histories* VI, 18) and Sallust (*Jugurthine War* XLI) deserve mention. It should be noted, however, that our emphasis on the outside world does not do full justice to Machiavelli's richer assessment of the Roman decline within the framework of his republican theory. For two excellent discussions, see Pocock (2003, 194–218) and Sasso (1993, 527–44).

Doyle, M. (1997). *Ways of War and Peace: Realism, Liberalism and Socialism.* New York: Norton.

Ercole, F. (1926). *La politica di Machiavelli.* Roma: A.R.E.

Fachard, D. (1996), 'Implicazioni politiche nell'*Arte della guerra*', in J.-J. Marchand (ed.), *Niccolò Machiavelli. Politico storico letterato.* Roma: Salerno, 149–73.

Fischer, M. (1995), 'Machiavelli's Theory of Foreign Politics', *Security Studies*, 5, 2:248–79.

Forde, S. (1992), 'Varieties of Realism: Thucydides and Machiavelli', *Journal of Politics*, 54, 2:372–93.

Forde, S. (1995), 'International Realism and the Science of Politics', *International Studies Quarterly*, 39, 2:141–60.

Gilbert, F. (1965). *Machiavelli and Guicciardini: Politics and History in Sixteenth-Century Florence.* Princeton: Princeton University Press.

Gilbert, F. (1969), 'Machiavelli e Venezia', *Lettere italiane*, 21, 4:389–98.

Gilbert, F. (1986), 'Machiavelli: The Renaissance of the Art of War', in P. Paret (ed.), *Makers of Modern Strategy from Machiavelli to the Nuclear Age.* Princeton: Princeton University Press, 11–31.

de Grazia, S. (1989). *Machiavelli in Hell.* Princeton: Princeton University Press.

Guidi, A. (2009). *Un Segretario militante: Politica, diplomazia e armi nel Cancelliere Machiavelli.* Bologna: il Mulino.

Hannaford, I. (1972), 'Machiavelli's Concept of *Virtù* in *The Prince* and *The Discourses* Reconsidered', *Political Studies*, 20, 2:185–9.

Holschki, L. (1945). *Machiavelli the Scientist.* Berkeley: The Gillick Press.

Hörnqvist, M. (2004). *Machiavelli and Empire.* Cambridge: Cambridge University Press.

Hulliung, M. (1983). *Citizen Machiavelli.* Princeton: Princeton University Press.

Lynch, C. (2012), 'War and Foreign Affairs in Machiavelli's *Florentine Histories*', *The Review of Politics*, 74, 1:1–26.

Mc Canles, M. (1984), 'Machiavelli and the Paradoxes of Deterrence', *Diacritics*, 14, 2:12–19.

Mallett, M. (1990), 'The Theory and Practice of Warfare in Machiavelli's Republic', in G. Bock, Q. Skinner, and M. Viroli (eds), *Machiavelli and Republicanism.* Cambridge: Cambridge University Press, 173–80.

Mansfield, H. C. (1996). *Machiavelli's Virtue.* Chicago: University of Chicago Press.

Marchand, J.-J. (1975). *Niccolò Machiavelli. I primi scritti politici (1499–1512).* Padova: Antenore.

Martelli, M. (1971), 'Il buon geomètra di questo mondo', in M. Martelli (ed.), *Tutte le opere di Machiavelli.* Firenze: Sansoni, XI–LX.

Matteucci, N. (1972), 'Machiavelli politologo', in M. P. Gilmore (ed.), *Studies on Machiavelli.* Firenze: Sansoni, 207–48.

Meinecke, F. (1962, originally 1924). *Machiavellism: The Doctrine of raison d'état and Its Place in Modern History.* Trans. D. Scott. New Haven: Yale University Press.

Mindle, G. B. (1985), 'Machiavelli's Realism', *Review of Politics*, 47, 2:212–30.

Najemy, J. M. (1993). *Between Friends: Discourses of Power and Desire in the Machiavelli–Vettori Letters of 1513–1515.* Princeton: Princeton University Press.

Norsa, A. (1936). *Il principio della forza nel pensiero politico di Niccolò Machiavelli*. Milano: Hoepli.

Pocock, J. G. A. (2003). *The Machiavellian Moment: Florentine Political Thought and the Atlantic Republican Tradition*. Princeton: Princeton University Press, 2nd edn.

Price, R. (1973), 'The Senses of *Virtù* in Machiavelli', *European Studies Review*, 3, 4:315–45.

Price, R. (1977), 'The Theme of Glory in Machiavelli', *Renaissance Quarterly*, 30, 4:588–631.

Price, R. (1982), '*Ambizione* in Machiavelli's Thought', *History of Political Thought*, 3, 3:383–445.

Regent, N. (2011), 'Machiavelli's Empire: *Virtù* and the Final Downfall', *History of Political Thought*, 32, 5:751–72.

Renaudet, A. (1956). *Machiavel*. Nouvelle édition revue et augmentée. Paris: Gallimard.

Rousseau, C. (1970). 'La doctrine de la guerre de Machiavel', *Annales de philosophie politique*, n. 9: *La guerre et ses théories*. Paris: Presses Universitaires de France, 15–28.

Sasso, G. (1967), 'Polibio e Machiavelli: costituzione, potenza, conquista', in *Studi su Machiavelli*. Napoli: Morano, 223–80.

Sasso, G. (1993). *Niccolò Machiavelli*. Bologna: il Mulino. Volume I: *Il pensiero politico*.

Skinner, Q. (1978). *The Foundations of Modern Political Thought*. Cambridge: Cambridge University Press. Volume 1: *The Renaissance*.

Skinner, Q. (1981). *Machiavelli*. Oxford: Oxford University Press.

Sobek, D. (2005), 'Machiavelli's Legacy: Domestic Politics and International Conflict', *International Studies Quarterly*, 49, 2:179–204.

Sullivan, R. R. (1973), 'Machiavelli's Balance of Power Theory', *Social Science Quarterly*, 54:258–70.

Viroli, M. (1998). *Machiavelli*. Oxford: Oxford University Press.

Von Albertini, R. (1995, originally 1955). *Firenze dalla repubblica al principato: Storia e coscienza politica*. Trans. C. Cristofolini. Torino: Einaudi.

Walker, R. B. J. (1993). *Inside/Outside: International Relations as Political Theory*. Cambridge: Cambridge University Press.

Waltz, K. N. (1959). *Man, the State and War: A Theoretical Analysis*. New York: Columbia University Press.

Whitfield, J. H. (1947). *Machiavelli*. Oxford: Blackwell.

Wight, M. (2005), 'Machiavelli', in *Four Seminal Thinkers in International Relations Theory*. Oxford: Oxford University Press, 3–28.

Wolin, S. S. (1960), 'Machiavelli: Politics and the Economy of Violence', in *Politics and Vision. Continuity and Innovation in Western Political Thought*. Boston: Little, Brown & Co., 195–238.

Wood, N. (1967), 'Machiavelli's Concept of *Virtù* Reconsidered', *Political Studies*, 15, 2:159–72.

Part I

A Way of Thinking and Some Basic Assumptions

1.1

A Compelling Logic

1.1.1 EITHER, OR

After a long decline throughout the fourteenth century, Pisa finally fell under the control of the Duke of Milan. A few years later, in 1405, the Duke's son sold the city to the Florentines, who imposed a harsh rule on her. Taking advantage of Charles VIII's descent into Italy, Pisa bought her independence back from the French in 1495. After her loss, the Florentines devoted their best efforts to retake her. Initially supported by several powers, the Pisans were gradually abandoned by all. In April 1499 even the Venetians agreed to evacuate the city in return for 180,000 florins from Florence. This is the general context in which the Speech was written—probably the outline for a more elaborate address to be given by some official. The Pisa affair went on for years. Although the issue was always intermingled with the complex international situation of that period, it was above all Venice, in her anti-Florentine stand, that helped Pisa defend her independence. In 1509, however, Venice had to face a formidable coalition (the League of Cambrai), while Florence could rely on the diplomatic support of the same coalition. The second excerpt is probably a synthesis of the opinions of military leaders and government officials on the eve of the decisive attack. The Speech is noteworthy because it is a very early example of Machiavelli's way of thinking, in which one alternative is set against another and no middle course is allowed. The Provisions relies on a similar logical structure: the situation is defined by two opposite extremes, each of which is sharply evaluated in its own merit.

Speech Concerning Pisa (1499)

I do not think I have to prove with arguments other than those you under-stand yourselves that retaking Pisa is necessary, if we want to preserve our independence, for nobody would doubt that. Thus, I will limit myself to examining the means through which that can be accomplished, that is either by force or by love. In the first case, Pisa would be taken back by siege; in the second case, it would give itself back to you voluntarily. And since the latter would be the safer, and therefore the more desirable, way, I will examine whether this is feasible or not [...]. You might lay your hands on Pisa without resorting to the use of force if the Pisans themselves were to come into your arms or if somebody were to give them to you without asking for anything in return. That the Pisans would be willing to submit again to your jurisdiction cannot be believed in light of the current situation: absolutely lacking in means of defence, isolated and extremely weak, turned down by the Duke of Milan, dismissed by the Genoese, disliked by the Pope, treated with little respect by the Sienese, they stubbornly resist, relying on the vain hope of receiving some help, and on your weakness and disunion. Their perfidy is such that they have always rejected the least overture or any embassy coming from you. They find themselves in so difficult a situation and they have not bent their spirit; therefore, one cannot and must not believe at all that they would ever come under your yoke voluntarily. As for Pisa being handed over to us by somebody who holds it, we must examine whether such a possessor has been called upon by them or has entered the city by force. In the latter case, there is no reason why he should grant the city to us, for if one has been strong enough to seize it, one will also be strong enough to defend it and keep it for himself; for Pisa is not a city that is to be given up gladly by anybody who happens to be its master. [... In the former case], looking at the fresh example of the Venetians, I do not believe that anyone [who holds it] would break faith with them and, under the pretext of defending them, betray them and hand them over to you as prisoners. And even if such a possessor were inclined to let Pisa come back under your rule, he would be more likely to desert it and leave it to you as a prey, just as the Venetians did. So that, for those reasons, it is difficult to see how Pisa could be retaken in any way short of war. Since the recourse to force is necessary, then, I will examine whether it is good to take that path at this time or not.

Provisions for Retaking Pisa (1509)

In order to succeed in the enterprise, Pisa must be taken by siege and hunger or by storm, pushing the artillery up to its walls. As far as the siege is concerned, one has first to examine whether the Lucchese would be willing, or able, to stop the flow of provisions from their country to Pisa. If they were, everyone agrees that it would suffice for us to keep an eye on the rivers;[1] to that purpose, one camp would do [...]. But since the Lucchese's intentions are

---

[1] The rivers Arno and Serchio.

doubtful, and one doubts that even if they were favourably disposed toward us they could actually seal up their country—the territory to be guarded is vast, and they cannot command the full obedience of their subjects—one comes to the conclusion that if Pisa is to be besieged effectively [. . .] a single camp would not be enough, but that one or two more would be needed [. . .].

[The military leaders] have also considered whether it is credible that the siege [. . .] would suffice, and have come to the conclusion that it would not, because the Pisans have enough provisions to sustain themselves until the next harvest [. . .]; thus they think that you will be forced to try and storm the city. It will probably be impossible for them to resist if you besiege them as tightly as you can for forty or fifty days, and meantime detach from them as many mercenaries as possible [. . .]. After that, you should enlist at once as much infantry as you can, set up two batteries and all that is needed to get close to the city walls, allow safe exit for women, children, the elderly, and anybody else who wants to leave—because everyone is good at defending the city. Thus the Pisans would find themselves deprived of defenders and attacked from two sides; they could not resist three or four assaults except by miracle [. . .].

1.1.2 WHAT DUKE VALENTINO WILL DO

Cesare Borgia (1475–1507), Duke of Valentinois (hence, the Italianized 'Valentino'), with the help of Pope Alexander VI (his father) and the King of France, has established a new state in the Romagna (see 3.3.2). Soon afterwards, his feudal lords and captains, along with the rulers of some neighbouring cities, plot against him. Florence too feels threatened by the Duke's rise, but she relies on the protection of the King of France. Machiavelli is thus sent to the Duke to express the Florentine desire to be on good terms with him. From the beginning, he observes the Duke's tactics in dealing with the rebels, his cunning and deception, and comes immediately to the conclusion that no amicable settlement is possible. In a very lucid analysis, Machiavelli underlines the incompatibility of the two parties' interests, points out the only possible—although unlikely—arrangement, and concludes with a precise prediction.

II Mission to Duke Valentino

Imola, 27 October 1502

[. . .] If we examine the characters of both the one and the other party, we shall find in the Duke [Valentino] a daring and fortunate man, full of hope, favoured by a pope and a king, and who finds himself assailed by the others, not only in a state that he wished to acquire, but also in one that he had already acquired.[2] The other party[3] will be seen to fear for their own states, and to have been afraid of the power of the Duke before they injured him; having done so now, they are much more afraid. And it is impossible to see how he can pardon the offence, or how they can dismiss their apprehensions; and consequently how the two parties can reach an agreement that is advantageous for all in their attempts against Bologna and the Duchy of Urbino.[4]

It is argued that an amicable arrangement between them would be possible only if they could unite their joint forces against some third party, in which case neither the Duke nor the rebel condottieri would lose their strength, and both would rather gain in renown and in real advantages [...]. However, if such an arrangement could be brought about, there would be no other power for them to turn against except Florence or Venice. An attack upon Florence is judged to be easier, so far as Florence itself is concerned, but more difficult on account of the King of France; an attempt upon Venice would be easier so far as the King of France is concerned, but more difficult on account of Venice itself. The latter would be the most agreeable to the Duke, and the former more acceptable to the rebels. Still it is not believed that either one or the other will be undertaken, although spoken of as a possible thing. And thus I can find no one who can definitely suggest a way for an agreement between the two. Those who nevertheless do have some definite idea on the subject believe that the Duke will split the rebels, and having thus broken up their alliance he would have nothing more to fear from them, and will then pursue his own enterprises. I am rather disposed to believe this [...].[5]

1.1.3 REASON GUIDES ANALYSIS

The King of France has been beaten, beyond the Alps, by Spain and England. The Emperor, the Swiss, and Venice are still his enemies. In short, he is in dire straits. Then, out of the blue, the King of Spain signs a truce with him. Francesco Vettori is puzzled. Machiavelli, in turn, invokes 'rational arguments': reason must shed light on circumstances that may otherwise look chancy and illogical. Although the soundness of Machiavelli's assessment is open to debate, what matters here is his deliberate effort to understand events rationally.

---

[2] Not only had the rebellion prevented the Duke from seizing Bologna, but it had also led to his loss of Urbino.

[3] The Orsini, Vitelli, and the other rebels.

[4] The Orsini supported the lord of Bologna, Giovanni Bentivoglio, and stirred up further troubles in the Marca of Ancona (where Urbino was located).

[5] This is, of course, precisely what happens two months later. Machiavelli wrote a famous piece on this affair, his *Description of the Manner in which Duke Valentino Proceeded to Kill Vitellozzo Vitelli, Oliverotto da Fermo, the Signor Paolo, and the Duke Gravina Orsini.*

Letter to Francesco Vettori, 29 April 1513

You wish to know [...] what I think moved the King of Spain [Ferdinand II] to make this truce with the King of France,[6] for when you look at the matter from all sides it seems to you that it is not to his interest. Since, therefore, you think on the one hand that King Ferdinand is wise, and on the other think he has made a mistake, you are obliged to suppose that something important is concealed under his act [...]. It seems to me that this uncertainty of yours depends chiefly on your belief in the prudence of the King of Spain. To this I answer: I am not able to deny that the King is wise, but all the same he appears to me more crafty and fortunate than wise. I do not intend to review his whole career, but will go directly to the enterprise he last attempted against France in Italy, before the King of England showed his intentions. Even though that undertaking came out well, it seemed to me and still seems to me that without necessity he endangered all his territories [...].[7]

I will never believe there is anything in his decision that is not plain to see, for I do not judge by appearances, nor do I intend to be influenced in this matter by any authoritative opinion that is not based upon rational arguments. Therefore I conclude that Ferdinand may have made an error [...], and planned badly and executed worse.

But let us drop this and admit that he is prudent [...]. [You argue] that he should have made complete peace with the King of France, and given Lombardy back to him, in order to oblige him to himself and take away from him any reason for leading an army to Italy. In such a way Ferdinand could have made himself secure. To this I answer that [...] one must observe that the King of Spain made that attempt against France because he hoped to conquer, and placed more reliance in the Pope, in England, and in the Emperor than, as it turned out, he saw he should have placed there [...]. From the Pope he obtained money at first in small amounts, and at last the Pope not merely did not give him money but every day sought to ruin him, and plotted against him. Nothing has come from the Emperor except the missions of the Bishop of Gurk,[8] slanders, and reproaches. From England he received only weak forces [...]. Hence he has thought it better to be beforehand with the King of France, as well as he could, rather than to remain in such great uncertainty and confusion, and subject to expense greater than he can bear [...]. And I believe that his design in this truce has been either to make his allies recognize their error and make them more eager for the war, since he has promised the ratification,[9] etc., or to get the war away from Spain and relieve himself of so

---

[6] The truce was signed in Orthez on 1 April 1513.

[7] Despite their victory over the Spanish army at Ravenna in April 1512, the French were defeated by the Swiss shortly afterwards and left Italy.

[8] Matthäus Lang von Wellenburg, secretary of Emperor Maximilian.

[9] Formally, the truce had to be ratified by his allies as well.

much expense and peril, for if Pamplona had been taken away from him this spring he would surely have lost Castile.[10]

As to affairs in Italy,[11] [...] I do not see that there is any utility in peace for him for the time being, because the French king would be powerful in Italy no matter how he got into Lombardy [...]. Today no attention is paid to faith and obligations, hence the King of Spain saw no security in them [... and] would have irritated against himself all other rulers in Italy and outside it, because, since he was the sole provoker of all of them against France, if he then abandoned them, it would be a very great injury. Hence if he had made peace according to your plan, he would have increased the power of the King of France for sure, aroused the anger of the confederates for sure, and still could not have felt sure of the faith of France. Yet this faith would have been the only thing on which he could rely: if he made France powerful and the others hostile, it would have been necessary to take his stand with France; but wise men never place themselves at the discretion of others except through necessity. Hence I conclude he may have made a better decision by making the truce, because that act shows his allies their error; he has made it impossible for them to complain, because he has given them time to ratify it; he has got the war away from his own country; he has stirred up new contests and confusion in Italian affairs, where he sees there is yet something to be torn up and a bone to pick [...]; and can believe that the Pope, the Emperor, and the Swiss will not be pleased with the greatness of the Venetians and of France in Italy. If they are not strong enough to keep France and Venice from occupying Lombardy,[12] at least with his help they are able to keep the two from going farther [...]. Hence he sees that this truce makes the victory of the King of France doubtful, he does not have to trust him and does not have to fear the alienation of his confederates, because the Emperor and England either will ratify it or will not. If they ratify it, they will do so thinking that this truce is beneficial to all; if they do not ratify it, they will probably wage war more vigorously, and assail France with larger forces than in the past year. In every one of these instances the King of Spain gets what he is looking for [...].

---

[10] In the second half of 1512, the French had launched an offensive in Navarre, only to be stopped at Pamplona.

[11] The truce affected military operations beyond the Alps, mainly in the Pyrenees. This is why Italian affairs must now be examined in their own merit.

[12] In the language of the time, 'Lombardy' still referred to the vast territory contained between the Apennines and the Alps, which is to the whole of Northern Italy.

1.2

On Human Nature

1.2.1 IF MEN WERE ALL GOOD

The following excerpts contain some of the best-known views of Machiavelli on human nature. Those thoughts constitute the foundations on which the 'truth of the matter' rests. The 'truth of the matter', as opposed to 'mere speculation', in turn, is the object of analysis. Several crude suggestions to the prince, therefore, far from being the expression of some gratuitous cynicism, reflect a deep anthropological pessimism that is portrayed here in its essential traits.

Prince XV, XVII, XVIII

XV—[...] As my aim is to write something that may be useful to those who wish to listen unbiasedly, it seems to me proper to pursue the real truth of the matter, rather than to indulge in mere speculation on the same; for many have imagined republics and principalities such as have never been known to exist in reality. For the manner in which men live is so different from the way in which they ought to live, that he who leaves the common course for that which he ought to follow will find that it leads him to ruin rather than to safety. For a man who always wishes to profess goodness will inevitably come to ruin amongst so many who are evil. A prince, therefore, who desires to maintain himself must learn to be able not to be good, but to be so or not as necessity may require [...].

I am well aware that it would be most praiseworthy for a prince to possess all the [...] qualities that are esteemed good; but as he cannot have them all, nor entirely observe them, because human nature does not permit it, he should be prudent enough to know how to avoid the infamy of those vices that would rob him of his state. As for the other qualities that entail no such risk [yet are dangerous nevertheless], he should guard against them, if possible; but if that be not possible, then he may with less hesitation follow his natural inclinations. Nor need he care about incurring censure for such vices, without which the preservation of his state may be difficult. For, all things considered, it will be found that some things that seem like virtue will lead you to ruin if you follow them; whilst others, that apparently are vices, will, if followed, result in your safety and well-being.

XVII—[...] This gives rise to the question whether it be better to be beloved than feared, or to be feared than beloved. It will be answered that it would be desirable to be both the one and the other; but as it is difficult to be both at the same time, it is much safer to be feared than to be loved, when you have to choose between the two.[1] For it may be said of men in general that they are ungrateful and fickle, dissemblers, avoiders of danger, and greedy of gain. So long as you shower benefits upon them, they are all yours; they offer you their blood, their substance, their lives, and their children, provided the necessity for it is far off, as I said above;[2] but when it is near at hand, then they refuse to obey you. And the Prince who relies entirely upon their words, without having otherwise provided for other precautions, comes to ruin; for friendships[3] that are won by rewards, and not by greatness and nobility of soul, may be claimed but are not had, and you cannot avail yourself of them in time of adversity. Besides, men have less hesitation in offending one who makes himself beloved than one who makes himself feared; for love holds by a bond of obligation which, as mankind is bad, is broken on every occasion whenever it is for the interest of the obliged party to break it. But fear holds by the apprehension of punishment, which never leaves men [...].

XVIII—[...] You must know, therefore, that there are two ways of carrying on a contest; the one by law, and the other by force. The first is practised by men, and the other by beasts; and as the first is often insufficient, it becomes necessary to resort to the second. A prince then should know how to employ the nature of man, and that of the beasts as well [...] as the one without the other cannot produce lasting results [...].

It being necessary then for a prince to know well how to employ the nature of the beasts, he should be able to assume both that of the fox and that of the lion; for whilst the latter cannot escape the traps laid for him, the former cannot defend himself against the wolves. A prince should be a fox, to know the traps and snares; and a lion, to be able to frighten the wolves; for those who simply hold to the nature of the lion do not understand how things go. A sagacious prince then cannot and should not fulfil his pledges when their observance is contrary to his interest, and when the causes that induced him to pledge his faith no longer exist. If men were all good, this precept would not be

---

[1] This is the general rule. However, fear should never degenerate into hatred, something that the prince must avoid (*Prince* XIX). On being beloved or feared, cf. 3.3.1 and 3.3.2.

[2] *Prince* IX.

[3] The 'friendships' mentioned here refer to the bonds between the prince and those who have helped him to seize power, and not between the prince and his subjects at large.

good; but as men are bad, and would not observe their faith towards you, you must, in the same way, not observe yours to them.[4] No prince ever lacked legitimate reasons with which to colour his want of good faith. Innumerable modern examples could be given of this; and it could easily be shown how many treaties of peace, and how many engagements, have been made null and void by the faithlessness of princes; and he who has best known how to play the fox has ever been the most successful [...].

And it must be understood that a prince, and especially one who has but recently acquired his state, cannot perform all those things which cause men to be esteemed as good; he being often obliged, for the sake of maintaining his state, to act contrary to faith, charity, humanity, and religion. And therefore is it necessary that he should have a versatile mind, capable of changing readily, according as the winds of fortune and the variation of things bid him; and [...] not to swerve from the good if he can, but to know how to resort to evil if he needs to.

A prince then should be very careful never to allow anything to escape his lips that does not abound in the above-named qualities, so that to see and to hear him he may seem all piety, faith, integrity, and religion. And more than all else is it necessary for a prince to seem to possess the last quality; for mankind in general judge more by what they see than by what they touch with their own hands, everyone being capable of the former, and but few of the latter. Everybody sees what you seem to be, but few really feel what you are; and these few dare not oppose the opinion of the many, who are protected by the majesty of the state; for the actions of all men, and especially those of princes, where there is no court to which to appeal, are judged by the result.

As long as a prince succeeds and maintains his state, the means which he employs for this will always be accounted honourable, and will be praised by everybody [...].

1.2.2 SOME MEN DESIRE, WHILST OTHERS FEAR

The desire to have more and the fear of losing what is possessed are two powerful motives of human action in Machiavelli's thought. While the role of fear— above all among states—will be examined in Part II, the brief excerpts below highlight the coexistence and the interplay between these two psychological forces.

---

[4] Cf. 2.1.3. Needless to say, this undermines the very foundation of international law. For a nice illustration of fox-like policies, see Count Sforza's rise in 5.1 (*Florentine Histories* VI, 17–22).

Discourses I, 37

It was a saying of ancient writers, that men afflict themselves in evil, and become weary of the good, and that both these dispositions produce the same effects.[5] For when men are no longer obliged to fight from necessity, they fight from ambition,[6] which passion is so powerful in the hearts of men that it never leaves them, no matter to what height they may rise. The reason for this is that nature has created men so that they desire everything, but are unable to attain it;[7] desire being thus always greater than the capacity of acquiring, discontent with what they have and dissatisfaction from it follow. This causes the changes in their fortunes; some men desire to have more, some others fear to lose what they have, and enmities and war are the consequences;[8] and this brings about the ruin of one province and the rise of another […].

Discourses I, 5

[…] On that occasion there was much discussion as to who is the most ambitious, he who wishes to preserve or he who wishes to acquire; as both the one and the other of these motives may be the cause of great troubles. It seems, however, that they are most frequently occasioned by those who possess; for the fear to lose stirs the same passions in men as the desire to gain, as men do not believe themselves sure of what they possess except by acquiring still more; and, moreover, those who possess much can provoke disorders more impetuously and vigorously […].

1.2.3 NATIONS PRESERVE FOR A LONG TIME THE SAME CHARACTER

As we have seen above, human beings are characterized by a set of (mostly) psychological features that we usually call 'human nature' and that provide the deepest foundations of the repetitiveness of behaviour. Similar features, we are now told, are the distinctive attributes not only of individuals but of entire peoples as well, and they help explain certain constant attitudes kept by a collectivity as a whole.

---

[5] Cf. 1.3.2, 4.2.1 (*Discourses* I, 33) and *Discourses* III, 21. This is why human beings always desire something new.

[6] Cf. *Discourses* I, 46, 4.1.3 (Letter to Francesco Vettori, 10 August 1513), and 4.1.4.

[7] Cf. 1.3.1 (*Discourses* II, 'Introduction').   [8] Cf. 3.2.1.

Discourses III, 43

Wise men say, and not without reason, that whoever wishes to foresee the future must consult the past; for all the human events, at any time, have their equivalent in the ancient times.[9] This arises from the fact that they are produced by men who are, and have always been, animated by the same passions, and thus they must necessarily lead to the same results. It is true that human actions are more or less excellent in one country or another,[10] according to the character of the education by which the various peoples have developed their manners and habits of life. It also facilitates a judgment of future by the past, to observe nations preserve for a long time the same character; ever exhibiting the same disposition to avarice, or bad faith, or to some other special vice or virtue. Whoever reads attentively the history of our city of Florence and observes the events of our more immediate times, will find that the Germans and the French are full of avarice, pride, cruelty, and bad faith,[11] from which four qualities our city has suffered greatly at various times. As for bad faith, everybody knows how often the Florentines have paid money to King Charles VIII upon his promising to restore to them the citadel of Pisa;[12] which promises, however, he never fulfilled, thereby exhibiting his want of good faith and his greed of money [...].

If Florence had not been constrained by necessity, or carried away by ambition, and had studied and known the ancient habits of the foreigners, she would not have allowed herself to have been deceived by them on this occasion, as well as on several others. For they have constantly preserved the same characteristics, and have on every occasion, and towards everybody, displayed the same conduct, as according to history they did in ancient times towards the Etruscans [... who] were deprived, by the avarice and bad faith of the Gauls, both of their money and of the assistance upon which they had counted from them.[13] So that we see from this example of the Etruscans, and by that of the Florentines, that the [Gauls of old and the modern] French have ever conducted themselves in the same manner; and thus we may readily judge to what extent princes may place confidence in them.

---

[9] Cf. 1.3.1 (*Discourses* I, 'Introduction').   [10] Cf. 1.3.1 (*Discourses* II, 'Introduction').
[11] In 1.2.1 similar features are attributed to human beings in general.
[12] In 1494–95. Cf. the Introduction to 1.1.1.
[13] In 299 BC the Etruscans offered the Cisalpine Gauls money for their help against the Romans. The Gauls pocketed the money and then refused to fight.

1.3

On Times and Affairs

1.3.1 THE WORLD REMAINS VERY MUCH IN THE SAME CONDITION

One can draw significant lessons and important rules of behaviour from a careful reading of history. Knowledge of the past allows one to see what is coming and thus act in time (cf. 1.2.3). Such a correspondence between the past and the future, via the present, relies in turn on the assumption of some immutable order of things—including a constant human nature—as emphasized not only in the excerpts below but in other writings as well (Discourses I, 11; Letter to Francesco Vettori, 20 December 1514; On the Mode of Dealing with the Rebellious Peoples of Valdichiana).

Discourses I, Introduction

[...] When we see [...] the prodigies of strength and of wisdom which, as history shows us, have been accomplished by ancient kingdoms and republics; the kings, captains, citizens, and legislators who have sacrificed themselves for their country—when we see these, I say, more admired than imitated (in fact, so much neglected by all that not the least trace of those ancient extraordinary qualities remains), we cannot but be at the same time as much surprised as afflicted. The more so as in the judiciary controversies which arise between citizens, or in the maladies to which men are subjected, we see that people have always had recourse to the judgments given and the remedies prescribed by the ancients. The civil laws are in fact nothing but decisions given by ancient jurisconsults, and which, reduced to a system, direct our modern jurisconsults in their decisions. Nor is the science of medicine but the experience of ancient physicians, which modern physicians have taken for their guide. And yet to give institutions to a republic, maintain states, to govern a kingdom, organize an army, conduct a war, dispense justice upon the subjects, and extend empires, you will find neither prince, nor republic, nor captain who has recourse to the examples of antiquity. This neglect, I am persuaded, is due less to the weakness to which our religion has reduced the world, or to the evils caused by the proud indolence which prevails in many Christian provinces and cities, than to the lack of real knowledge of history, the true sense of which is not drawn, nor the taste of which appreciated, from mere reading. Thus the majority of those who read it take pleasure in the variety of the events which history relates, without thinking at all of imitating the ancient examples, deeming that not only difficult, but impossible; as though heaven, the sun, the elements, and men had changed their motions, regularities and strength, and were different from what they were in ancient times [...].[1]

Discourses I, 39

Whoever considers the past and the present will readily observe that all cities and all peoples are and ever have been animated by the same desires and the same ferments; so that it is easy, by diligent study of the past, to foresee what is likely to happen in the future in any republic, and to prepare those remedies that were used by the ancients, or, not finding any that were employed by them, to devise new ones from the similarity of the events. But as such considerations are neglected or not understood by most of those who read history, or, if understood by these, are unknown by those who govern, it follows that the same troubles always recur in all ages [...].

Discourses II, Introduction

Men ever praise the olden times, and find fault with the present [...]. Their opinion is generally erroneous in that respect, and I think the reasons which cause this illusion are various. The first I believe to be the fact that we never know the whole truth about the past [... as] most writers obey the fortune of conquerors to that degree that, by way of rendering their victories more glorious, they exaggerate not only the valiant deeds of the victor, but also of the vanquished [...]. Another reason is that men's hatreds spring from fear or envy. Now, these two powerful reasons of hatred do not exist for us with regard to the past, which cannot injure us or make us envious [...].

This practice of praising and decrying is very general, though it cannot be said that it is always erroneous; for sometimes our judgment is of necessity correct, human affairs being in a state of perpetual movement, always either ascending or declining [...]. I think that, as a whole, the world remains very much in the same condition, and that there has been both some good and

---

[1] Cf. 1.2.3.

some bad in it; but the good and the bad move from one country to another, as we learn from what we know of those ancient kingdoms that would pass primacy on to each other due to the variations in their customs,[2] whilst the world remained the same. The only difference being, that while the world had first located its *virtù* in Assyria, it thence moved it to Media, and afterwards to Persia, until it came into Italy and to Rome. And if after the fall of the Roman Empire none other sprung up that endured for any length of time, and where the world kept its *virtù* concentrated together, we nevertheless see it scattered amongst many nations where people would live according to *virtù*, as, for instance, in the Empire of Charlemagne, the Turkish empire, the Sultanate of Egypt, and the Swiss and German free cities [...]. And those who live in those countries and praise the past more than the present may deceive themselves; but whoever is born in Italy and Greece [...] has good reason to find fault with his own and to praise the olden times [...].

If men's judgment is at fault upon the point whether the present age be better than the past [...], the judgment of old men of what they have seen in their youth and in their old age should not be false, inasmuch as they have equally seen both the one and the other. This would be true, if men at the different periods of their lives had the same wisdom and the same desires. But as the latter vary—though the times do not—those different periods cannot appear the same to men who have other desires, other delights, and other considerations in old age from what they had in youth. For as men when they age lose their strength, whilst their wisdom and prudence improve, so the same things that in youth appeared to them supportable and good, will of necessity, when they have grown old, seem to them insupportable and bad; and when they should blame their own wisdom they find fault with the times. Moreover, as human desires are insatiable (because nature has given men the faculty of being able to, and of wishing to, desire everything whilst fortune has given them the faculty of achieving only a few things), this gives rise to a constant discontent in the human mind and a dissatisfaction for the things we possess;[3] and it is this which makes us decry the present, praise the past, and desire the future, and all this without any reasonable motive [...].

1.3.2 TIMES, THE CONDITIONS OF THINGS, WISDOM, AND FORTUNE

In this draft of a letter that was probably never sent, Machiavelli touches upon a crucial issue that he will elaborate years later in the Prince *(cf. 1.3.3) and the*

---

[2] Good or bad customs, as stated above. These adjectives, just as the nouns 'customs' and *virtù*, are to be understood in their political meaning.
[3] Cf. 1.2.2 (*Discourses* I, 37).

Discourses *(cf. 3.4.5), i.e. the problem of the relations between the individual and the context in which he acts. Success is explained in terms of a coincidence between one's ways and the nature of the situation in which one finds oneself. Not only can human beings not modify the natural course of things, but they cannot even adapt themselves to the situation, when the latter is not propitious, because they cannot alter their natural inclinations and predispositions.*

Letter to Giovan Battista Soderini, 13–21 September 1506

[...] The same thing results from different methods of proceeding, and many who work in different ways get to the same end [...].[4] Lorenzo de' Medici disarmed the people in order to hold Florence; Giovanni Bentivoglio armed them in order to hold Bologna; the Vitelli in Città di Castello and the present Duke of Urbino[5] in his province demolished their fortresses in order to hold those states; Count Francesco [Sforza] and many others built fortresses to make themselves secure of their states [...]. Many who think over and measure everything fail in their designs [...]. Such men as those mentioned above and many others who can be cited on this subject have been seen and can be seen every day either obtaining kingdoms or taming them or being driven out of them, according to circumstances; and sometimes the mode of proceeding that was praised when it was bringing gain is reviled when it causes loss [...]. But why it is that opposite methods lead, equally, sometimes to success and sometimes to failure, I do not know, but I should be very glad to know. Still, in order to get your opinion, I shall be so bold as to state mine.

I believe that as nature has given men different faces, so she has given them different temperaments and imaginations.[6] From this comes that every man conducts himself according to his temperament and imagination. And because on the other hand the times vary and the situations are different, one man's efforts result just as he wishes them to, and he is successful whose mode of proceeding finds a correspondence with the time; and, quite the other way, he is unsuccessful whose actions do not find such a correspondence with the time and the situation. Hence it can very well happen that two men, working quite differently, come to the same end, because each of them can find a correspondence with the situation in which he finds himself, for there are as many types of conditions as there are provinces and states. But because times and things both in general and in particular change frequently, and men do not change their imagination or their mode of proceeding, it comes about that the

---

[4] Cf. 1.3.3 *(Prince XXV)*.   [5] Guidobaldo di Montefeltro.
[6] Cf. *Prince XXV, Discourses* III, 8 and 3.4.5.

same man has at one period good fortune, and at another bad fortune. And certainly anyone wise enough to understand the times and the conditions of things, and who fits himself to them, would always have good fortune, or would always protect himself from misfortune, and it would seem to be true that the wise man rules the stars and the fates. But a man so wise as this is never found, because in the first place men are short-sighted and in the second cannot command their temperament;[7] as a result fortune varies, and controls men, and keeps them under her yoke [...].

1.3.3 WHAT CAN—AND CANNOT—BE DONE ABOUT FORTUNE

Machiavelli entertains two different views on the role of Fortune in human affairs. The first finds its classical statement in the excerpt from the Prince *below: Fortune is the arbiter of half of our actions, the other half remaining in our hands. Hence the importance of taking precautions well in advance. Such a perspective entails an immediate practical consequence: we should never give in to events; on the contrary, we should react and fight back. The second view— expressed in the* Discourses—*is almost fatalistic: you succeed or fail independently of what you do. Here Fortune looks like a force that cannot be resisted. Yet, even in this case, we should not adopt a passive attitude, for we can never know in advance what Fortune reserves for us.*

Prince XXV

I am well aware that many have held and still hold the opinion, that the affairs of this world are so controlled by Fortune and by God that human wisdom and foresight cannot modify them; that, in fact, men can do nothing about it, and that they might just as well come to the conclusion that they should not even make much of an effort, but yield to Fortune [...].

In reflecting upon this at times, I am myself in some measure inclined to that belief; nevertheless, as our free will is not entirely destroyed, I judge that it may be assumed as true that Fortune to the extent of one half is the arbiter of our actions, but that she permits us to direct the other half or so ourselves.[8] I compare Fortune to one of those swollen rivers which, when they rage, overflow the plains, tear up the trees and buildings, and sweep the earth from

---

[7] Cf. 1.3.3 (*Prince* XXV) and 3.4.5.

[8] In a similar vein, *Discourses* I, 4; II, 30; and 4.3.1.

one place and deposits it in another. Every one flees before the flood, and yields to its fury, unable to resist it. Although those rivers do such things, one could nevertheless provide against their overflow by dykes and walls when they are in their ordinary condition, so that when they rise they would flow either in the channel thus provided for it, or that at any rate their violence would not be entirely unchecked, nor their effects prove so injurious. It is the same with Fortune, who displays her power where there is no organized *virtù* to resist her and directs her blows where she knows that there are no walls or dikes to contain her [. . .].

We see a prince succeed one day, and brought to ruin the next, without his nature or any aspect of his personality being changed. I believe this results mainly from the causes which have been discussed at length above;[9] namely, that the prince who relies entirely upon fortune will come to ruin as fortune varies. I believe, further, that the prince who finds a correspondence between his mode of proceeding and the character of the situation will be prosperous; and in the same way will he be failed, if the situation diverges from his mode of conduct. For we see men proceed in various ways to attain the end they aim at, that is glory and riches: the one with circumspection, the other with rashness; one with violence, another with cunning; one with patience, and another with impetuosity; and all may succeed in their different ways. We also see that, of two men equally prudent, the one accomplishes his designs, whilst the other fails; and in the same way we see two men succeed equally well by two entirely different methods, the one being prudent and the other rash; which is due to nothing else than the character of the situation, which either conforms to their mode of proceeding or not [. . .]. If one man who acts with caution and patience finds himself in such a time and situation that reward his conduct, he will succeed; but if these change, he will come to ruin, because he has not changed his conduct accordingly. Nor is there any man so sagacious that he will always know how to adapt himself to such change of times and circumstances; for men do not readily deviate from the course to which their nature inclines them; and, moreover, if they have generally been prosperous by following one course, they cannot persuade themselves that it would be well to depart from it. Thus the cautious man, when the moment comes for him to strike a bold blow, will not know how to do it, and thence will he fail; for if one could change one's own nature according to the times and circumstances, fortune would not change [. . .].[10]

[Pope] Julius [II], then, achieved by his impetuous moves what no other Pontiff could have accomplished with all possible human prudence [. . .]. The shortness of his life saved him from experiencing any reverses; for if times had supervened that would have made it necessary for him to proceed with caution

---

[9] *Prince* VII.   [10] Cf. 1.3.2 and 3.4.5.

and prudence, he would assuredly have come to ruin; for he could never have deviated from the course to which his nature inclined him.

I conclude, then, inasmuch as fortune is changeable and men persist obstinately in their own ways, one will be successful only so long as one's ways coincide with those of fortune; and whenever these differ, one will fail. I judge impetuosity to be better than caution; for Fortune is a woman, and if you wish to master her, you must strike and beat her, and you will see that she allows herself to be more easily vanquished by the impetuous than by those who proceed coldly. For, as a woman, she ever favours the young, because they are less cautious and more impetuous, and command her with greater audacity.[11]

Discourses II, 29

[According to] Livy [. . .], 'fortune thus blinds the minds of men when she does not wish them to resist her impending power'. This conclusion could not be truer; therefore, in general, men who live in great adversity or prosperity deserve less blame or less praise. For it will most of the time be found that they have been brought to their ruin or their greatness by some great occasion offered by heaven, which has given them, or has deprived them of, the opportunity to conduct themselves with *virtù*.[12]

When fortune wishes to effect some great result, she selects for her instrument a man of such strength of mind and *virtù* that he will recognize the opportunity which she offers him. And thus, in the same way, when she wishes to effect some great ruin, she places men at the head who hasten such ruin. And if there be anyone who could prevent that ruin, either she has him killed, or she deprives him of all means of doing any good. The instances cited by Livy show clearly how fortune, by way of elevating Rome and carrying her to that greatness which she attained, deemed it necessary to strike her [. . .] but did not wish to ruin her entirely.[13] And therefore we see how she caused Camillus to be exiled, but not killed; how she caused the city of Rome to be taken by the Gauls, but not the Capitoline citadel; how she caused the Romans to do nothing well for the protection of the city, whilst in their preparations for the defence of the citadel they omitted no good provision. To permit Rome to be taken, fortune caused the greater part of the troops who were beaten on the

---

[11] Machiavelli expresses his preference for 'impetuosity' also in *Discourses* III, 44.

[12] At the opening of his *Life of Castruccio Castracani* Machiavelli writes: 'Being fortune desirous of showing to the world that great men owe much to her and little to wisdom, she begins to show her hand when wisdom can really play no role [i.e. right from their birth]: thus all success must be attributed to her'. See also 2.1.2.

[13] The episode mentioned here took place in 390 BC, as Rome was attacked by the Gauls.

River Allia to go to Veii, and thus cut off all means for saving the city. And yet, whilst doing all this, she prepared everything for the recovery of Rome, for she caused an entire Roman army to go to Veii, and Camillus to be exiled to Ardea, so that, under the command of a general untarnished by the disgrace of defeat and intact in his reputation, a large body of troops might be brought together for the recapture of the city.

I might cite some modern examples in confirmation of the views I have advanced, but do not deem it necessary, as that of the Romans suffices. I repeat, then, as an incontrovertible truth, proved by all history, that men may second fortune, but not oppose her; they may weave her warps, but not break them.[14] Yet men should never despair on that account; for, not knowing her aims, which she pursues by devious and unknown ways, they must always be hopeful, and hoping on, never yield to despair, whatever situation or troubles may befall them.

---

[14] Fortune provides the warp, a set of yarns arranged lengthways on a loom, that cannot be broken but can only be completed with horizontal threads. In other words, Fortune sets the stage and decides the direction that things will take; human beings can only carry out what has been initiated by her.

Part II

The International Context:
Fear and Self-Help

2.1

Survival and Security

2.1.1 ONLY FORCE MAKES STATES KEEP THEIR WORD

In early 1503, Florence was in a very delicate position: while her French ally was engaged in the Kingdom of Naples, Duke Valentino, at the peak of his power, had practically surrounded Tuscany, Lucca and Genoa were helping Pisa in her resistance to Florentine efforts, and Venice was more hostile than ever. The government intended to raise new taxes for military readiness, but the general mood was against a heavier fiscal burden. The speech was probably given by Gonfalonier Soderini, and the appropriation was eventually passed in late March. The binomial force–prudence, just as the sharp distinction between the domestic setting and the international setting, will be further developed years later in Machiavelli's major works.

Words to Be Spoken on the Law for Appropriating Money, after Giving a Little Introduction and Excuse (1503)

All the cities that have ever, at any time, been ruled by an absolute prince, by aristocrats, or by the people [...], have relied for their own defence on a combination of force with prudence; alone, prudence is not enough, and force does not make a policy successful, and, even if it does, it cannot maintain what has been achieved. Force and prudence are thus the very nerve of all states that have ever existed and that always will exist. And if one has observed how kingdoms have succeeded each other, and how provinces and cities have become ruined, one has seen that all this has been caused by nothing but the want of arms or wisdom [...].

Without armed forces, cities are not preserved but meet their end. Such an end is either by destruction or servitude. You have come close to both, last year, and you will again, if you do not change your mind [...]. And if you argued, 'What need do we have for armed forces? We are under the protection of the King of France! Our enemies have been eliminated![1] And Duke Valentino has no reason for injuring us', one would reply that your view could not be more reckless, because every city, every state must consider as enemies all those who can hope to seize what belongs to it and against whom it cannot defend itself. Never was there a wise princedom or republic that was willing to keep its own territory at the discretion of others, or that, upon doing so, thought it held it securely [...].

Let us examine our situation thoroughly. Let us start by looking at home. You will see that you are unarmed, and that your subjects are disloyal as you experienced a few months ago.[2] It is understandable that they should be so, because men cannot and must not be faithful servants of a master by whom they can be neither defended nor governed [...].

Now leave home, and look at those whom you have around you; you will see that you are caught between two or three cities that wish less for their own life than for your death.[3] Move a bit further, leave Tuscany and consider all of Italy; you will see that it is revolving under the King of France, the Venetians, the Pope, and Duke Valentino. Start with the King. Here it is necessary to tell the truth, and I intend to do so. Either the King will run into no other impediment or constraint in Italy than what you offer—in which case there is no remedy, because all forces, all measures will not save you; or he will run into some impediments, as seems to be the case,[4] and then a remedy may or may not be there, depending on what you will or will not. The remedy consists of organizing your military forces in such a way that in all his decisions he will have to take you into consideration, just as he does with the others of Italy; of not encouraging, by remaining unarmed, somebody powerful to ask the King to leave you to him as a prey; of not inducing the King to count you among the unimportant, but doing such things that he will be forced to respect you and that no one will entertain the idea of subjugating you. Look at the Venetians now. This will not be much trouble: everyone knows their ambition, that you owe them 180,000 ducats,[5] that they are waiting for the right opportunity, and that it is better to spend that money to wage war on them rather than give it to them so that they will injure you with it. Let's now move to the Pope and his Duke. There is little need to comment on this: everyone knows of what sort their nature and appetite are, and of what kind their ways, and what faith can be given or received. I will only say that no agreement has been made with them yet [...]. But let us assume that a deal should be made tomorrow: I have told you that only the

---

[1] In particular, Vitellozzo Vitelli, killed by Duke Valentino a few months earlier (cf. 1.1.2 and 4.4.4, ft. 101).

[2] For example, the rebellion of Arezzo in 1502.

[3] Siena, Pisa, and Lucca.

[4] Louis XII was fighting against Spain in the Kingdom of Naples while the Emperor and the Swiss challenged the French occupation of Milan.

[5] Cf. the Introduction to 1.1.1.

rulers who cannot harm you will be your friends, and I am telling you again; for among private individuals laws, contracts, and agreements make them keep faith, but among sovereigns only force does [...].[6]

Many of you must remember when Constantinople was taken by the Turks. That Emperor saw his ruin coming.[7] Not being able to take proper measures with his regular revenues, he called upon his citizens, and showed them the dangers and the remedies; and they made fun of him. The siege came. Those citizens who earlier had underestimated the warnings of their lord, as soon as they heard within their walls the sound of artillery and the surging fury of the army of their enemies, rushed crying to the Emperor with their bosoms full of money. But he chased them away, saying: 'Go and die with that money, for you have not wished to live without it'.

But there is no need to go to Greece for examples, having them in Florence. In September 1500, Duke Valentino left Rome with his armies; nobody knew whether he would enter Tuscany or the Romagna. Being unprepared, the entire city was in suspense, and everyone prayed to God for time. But as soon as he showed us his back and moved towards Pesaro [...] a mood of rash confidence prevailed, so that it proved impossible to convince you to vote in favour of any appropriation [...] until when, gathered in this place on 26 April 1501, you heard about the loss of Faenza [...]. Had the appropriation been passed six months earlier, it would have been effective; but having been passed six days earlier, there was little it could do for your safety. In fact, on 4 May you heard that the enemy army was in Firenzuola [...] and you saw your houses burned down, your property plundered, your subjects slain and led prisoner [...]. And those who, six months earlier, had not wished to pay twenty ducats, must now pay 200 [...]. As you see the sun, you do not believe that it would ever rain, as it happens now. You do not consider that Duke Valentino can be with his army in your state in eight days; the Venetians, in two. You do not consider that the King of France is still entangled with the Swiss in Lombardy, that he has not settled things yet either with the Emperor or with the King of Spain and that he finds himself in a difficult position in the Kingdom of Naples. You do not see your weakness, as things stand now, or the mutations of fortune.

Other people often grow wise with their neighbours' dangers; you do not, with your own; nor do you trust yourselves, nor do you realize how much time you are wasting and have wasted. Such time you will regret again, and to no avail, unless you change your mind. For I tell you that fortune does not change her verdict when there is no change in the mode of proceeding; nor do the heavens wish to, nor can they, sustain something that intends to fall anyway.

---

[6] In a similar vein, 2.2.5 (*Florentine Histories* VIII, 22), 1.2.1 (*Prince* XVIII), 2.1.3 (*Discourses* III, 42), 3.4.6 and 4.4.4.

[7] In 1453. The last Byzantine Emperor was Constantine XI.

This I cannot believe is the case, seeing that you are free Florentines and resting your liberty in your own hands. I believe that you will treat that liberty with the respect that those who are born free and wish to live free have always had.

2.1.2 SECURITY IS MORE IMPORTANT THAN GLORY

Castruccio Castracani (1281–1328), Ghibellin leader and lord of Lucca, is transformed by Machiavelli into an ideal prince: the cunning of Duke Valentino and the military competence of Fabrizio Colonna (the main character in the Art of War*) are blended into one profile. A daring, brave, ruthless, gallant man, Castruccio keeps expanding his dominions, until death suddenly strikes him. As he is about to die, his last words to Paolo, his pupil, reveal that he regrets not having looked for less glory and more security, for the state he leaves to him is vulnerable and shaky, its greatness and size notwithstanding.*

Life of Castruccio Castracani of Lucca (1520)

[...] But fortune, growing envious of the glory of Castruccio, took away his life just at the time when she should have preserved it, and thus ruined all those plans which for so long a time he had worked to carry into effect, and in the successful prosecution of which nothing but death could have stopped him. Castruccio was in the thick of the battle the whole of the day; and when the end of it came, although fatigued and overheated, he stood at the gate of Fucecchio to wait for his men on their return from victory and personally welcome and thank them [...]. Here Castruccio stood exposed to a wind which often rises at midday on the banks of the River Arno, and which is often very unhealthy; from this he took a chill, of which he thought nothing, as he was accustomed to such troubles; but it was the cause of his death. On the following night he was attacked with high fever, which increased so rapidly that the doctors saw it must prove fatal. Castruccio, realizing this, called Paolo Guinigi to him, and addressed him as follows: 'If I could have believed, my son, that fortune would have cut me off in the midst of the path which was leading to that glory which I intended to achieve with all my successes, I should have laboured less, and I should have left you, if a smaller state, at least with fewer enemies and less hostility. For, being content with the governorships of Lucca and Pisa, I would neither have subjugated the Pistoians, nor outraged the Florentines with so many injuries. On the contrary, after making both these peoples my friends, I would have led, if not a longer, at least a quieter life, and have left you a state without a doubt smaller, but one more secure and solid. But fortune, who insists upon being the arbiter of all human affairs,[8] did not endow me with sufficient judgment to recognize this from the first, nor the time to surmount it [. . .].

'Thus I leave you a vast territory, of which I am well content; but as I leave it to you feeble and unsettled, I am deeply concerned. You have the city of Lucca, which will never rest contented under your government. You have Pisa, where the men are of nature changeable and unreliable; and the Pisans, although they are accustomed to be held sometimes in subjection, will ever disdain to serve under a Lucchese. Pistoia is also disloyal to you, she being divided into factions and incensed against our family by reason of the wrongs recently inflicted upon her. You have for neighbours the offended Florentines, injured by us in a thousand ways, but not utterly destroyed, who will hail the news of my death with more delight than they would the acquisition of all Tuscany. In the Emperor and in the princes of Milan you can place no reliance, for they are far distant, slow, and their help is very long in coming. Therefore, you have no hope in anything but in your own abilities, and in the memory of my *virtù*, and in the prestige which this latest victory has brought you; which, if you know how to use it with prudence, will assist you to come to terms with the Florentines, who, as they are suffering under this great defeat, should be inclined to listen to you. And whereas I have sought to make them my enemies, because I believed that their hostility would conduce to my power and glory, you have every inducement to make friends of them, because their alliance will bring you advantages and security. It is of the greatest importance in this world that a man should know himself, and be able to measure the strength of both his mind and his state; and he who knows that he has not a genius for fighting must learn how to govern by the arts of peace' [. . .].

2.1.3 ALL MEANS ARE ACCEPTABLE WHEN THE SURVIVAL OF THE STATE IS AT STAKE

When it comes to state survival, honour and dishonour, glory and shame, justice and injustice simply have no place. More particularly, promises that have been extorted by force will not—and must not—be kept. The well-known episode of the Caudine Forks (events take place during the Second Samnite War, in 321 BC) is a vivid illustration of this basic principle of raison d'état.

Discourses III, 41–2

41. As stated above,[9] the Roman consul and his army were shut in by the Samnites, who proposed to him the most ignominious conditions, such as to

---

[8] In 1.3.3, however, it is argued that fortune is the arbiter of one half of human actions.
[9] *Discourses* III, 40.

pass under a yoke, and to send the army back to Rome disarmed; which filled the consuls with consternation and the army with despair. But Legate Lentulus said, that for the purpose of saving the country no propositions ought to be rejected. The safety of Rome depended upon that army, and he maintained that it ought to be saved at any price; and that their country was well defended no matter how it was defended, whether by ignominious or honourable means. For, if the army were saved, Rome would have the opportunity to wipe out that disgrace; but if the army were lost, even if they died gloriously, Rome and her liberties would also be lost. This advice of Lentulus was followed. And the case deserves to be noted and imitated by every citizen who finds himself called upon to counsel his country. For where the very safety of the country depends entirely upon the resolution to be taken, no consider-ations of justice or injustice, mercy or cruelty, nor of glory or of shame, should be allowed to prevail. In fact, putting all other considerations aside, one must follow the decision that will save the life and liberty of the country [...].

42. When the consuls returned to Rome with their troops disarmed and the insult to which they had been subjected at the Caudine Forks, Consul Spurius Posthumius was the first who said in the senate that the peace agreed to at Caudium ought not to be observed. He maintained that this peace did not bind the Roman people, but only himself individually and those others who had assisted in concluding it. And, therefore, if the people wished to free them-selves from all its obligations, they need only send him and the others back as prisoners to the Samnites. He urged this advice so persistently that the senate agreed to it, and sending him and the others as prisoners to the Samnites, protested against the validity of the peace. And fortune so favoured Posthu-mius in this matter that the Samnites declined to keep him, so that when he returned to Rome he was more honoured there for the defeat he had suffered, than was Pontius by the Samnites for the victory he had gained.

This case suggests two points for reflection: first, that one may acquire glory in any action. In victory it follows as a matter of course, and in defeat it may be acquired, either by showing that it was not due to any fault of his, or by promptly doing some brave act that neutralizes the effects of the defeat. Second, that there is no disgrace in disregarding promises that have been exacted by force. Promises touching public affairs, and which have been made under constraint, will always be disregarded when that constraint no longer exists, and this involves no dishonour for those who break them. History offers us many examples of this, and even in the present times we have daily instances of it. Not only do princes pay no attention to pledges which they have been forced to give, when that force has ceased to exist, but they frequently disregard equally all other promises as well, when the motives that induced them no longer prevail.[10] Whether such conduct be praiseworthy

---

[10] Cf. 2.1.1, fn. 6.

or not, or whether princes should follow such proceedings, has been so fully discussed in our treatise of *The Prince*, that we will not touch upon that question any further here.[11]

2.1.4 THE ANTAGONISM OF OPPOSING FORCES

In the Spring of 1513, the French, allied with the Venetians, try to take the duchy of Milan once more. On 6 June, they are severely defeated next to Novara by the Swiss, who have been holding Milan as a protectorate since 1512. In his effort to assess the consequence of this new French setback and anticipate the terms of a possible settlement, Machiavelli engages in an analysis of the international situation in which considerations of fear and security play a major role. The general arrangement he has in mind would satisfy some and dissatisfy others; it is the pressure exerted by the latter that, paradoxical as it may sound, would bring about stability for the system as a whole (see also 4.1.2).

Letter to Francesco Vettori, 20 June 1513

[...] You have seen the result of the King of France's campaign in Italy [...]. And since I believe that a prudent man must always think about what might harm him and anticipate things well in advance,[12] and second what is good and oppose in time what is bad, I have put myself in the Pope's shoes and I have thoroughly examined what I would fear now and the remedies that I would adopt [...].

If I were the Pope, I would wait and see until an agreement is reached according to which all arms, or most of them, would be deposed. I would not feel secure from the Spaniards, should they be less constrained in Italy than they are now; or from the Swiss, should they not fear France or Spain; or from anybody else who happened to be powerful in Italy. On the contrary, I would not fear the King of France, as long as he stayed on the other side of the Alps or entered Lombardy again in agreement with me. And reflecting upon the current situation, I would be concerned about both a new settlement and a new war. A new war, which would drive me back to the fear I felt only a few days ago, is not likely unless the King of France achieves a great victory against the English.[13] As for the settlement, I would be concerned if the King of France

---

[11] Cf. 1.2.1 (*Prince* XVIII).

[12] 'When the evils that arise [...] are seen far ahead [...] then they are easily remedied' (*Prince* III).

[13] Prior to the Battle of Novara, the Pope was weary of France. Now, he must fear Spain—the only great power left in Italy—and the Swiss. A certain balance might be restored only if France defeated England beyond the Alps. But Louis XII will be beaten again at Guinegate, in August.

reached an agreement with the King of England or the King of Spain without me [...]. While a deal with England is hard, a deal with Spain is possible and reasonable [...], for the following reasons. I have always believed [...] that Spain would like [...] to see the King of France out of Italy, provided it is the King of Spain himself, with his own armies and reputation, who drives him out. I have never believed [...] that the victory the Swiss achieved over France last year pleased the King of Spain much.[14] This view of mine is based upon what reason shows—the Pope and the Swiss would be too powerful in Italy— and upon information—I was told that the King of Spain was complaining about the Pope as well, blaming him for having given too much power to the Swiss. And I believe that this was one of the reasons why he made a truce with the King of France.[15] Now, if he disliked that Swiss victory, I guess he likes this second victory even less, because he sees that he is alone in Italy; that the Swiss enjoy a great reputation here; that the Pope is young, rich, and understandably eager for glory and willing to prove himself no less worthy than his predecessors; and that the Pope's brothers and nephews do not have a state of their own. The King of Spain, therefore, must rightly fear the Pope who, in alliance with the Swiss, can seize his possessions; if the Pope were willing to do so, not many impediments would keep him from it. And the safest countermeasure for the King of Spain is a deal with the King of France, whereby the former would easily gain Navarre,[16] and the latter would be given a territory hard to defend, due to its proximity to the Swiss;[17] the Swiss would be deprived of their easy access to Italy and the Pope would be deprived, in turn, of the opportunity to avail himself of them. In light of the situation in which he finds himself now, the King of France is not likely to reject such a deal; in fact, he should ask for it himself.

Thus, if I were the Pope, and if I believed that a deal like this could be made, I should want either to thwart it or to promote it myself. And it seems to me that under the current conditions it would be easy to conclude a peace between the King of France, the King of Spain, the Pope and the Venetians. I am leaving out the Swiss, the Emperor, and the King of England because in my view the latter will follow the King of Spain's lead; I do not see how the Emperor might be in agreement with the Venetians, or how the King of France might find a compromise with the Swiss [...]. Such an arrangement would be advantageous for all four of them: the Venetians should be satisfied with Verona, Vicenza, Padua, and Treviso; the King of France with Lombardy; the Pope with his own state; Spain with the Kingdom of Naples. Such a settlement would harm only the Duke of Milan, who is a puppet,[18] the Swiss

---

[14] June 1512.   [15] This is the truce of 1 April 1513, debated in 1.1.3.

[16] In 1512 Ferdinand had seized, by surprise, the Iberian part of the Kingdom of Navarre.

[17] The duchy of Milan.

[18] Massimiliano Sforza, placed as a duke by the Swiss in 1512.

and the Emperor. The latter two would be left as a thorn in the side of the King of France, and he, in order to defend himself, would always have to be ready for war against them, which would make all the others secure from him, and each of them would keep an eye on the other. Thus, I see a good deal of security and ease in this agreement, because the parties would share a common fear of the Germans,[19] which would be the glue that would make them stick together, and because none of them would have reason to complain, except for the Venetians,[20] who would have to bear [...].

[19] The Swiss and the Emperor combined.
[20] In this arrangement, the Romagna—an object of Venetian expansionism—would remain in the Pope's hands.

2.2

'Fear Is the Greatest Master'

2.2.1 THE POPES

The State of the Church was established in the first half of the eighth century. Moving from its core, that is the duchy of Rome, it soon extended to the Exarchate and the Pentapolis thanks to the Frankish kings' donations. On various occasions—the last time during the fifteenth century—the popes tried to transform a conglomerate of fiefs and cities into a solid principality, always to no avail. Their intrinsic weakness, as well as their geopolitical location in Central Italy, made them constantly fear that Northern and Southern Italy might be united under a single ruler. The result of such a fear was the policy described below.

Discourses I, 12

[...] A country can never be united and happy, except when it obeys wholly one government, whether a republic or a monarchy, as is the case in France and in Spain; and the sole cause why Italy is not in the same condition, and is not governed by either one republic or one prince, is the Church; for having acquired and held a temporal dominion, she has never had sufficient power or political ability to enable her to achieve undisputed primacy and make herself sole sovereign of all Italy. And on the other hand she has not been so feeble that the fear of losing her temporal power prevented her from calling in the aid of a foreign power to defend her against such others as had become too powerful in Italy; as was seen in former days by many experiences, when through the intervention of Charlemagne she drove out the Langobards, who were masters of nearly all Italy;[1] and when in our times she crushed the power of the Venetians by the aid of France,[2] and afterwards with the assistance of the Swiss drove out, in turn, the French.[3] The Church, then, not having been

---

[1] In the second half of the eighth century.
[2] The League of Cambrai (1508).   [3] The Holy League (1511).

powerful enough to be able to master all Italy, nor having permitted any other power to do so, has been the reason Italy has never been able to unite under one head, but has always remained under a number of princes and lords, which has occasioned her so many dissensions and so much weakness that she has become a prey not only to powerful foreigners, but of whoever chooses to assail her [. . .].

Florentine Histories II, 10

[. . .] As the popes always feared anyone who had attained great power in Italy, even though he had acquired it by the support of the Church, so they fought to abate that power, which gave rise to frequent disturbances and consequent changes. For the fear of a powerful state or individual made the pontiffs raise up a weak one to keep the other in check; and when the one had become powerful in turn, they again feared him, and sought to put him down. This made them take the Kingdom of Naples from Manfred and give it to Charles [of Anjou];[4] this, in turn, made them fear Charles and seek to bring him to ruin. Pope Nicholas III, influenced by these considerations, laboured so effectually that Charles was deprived of the government of Tuscany by means of the Emperor [. . .].[5]

2.2.2 FRANCE

This excerpt is taken from what was probably a comprehensive report to the Florentine government written by Machiavelli after his third and fourth missions to France, in 1510 and 1511, respectively. The part on French foreign relations corresponds to the situation in 1511, prior to the creation of the Holy League (October), and this is why the overall position of France sounds so safe.

An Account of the Affairs of France (1511–12)

[. . .] France fears the English quite a lot, because she remembers the incursions and devastations by the latter in the realm; so that the very name of the English is a terror to the people, who do not realize that France is nowadays in a very different position from what she was in those times. For she is armed,

---

[4] Manfred, illegitimate son of Frederick II, pursued the traditional anti-papal policy of the House of Swabia. In 1266 he was defeated and killed by Charles, who had been called upon by Pope Clement IV.

[5] Charles was also imperial Vicar of Tuscany.

experienced in war, and united, and holds those very provinces on which the English relied, such as the duchies of Brittany and Bourgogne. Moreover, the English are no longer disciplined, for it is a long while since they have had a war, so that none of the people now living have ever seen an enemy's face; and then there is no one save the Archduke[6] who would be willing to ally with them on the Continent.

The French would be much afraid of the Spaniards on account of their sagacity and vigilance. But every time that the King of Spain would attack France, he would have to do it at great disadvantage; for from that point in his kingdom from which his troops would have to start to the passes of the Pyrenees which stretch into France, the distance is so great and the country so sterile that if the French make a stand at such passes and at those towards Perpignan or Guyenne, the enemy's army would be disorganized, if not from want of reinforcements, at least from want of provisions which would have to be brought from a great distance [...].

The French do not fear the Flemish, whose country is so cold that they cannot raise sufficient provisions, and particularly grain and wine, which they have to procure from Burgundy, Picardy, and some other provinces of France. Moreover, the people of Flanders live on their manufactures, and they sell their goods and merchandise at the French fairs in Lyons and Paris [...]. Thus, whenever their trade with France was interrupted, they would have no other market; so that not only could they not purchase provisions, but their products would remain on their hands. Therefore the Flemish will never have war with France, unless they are forced to it.

The Swiss are much feared by the French, owing to their close proximity, and the sudden attacks they can launch, against which, owing to their rapidity, it is impossible to provide in time. These incursions of the Swiss, however, are mere predatory raids; for as they have neither artillery nor horses, and as the strong places which the French hold near the frontier are well supplied with munitions, the Swiss are not able to make much progress [...].

There is nothing to be feared from the side towards Italy, for the Apennine Mountains and the fortified cities the French hold at their base[7] would arrest anyone who wished to attack the Kingdom of France. And the country behind them is so unproductive that they would starve; or they would have to leave these strongholds behind them, which would be great folly; or they would have to go to work and take these fortresses. [... In addition,] there is not in all Italy a prince capable of assaulting France, and Italy herself is not united, as she was in the time of the Romans.

On the south side, France has nothing to fear, due to the sea in whose ports there are always vessels enough, belonging to the King and to the barons, to be

---

[6] Charles of Habsburg, the future Emperor Charles V.
[7] In Provence and the Dauphiné.

able to defend that part of the kingdom from any unexpected attack; against a premeditated attack there is always time to take measures, for whoever contemplates it needs time to make the necessary preparations and arrangements, and this will quickly become known to everybody. And all these provinces are generally provided with a garrison of men-at-arms,[8] for the greater security [...].

2.2.3 SPAIN

In March 1514, France and Spain signed a new truce. This alarmed the Pope, who tried a rapprochement with France, in order to prevent the two great powers from arriving at such an arrangement over Lombardy that would lead to the primacy of Spain in Italy. In this letter, Machiavelli analyses the predicaments in which Spain finds herself at this particular time, including her shaky relations with the Pope, the Emperor, and the King of France.

Letter to Francesco Vettori, 16 April 1514

[...] In my view, the King of Spain [...] is currently in the midst of many difficulties. I do not believe he finds the present arrangement of Italy congenial, nor can he tolerate the remarkable power of the Church and the Swiss, because he has more to fear for the state of Naples now than when the French were around.[9] At that time, the Pope was a buffer between Milan and Naples, and he could not allow the French to take over the Kingdom of Naples lest he be caught in the middle; but now nobody stands in between the Pope, the Swiss and the King of Spain. In addition, I do not believe he finds the war on the other side of the Alps congenial, because warfare cannot always end in a stalemate, as it did last year. In the long run, the King of France will either win or lose; in neither case will Spain be left secure. And if a third case comes up in which they [the belligerents] get tired of fighting each other, they might all turn against the source of their troubles, because it is to be believed that his snares are known to all and have begun to generate hatred and annoyance in the minds of his friends and enemies alike.

Therefore, since he does not find the current situation congenial, he must figure out how to change it. If he wants to reshape the Italian affairs so as to increase his own security, he must expel the Swiss from Milan without replacing them with the French. In doing so, he faces two problems; first, how can he expel the Swiss if not with French help; second, whom does he

---

[8] Fully armoured men on armoured horses.   [9] From 1501 to 1504.

have to place there? Going back to the first point, I believe that the King of France will never agree to come down to Lombardy in full force unless he is to stay as master. And even if there was a treaty according to which the King of France should come down or should hand Milan over to [...] others, I do not see how he, being more powerful, could comply with the agreement, unless he is a fool, nor do I see how the King of Spain could trust such a promise. Everybody will agree that the Swiss cannot be taken out of Milan without French help [...], given who they are, where they are, how many they are, and the awareness they have developed of their own strength. As to the second problem, I do not believe that the King of Spain would be willing to hand Milan over to the Church, or, even less so, to the Venetians; for himself, he cannot take it. He might hand it, according to some, to his grandson, which sounds quite reasonable; however, there would be no security at all for him in such an arrangement, because for the time being he would have to give Milan to the Emperor;[10] and should the Emperor become the ruler of Milan, he would immediately desire to rule all of Italy, and he would start with Naples, to which the Germans have more ancient claims than the Spaniards [...].

2.2.4 FLORENCE

Driven by her desire to take Lucca, Florence has suddenly to cope with an unexpected fear. The latter prevails, 'as is always the case'. Events take place in 1437; for the general context, see 4.2.2 (Florentine Histories V, 10).

Florentine Histories V, 12–13

12. The Florentine army [...] after doing infinite damage to the country [...] went into camp at Nozzano;[11] so that the people of Lucca, hemmed in on all sides and deprived of all hopes of succour, should surrender under the pressure of hunger [...]. The Lucchese, as was most natural, finding themselves so closely pressed, had recourse to the Duke of Milan [Filippo Maria Visconti] [... and he], adding to his inveterate hatred of the Florentines the new obligations he owed to the Lucchese, and being above all desirous that the Florentines should not aggrandize their power by so important a conquest, resolved to send a large force into Tuscany, or to make so vigorous an attack upon the Venetians that the Florentines would be compelled to desist from

---

[10] The Archduke Ferdinand II of Habsburg, born in 1503, grandson of the King of Spain, was not of age yet. His other grandfather was Emperor Maximilian.

[11] About 4 miles west of Lucca.

their attempt upon Lucca for the sake of going to the assistance of the Venetians.[12]

13. [...] This made the Florentines begin to lose the hope of taking Lucca; and in order to keep the Duke occupied in Lombardy, they urged the Venetians to attack him with all their forces. But these were also alarmed because their commander, the Marquis of Mantua,[13] had left them, and had entered the service of Duke Filippo. Finding themselves thus as it were disarmed, they replied to the Florentines, that, far from being able to increase their efforts, they could hardly continue the war unless the Florentines sent them Count Francesco Sforza to command their army [...]. The Florentines considered it necessary that the war should be pushed with vigour in Lombardy; at the same time, they felt that their attack upon Lucca would prove in vain, should they be deprived of the Count; and they knew perfectly well that the Venetians made this demand for Sforza, not so much because he was indispensable to them as for the purpose of preventing them from succeeding in their attempt against Lucca [...]. The Florentines were thus agitated by two different feelings; the one the desire to possess Lucca, and the other the fear of war with the Duke of Milan. Fear, however, prevailed, as is always the case; and they consented that, after the capture of Nozzano, Count Sforza should go into Lombardy [...].

2.2.5 NAPLES

In 1478 war breaks out between Florence and the Pope, who is allied with the King of Naples. The King's son, the Duke of Calabria, invades Tuscany. Although Florence manages to sign a separate peace with Naples in March 1480, the terms of the agreement leave the King free to decide whether or not to return the territories seized in Tuscany. The Duke of Calabria is strongly tempted to keep what he has taken. But just like Florence in the previous excerpt, the King of Naples is now forced to give up a gain within reach under the pressure of an impending threat.

Florentine Histories VIII, 19–22

19. [...] Notwithstanding the treaty of peace, however, Alfonso, Duke of Calabria,[14] remained with his army at Siena, assigning as the reason for his

---

[12] Venice and Florence had been allies against Milan for a long time.

[13] Gian Francesco Gonzaga.

[14] The Duke of Calabria—in this case Alfonso—is the official title of the heir to the throne of the Kingdom of Naples.

not leaving the civil dissensions that agitated that city, [...] so that [...] he excited the suspicions not only of the Sienese, but also of the Florentines, that he desired to make himself prince of the city. Florence seemed to be powerless to prevent it, because of the new alliance with the King of Naples, and the resentment of the Pope and the Venetians [...]. But God, who in similar extreme circumstances has always taken the city of Florence under his special protection, caused an unexpected event, which gave the Pope and the King of Naples, as well as the Venetians, more important things to think of than the affairs of Florence.

20. [...] Whilst returning from Rhodes, a portion of Mehmed II's[15] fleet under Gedik Ahmed Pasha turned towards Valona; and either because he was tempted by the facility of the undertaking, or because his master had so ordered him, in sailing along the coast of Italy he suddenly landed 4,000 men and attacked the city of Otranto, which he quickly took and sacked, slaying all the inhabitants [August 1480]. Thereupon, with such means as were most conveniently at hand, he fortified himself in that city and port, and having collected a good body of cavalry he scoured and pillaged the surrounding country. The King of Naples, hearing of this attack and knowing the power of the assailant, despatched messengers in every direction to make it known, and to ask for help against the common enemy; and in the most pressing manner ordered the immediate return of the Duke of Calabria and his forces from Siena.

21. This attack of the Turks troubled Duke Alfonso and the rest of Italy just as much as it caused joy to the Florentine and the Sienese. The latter felt as though they had recovered their liberty, and the former that they had escaped from the danger of losing theirs. This opinion was confirmed by the regrets of the Duke at being obliged to leave Siena, for he blamed fortune for having, by an unexpected and untoward occurrence, deprived him of the opportunity of making himself master of Tuscany. This same event caused the Pope to change his course; and whilst before he would not listen to any Florentine ambassadors, he suddenly became so affable that he gave ear to anyone that would speak to him on the subject of a general peace [...].

22. The affairs with the Pope being thus settled, and the departure of the Duke of Calabria from Tuscany having relieved both Florence and Siena of all apprehensions of the King of Naples, the Florentines availed of the continuance of the war with the Turks to press King Ferdinand for the restitution of their castles, which the Duke of Calabria upon his withdrawal had left in the hands of the Sienese. The King feared lest the Florentines should leave him in his necessity and declare a fresh war against the Sienese, and thereby prevent him from obtaining the assistance he looked for from the Pope and the other

---

[15] Mehmed II the Conqueror was the Sultan of the Ottoman Empire.

Italian princes; he therefore consented to the restoration of the castles [March 1481], and thus bound the Florentines to him with new clauses of agreement. It is thus that force and necessity, and not written treaty obligations, cause princes to observe their faith [...].[16]

2.2.6 VENICE

Fear runs across Venice's history, from her birth to her rise, down to her decline. Fear was the force driving various peoples to found Venice, in the fifth century, and to consolidate the new city; fear, or better still, terror, was what Venice inspired to all at the peak of her power; and fear was the rationale behind the grand anti-Venetian coalition of 1508 that destroyed that power.

Florentine Histories I, 29

When Attila, King of the Huns, besieged Aquileia,[17] its inhabitants, after defending themselves a long time, despaired of their safety, and took refuge as best they could, with their movables, upon those rocky shoals that lay unoccupied near the head of the Adriatic Sea. The Paduans, also, seeing the war approach, and fearing that, after Aquileia had been taken, Attila would attack them too, carried all their movables of greatest value to a point on the same sea called Rivo Alto,[18] where they also sent their women and children and old men, keeping the young men in Padua for its defence. Besides these, the people of Monselice, together with the inhabitants of the hills around, pushed by the same terror, took refuge on rocky shoals of the same sea. But after Aquileia was taken and after Attila had destroyed Padua, Monselice, Vicenza, and Verona, the Paduans and the richest people of the other cities remained to inhabit the swamps around Rivo Alto. Similarly, all the people of the vicinity of that province, which was anciently called Venetia,[19] put to flight by the same fears, in like manner took refuge in those marshes. Thus constrained by necessity, they left the most agreeable and fertile places to dwell in sterile and unsettled ones, deprived of all comforts. A great many people being thus suddenly brought together there, they made those places in a very short time, not only fertile, but most delightful; and having established laws and institutions amongst themselves, they lived securely whilst there was so much ruin and distress throughout Italy, and in a little while they grew in reputation and power. For, besides the above-mentioned

---

[16] Cf. 2.1.1.   [17] In 452.   [18] Rialto.
[19] The Roman name of north-eastern Italy.

inhabitants, many others took refuge there from the cities of Lombardy, mostly driven away by the cruelties of Cleph, King of the Langobards;[20] and which caused the new city to increase so considerably [...]. As necessity had obliged them to live as it were in the water, so, unable to avail of the land, they were forced to see how they could gain an honest living by sea; and going with their vessels to all parts of the world, they filled their city with various kinds of merchandise, of which other people being in need caused them frequently to resort there for their supplies. Nor did the Venetians for many years think of any other dominion than that which facilitated the transport of their merchandise; and therefore they acquired many ports in Greece and in Syria.[21] And as the French in their crusades availed of the vessels of the Venetians, they assigned to them the island of Candia as a reward.[22] And so long as they lived in this way their name became feared on the seas, whilst in Italy it was venerated, so that in most of the controversies that arose the Venetians for the most part became the arbiters [...]. But as the Venetians, urged on by the lust of conquest,[23] had in the course of time obtained possession of Vicenza, Treviso, and Padua,[24] and afterwards of Verona, Bergamo, and Brescia,[25] and of a number of places in the Kingdom of Naples[26] and in the Romagna,[27] they acquired such a reputation for power that they became a terror not only to the princes of Italy, but also to the kings beyond the Alps. In consequence of which these combined against the Venetians, who thereupon lost in one day[28] that state and power which they had achieved in so many years and at such infinite expense. And although they have recently reacquired it in part, yet not having recovered their former reputation or power, they exist, like all the other Italian states, at the discretion of others.

2.2.7 MILAN

The Duke of Milan has a great opportunity to further increase his power, being the arbiter of the Neapolitan succession. The pretender to whom he is

---

[20] Cleph ruled from 572 to 574.

[21] The Middle East at large. After the First Crusade (1096–1099), Venice established commercial bases and emporia in Egypt, Lebanon, Palestine, Cyprus, and Turkey.

[22] In 1204, after the Fourth Crusade.

[23] Machiavelli always condemns Venice's expansionism on the mainland. Although, to him, the desire to expand is 'only natural' (cf. 4.1.3, 4.1.4, and 4.3.4), Venice's policy is disapproved of because the way in which her political system is organized is far from being congenial to expansion: cf. *Discourses* I, 6; III, 31; and 4.1.4.

[24] In 1404, 1339, and 1405 respectively.

[25] Verona in 1405, Bergamo and Brescia in 1428.

[26] Some ports on the Apulian coast, in 1501.

[27] Ravenna and Cervia, in 1441.　　　[28] Battle of Agnadello, 14 May 1509.

hostile—Alfonso of Aragon—falls into his hands. The two men meet, and Alfonso makes the Duke realize that the policy he has adopted would weaken his position, make him vulnerable, and jeopardize his security. Convinced by these arguments, the Duke changes his mind and sets Alfonso free.

Florentine Histories V, 5

Whilst the affairs of Florence were in this condition, Joan, Queen of Naples, died [February 1435], leaving by her will René of Anjou heir to the kingdom. Alfonso, King of Aragon, happened to be at that time in Sicily, and, having friendly relations with many of the Neapolitan barons, he prepared to take possession of that kingdom. The Neapolitans and many of the barons favoured René; the Pope,[29] on the other hand, wanted neither René nor Alfonso to have the kingdom, but desired that it should be administered by a governor of his own.[30] Meanwhile, Alfonso came into the kingdom [...] to compel the Neapolitans to acknowledge him as sovereign and sent his fleet to attack Gaeta, which was held by the Neapolitans. In consequence of this, the Neapolitans applied for assistance to [the] Duke [of Milan] Filippo [Visconti], who persuaded the Genoese to take the enterprise in hand. These promptly armed a large fleet for the purpose not only of complying with the wishes of the Duke, their lord, but also to save the merchandise which they had in Naples and in Gaeta. Alfonso, on the other hand, hearing of this, increased his own fleet, and went in person with it to meet the Genoese; and having encountered them above the island of Ponza, the Aragonese fleet was defeated, and Alfonso together with many other princes were made prisoners, and delivered by the Genoese into the hands of Filippo. This victory alarmed all the princes of Italy who feared the power of Filippo, for they judged the opportunity favourable for him to make himself master of the whole country. But—so different are human predictions from the actual outcome of events— Filippo took exactly the opposite course. Alfonso was a man of sagacity, and so soon as he had an opportunity of speaking with Filippo, he demonstrated to him that it was a great error on his part to support René in opposition to himself. For, argued he, if René should become King of Naples, he would make every effort to have Milan become the property of the King of France, so as to have friendly support near at hand, and not to be obliged, in a moment of need, to labour for the passage of his allies; and René could not secure this advantage for himself except by causing Milan to become French thanks to the ruin of Filippo. But if, on the contrary, he, Alfonso, should become King of

---

[29] Eugene IV.
[30] The Church still enjoyed feudal rights over the Kingdom of Naples.

Naples, he would intervene in favour of Filippo; for having no other enemy to fear except the French, he would of necessity be obliged to love and please, if not obey, him, who had it in his power to open the way to his enemies. Thus, although the title of king would be Alfonso's, yet the authority and power would really be Filippo's. So it really concerned Filippo more than Alfonso to reflect upon the danger of the one course and the advantage of the other, unless Alfonso preferred to gratify some desire of his rather than to assure the security of his state. For in the one case he would really be prince, and free; and in the other, being between two most powerful princes, he would either lose his state, or he would live in perpetual apprehension, and obey them like a slave. These arguments had such an effect upon the mind of the Duke that, having changed his purpose, he set Alfonso at liberty, and sent him honourably back to Genoa, and thence to the Kingdom of Naples [...].

2.3

Good Laws and Good Armies

2.3.1 THE FOUNDATIONS OF ALL STATES

In order to survive and flourish in a conflictual international system, all states must have solid military institutions. Machiavelli's preference for a militia, as opposed to mercenaries (the common practice throughout the fifteenth century), is based upon several considerations. To begin with, the condottieri and their troops are utterly unreliable. In addition, dependence on external support drastically reduces one's freedom of movement. Finally, mercenaries are expensive, and the city that relies on them will inevitably witness a pervasive influence of the wealthy. A good army requires first of all regular training. But just as essential is some close relationship between political and military institutions, for soldiers can be asked to sacrifice themselves only if they fight for a society in which they play an active role as citizens.

Prince XII

[...] The main foundations which all states must have, whether new, or hereditary, or mixed, are good laws and good armies. And as there can be no good laws where there are not good armies, and the laws will be apt to be good where the armies are so, I will leave the question of the laws, and talk about the armies.

I say, then, that the armies with which a prince defends his state are either his own, or they are mercenaries or auxiliaries, or they are mixed. Mercenary and auxiliary troops are both harmful and dangerous; and if anyone attempts to found his state upon mercenaries, it will never be stable or secure [...]; so that the ruin of the prince who depends on them will be deferred only just so long as attack is delayed; and in peace he will be despoiled by his mercenaries, and in war by his enemies. The reason of all this is that mercenary troops are not kept in the field by any other affection, or by any other consideration except their small stipend, which is not enough to make them willing to die for you. They are ready to serve you as soldiers so long as you are at peace; but when war comes, they will either run away or march off. There is no difficulty in demonstrating the truth of this; for the present ruin of Italy can be attributed to nothing else but to the fact that she has for many years depended upon mercenary armies, who for a time had some success, and seemed valorous enough amongst themselves, but so soon as a foreign enemy came they showed what stuff they were made of. This was the reason why Charles VIII, King of France, was allowed to take Italy with merely a piece of chalk [...].[1]

Their commanders are either competent, or they are not; if they are, you cannot trust them, because their chief aim will always be their own aggrandizement, either by imposing upon you, who are their employer, or by oppressing others beyond your intentions; and if they are incompetent, they normally bring you to ruin [...]. Experience has shown that princes as well as republics achieve the greatest success only when they are armed [...], and that a republic that has armies of her own is less easily subjected to servitude by one of her own citizens, than one that depends upon foreign troops. Rome and Sparta were for many centuries armed and free; the Swiss are most thoroughly armed and enjoy the greatest freedom [...].

Discourses III, 31

[...] Insolence in prosperity and abjectness in adversity are the result of habit and education. If this be feeble and vile, then your conduct will likewise be without energy. But if the education be of an opposite nature, then it will produce men of a different character; since it enables you to know the world better, it teaches you to be less elated in good fortune, and less depressed by adversity. And what we say of individuals applies equally to the many who constitute a republic, who achieve the same level of excellence as that of the manners and institutions that prevail there.

Although I have elsewhere maintained[2] that the foundation of states is a good military organization, and that without such a military organization there can neither be good laws nor anything else good, yet it seems to me not superfluous to repeat myself, because the necessity of this appears on every page of Livy's history. We also see that troops cannot be good unless they are well disciplined and trained, and this cannot be done with any troops other than natives of the country. A state is not and cannot be always engaged in war; therefore troops must be trained and disciplined in times of peace, and this can only be done with subjects of the state, on account of the

---

[1] When the French descended into Italy in 1494–95, according to Pope Alexander VI (as reported by Philippe de Commynes) all it took for Charles VIII to conquer the country was the chalk needed to mark the buildings that were to be used as lodgements for his troops.

[2] Cf. *Discourses* I, 4.

expense [...]. Now, any city that adopts the military organization and the institutions of the Romans, and whose citizens, both as private individuals and as members of the state, experience on a daily basis their own *virtù* as well as the power of fortune, will always find them to have the same inner strength and to display the same dignity under all circumstances. But a republic unprovided with such military force, and which relies only upon the chances of fortune, and not upon the *virtù* of her citizens, will vary according to the varying of fortune [...].

2.3.2 EXTERNAL THREATS AND MILITARY ORGANIZATIONS

Fabrizio Colonna (fl. 1455–1520) was a renowned condottiero, whose reputation induced Machiavelli to adopt him as the main character in the Art of War. *The work is structured as a dialogue between Fabrizio and a group of Florentine patricians. In this excerpt, Colonna argues that the quality of military institutions is a precipitate of the international context, and above all of the fear that it generates.*

Art of War II

FABRIZIO:
[...] You know of the men excellent in war there have been many famed in Europe, few in Africa, and less in Asia. This results from the fact that these last two parts of the world have had a principality or two, and few republics; but Europe alone has had several principalities and countless republics [...]. Where there are a number of states, a number of able men spring up; where there are only a few, a few [...]. Few men, therefore, sprang up in Asia, because that region was entirely subject to one kingdom in which—being it for most of the time indolent due to its size—men excellent in their dealings could not be born. The same happened in Africa; yet more able men, thanks to the Carthaginian Republic, did arise. More excellent men come out of republics than from kingdoms, because in the former individual qualities are honoured most of the time, in the kingdoms they are feared; whence it results that in the former, men of talent are raised, in the latter they are extinguished. Whoever, therefore, considers the part of [the world that is called] Europe, will find it to have been full of republics and principalities, which from the fear one had of the other, were forced to keep alive their military organizations, and honour those who greatly prevailed in them. For in Greece, in addition to the Kingdom of the Macedonians, there were many republics, and most excellent men arose in each of them. In Italy, there were the Romans, the Samnites, the

Etruscans, the Cisalpine Gauls. France and Germany were full of republics and princes. Spain, the very same. And although in comparison with the Romans, very few others are named, this results from the malignity of the writers, who follow fortune and to whom it was most of the time enough to honour the victors [...]. And since it is true, therefore, that where there are many states, more valiant men spring up, it follows, of necessity, that those being extinguished, *virtù* is extinguished little by little, as there is less reason which causes men to become excellent. And having the Roman Empire later grown and extinguished all the republics and principalities of Europe and Africa, and for the most part those of Asia, no other path to *virtù* was left, except Rome. Whence it resulted that men of *virtù* began to be few in Europe as in Asia; and *virtù* itself ultimately went in to an extreme decline; for all the *virtù* being concentrated in Rome, as Rome was corrupted, so almost the whole world came to be corrupted [...]. And although afterwards that Empire, because of the inundation of [... the] barbarians, became divided into several parts, this *virtù* was not renewed: first, because it takes quite some time to recover institutions when they are spoiled; second, because the way of living today, due to the Christian religion, does not impose the same necessity to defend ourselves that anciently existed. Back then, those defeated in war were either put to death or remained slaves in perpetuity where they led lives of misery; the conquered lands were laid waste or their inhabitants were driven out, their goods taken away, and they were sent dispersed throughout the world so that those overcome in war suffered every extreme misery. Men were terrified from the fear of this, and they kept their military exercises alive, and honoured those who were excellent in them. But today, this fear in large part is lost, and few of the defeated are put to death, and no one is kept prisoner long, for they are easily liberated. Cities, although they have rebelled a thousand times, are not destroyed, goods are left to their people, so that the greatest evil that is feared is a ransom; so that men do not want to subject themselves to military institutions and to endure steady hardships under them in order to escape dangers which they little fear. In addition, these provinces of Europe exist under very few rulers as compared to the past, for all of France obeys a king, all of Spain another, and Italy is divided into a few parts; so that weak cities defend themselves by allying themselves with the victors, and strong states, for the reasons mentioned, do not fear destruction.

COSIMO:
Yet, in the last twenty five years, many cities have been seen to be pillaged, and several kingdoms to be lost; which examples ought to teach others how to live and to resume some of the ancient military institutions?

FABRIZIO:
That is what you say, but if you would note which cities have been pillaged, you would not find them to be the capitals, but only subject towns, as is seen in the

sacking of Tortona and not Milan, Capua and not Naples, Brescia and not Venice, Ravenna and not Rome.³ Which examples do not make the rulers change their mind; in fact, they make them to remain all the more in their opinion of being able to recover themselves by ransom. And because of this, they do not want to subject themselves to the bother of military training, as it appears to them partly unnecessary, partly a tangle they do not understand. The subjects, to whom such examples ought to cause fear, cannot remedy matters; some princes, having lost their state, are no longer in time, and those who still hold it do not know how to remedy matters nor do they want to. For they want without any hardship to remain in power through fortune, not through their own *virtù*; they see that, because there is so little *virtù*, fortune governs everything, and they want it to master them, not they master it. And that what I have discussed is true is shown by considering Germany, in which, because there are many principalities and republics, there is much *virtù*, and all that is good in current military institutions, depends on the example of those people, who, being utterly jealous of their state and fearing servitude (which elsewhere is not feared), maintain themselves masters and in honour [...].

2.3.3 MILITARY FORCE IS AT THE SERVICE OF SECURITY

Machiavelli is quite sensitive to the themes of glory and honour, and he looks at successful military enterprises as instrumental in bringing about renown and reputation. Despite all this, however, the main function of military power is to provide security. The point is significantly made in the Introduction of Machiavelli's main work on military affairs. Those who neglect security—just as the Italian princes have—are bound to be destroyed, as can be seen in the second excerpt.

Art of War, Introduction

Many [...] have held and still hold the opinion that there is nothing which has less in common with another, and that is so dissimilar, as civilian life is from the military. Whence it is often observed, if anyone designs to excel in the military profession, that not only he soon changes his clothes, but also that

---

³ By the French in 1499 (Tortona), 1501 (Capua), and 1512 (Brescia and Ravenna).

he departs from any civilian custom in his habits, manners, voice, and presence [...].

But if one should consider the ancient institutions, one would not find matters more united, more in conformity, and which, of necessity, should love each other as much as these; for in all the professions that are established in a society for the sake of the common good of men, all the institutions created to live in fear of the laws and of God would be in vain if their defence were not provided for; such defence, if well arranged, maintains those institutions, even if the latter are not well arranged. And so, on the contrary, good institutions without the help of the military are not much differently disordered than the rooms of a superb and regal palace, even though adorned with gems and gold, when, not being roofed over, they would not have anything to protect them from the rain. And if in any other institution of a city and of a republic every diligence was employed in keeping men loyal, peaceful, and full of the fear of God, it was doubled in the military; for in what man ought the country look for greater loyalty than in that man who has to promise to die for her? In whom ought there to be a greater love of peace than in him who can only be injured by war? In whom ought there to be a greater fear of God than in him who, undergoing infinite dangers every day, has more need for his aid? This necessity, well considered both by those who gave laws to states and by those in charge of military training, brought it about that the life of soldiers was praised by the other men and followed and imitated with all diligence. But because military institutions have become completely corrupt and far removed from the ancient ways, these wrong opinions have arisen which make the military hated and intercourse with those who engage in it avoided [...].

Art of War VII

[...] The Italians, because they have not had wise princes, have not produced any good military organization; and because they did not have the necessity that the Spaniards had,[4] have not produced it by themselves, so that they remain the shame of the world. And the people are not to blame, but their princes are, who have been castigated, and for their ignorance have received a just punishment, ignominiously losing the state, and without any show of *virtù*. Do you want to see if what I tell you is true? Consider how many wars have been waged in Italy, from the passage of King Charles [VIII of France][5]

---

[4] A few lines above: 'They [the Spaniards] fight in a foreign country, and it seems to them that they are constrained to win or die, and as no place appeared to them where they might flee, they became good'.

[5] In 1494.

until today; and wars usually make men warlike and acquire reputation; these, as much as they have been great and cruel, so much more have caused the people and their leaders to lose reputation [...].

Our Italian princes, before they tasted the blows of the ultramontane wars, believed it was enough for them to think of a sharp reply in their study, write a beautiful letter, show wit and promptness in their sayings and in their words, know how to weave a deception, ornament themselves with gems and gold, sleep and eat with greater splendour than others, keep many lascivious women around, conduct themselves avariciously and haughtily toward their subjects, become rotten with idleness, hand out military ranks at will, express contempt for anyone who may have suggested any praiseworthy reform, want their words should be the responses of oracles; nor were these petty men aware that they were preparing themselves to be the prey of anyone who assaulted them. From this, then, in the year 1494, there arose the great frights, the sudden flights, and the astonishing losses: thus, three very powerful states of Italy[6] were several times sacked and despoiled. But what is worse is that the others persist in the same error, and live in the same disorder; and they do not consider that those who in antiquity wished to hold their state, did all those things we discussed, and had them done, and that they thoroughly concentrated on preparing the body for hardships and the mind not to be afraid of danger [...].

[6] The duchy of Milan, the Venetian Republic and the Kingdom of Naples.

Part III

Domestic Orders, Disorders, and Foreign Affairs

3.1

The Great Powers Compared

3.1.1 FRANCE

(See also the Introduction to 2.2.2). France and the Empire (on which see the next excerpt) represent two opposite constitutional models. Their institutional dissimilarities contribute to explain their different foreign policy style. The Kingdom of France is a centralized state in which the consolidation of the Crown makes it possible to preserve national unity even in case of dynastic turbulences. In addition, the Crown has succeeded in taming the territorial lords, and much of the administration is in the hands of the king or of individuals appointed by him. As a result, the French king can avail himself of vast resources and relies on a stable domestic front.

An Account of the Affairs of France (1511–12)

The Crown and the King of France are at this time more flourishing, rich, and powerful than they have ever been; and for the following reasons.

The Crown, being based upon hereditary succession, has become rich; for as it has happened sometimes that the king had no sons nor heirs to his properties, his territories and substance have fallen to the Crown. As this has been the case with several kings, the Crown has been greatly enriched by the many territories that have thus come to her [. . .]; so that at this time all the good fiefs of France belong to the Crown, and not to private barons.

Another and most important cause of the power of this king is that formerly France was kept disunited by the powerful barons, who dared, and did not hesitate, to undertake anything against the king; as was the case with the dukes of Guyenne and of Bourbon, who are now most submissive [. . .].

A further reason is that every neighbouring prince did not hesitate to attack the Kingdom of France; for there was always either a duke of Brittany, or a duke of Guyenne, or of Burgundy, or of Flanders, ready to aid him, and to grant him passage through, and asylum in, his territory. This happened whenever the English were at war with France[1] [...]. But now that Brittany, Guyenne, and the Bourbons, as well as the greater part of Burgundy, are the most submissive provinces of France, the neighbouring princes have no longer the same facilities for attacking the Kingdom of France; on the contrary, these provinces would now prove hostile to such an invader. And the king, having acquired these provinces, has himself become more powerful thereby, whilst the enemy has become weaker.

There is still the further reason that nowadays the richest and most powerful barons of France are of royal blood and lineage, so that, if the superior branch were to lack heirs, the Crown may descend to them. And therefore each maintains his good relations to the Crown, hoping that either himself or his children may someday attain that high rank [...].

The final reason is that the properties of the barons of France are not divided amongst the heirs, as is the case in Germany and in the greater part of Italy; but they go entirely to the oldest sons, who are the real heirs. The other brothers submit patiently, and, aided by the older brother, they nearly all take to the profession of arms, and strive in that career to achieve a rank and wealth that will enable them also to purchase a territory, and in this hope they live. And thence it comes that the French men-at-arms are nowadays the best, for they are all nobles or sons of lords, and they get ready to achieve the same rank as their fathers.

The infantry that is raised in France cannot be good for much, for it is a long time since they have had a war, and therefore they have no experience whatever. They are moreover all of the lower order and craftsmen from the country, and are so subordinated to the nobles and so humble in all their actions as to have become actually debased; and for that reason the king does not employ them in war, for they have proved themselves bad [...]. If the French infantry equalled in goodness their men-at-arms, then there can be no doubt that they would defend themselves successfully against all other princes.

The French are by nature more ferocious than vigorous and adroit; and if you can resist the fury of their first assault, you will find them so depressed and so entirely discouraged, that they become cowardly like women. They do not support fatigue nor discomforts, and soon become neglectful of everything, so that it is easy to surprise them in disorder, and to overcome them [...].

By the extent of her territory and the advantages derived from her large rivers, France is very fertile and opulent; but foodstuffs, as well as manual labour, have little or no value, owing to the scarcity of money amongst the people, who can barely get enough together to pay their dues to the lord proprietor, although the amounts are but very small [...]. And of the money which the gentlemen draw from their tenants, they spend nothing except for

---

[1] The Hundred Years War (1337–1453).

their clothing; for they have cattle enough to give them meat, innumerable fowls, lakes, and parks with an abundance of every variety of game; thus all the money is concentrated in the hands of the gentlemen, which amounts to large sums these days [...].

In the process of consulting about and managing of the affairs of the Crown and the state of France, the prelates always constitute the majority; the other lords care nothing about this, for they know that the execution of the decisions always devolves upon them; and thus both are satisfied, the former with the direction, and the latter with the execution; although at times old officers are called upon, when military matters have to be discussed, so that they may guide the prelates, who have no practical experience in these matters [...].

Little is spent in guarding the cities, for the people are most obedient, so that fortresses are not needed for the preservation of quiet within the realm; and on the frontiers, where there would otherwise be some occasion for such expenditure, the garrisons of men-at-arms make such expense unnecessary. For against a great invasion there is always time to prepare, as the invader himself would need time to gather his forces for such an attempt [...].

I have not been able to ascertain the ordinary or extraordinary revenues of the Crown; I have asked a great many persons, and they have all replied that the revenue depended entirely on the will of the king. Someone, however, has told me that a portion of the ordinary revenue, that is to say, that part which is called 'the king's cash', and which is derived from gabels (on bread, wine, meat, and the like), yields about 1,700,000 écus. The extraordinary revenue is derived from taxes, and these are fixed high or low according to the king's will. And if these revenues are insufficient, then loans are resorted to, which are, however, rarely repaid [...].

The authority of the barons over their subjects is complete. Their revenues consist of bread, wine, and meat, the same as those stated above, and so much for every family per year [...]. The barons cannot raise taxes nor loans without the king's consent, which he rarely grants.

The Crown exacts from the barons nothing but the impost upon salt, and never imposes extraordinary taxes upon them except in case of some extraordinary necessity [...].

The number of governors of provinces depends upon the will of the king, who pays them what he pleases; they are named by him for life or for a year, according to his pleasure [...]. In fact all the offices of the realm are bestowed or sold by the king, and by no one else.

Every year the provincial parliaments are convened [...], according to the pleasure of the king. The Generals [of Finance] present an account of the expenses and of the ordinary revenues of the year, and then the level of taxation is decided according to the expenses, and the amount of the pensions and the number of the pensioners are increased or diminished according to the king's orders [...].

Garrisons are placed wherever the king wills it, and as many men and pieces of artillery as seems good to him. Nevertheless, all the places have a few pieces of artillery in store. And within the last two years they have established them in a great many places in the kingdom, at the cost of the cities where such depots have been formed, by increasing the taxes one penny per head of cattle or per measure of grain. Ordinarily, when the kingdom is secure, there are only four places that are garrisoned; these are Guyenne, Picardy, Burgundy, and Provence. These garrisons change places, and are increased in numbers, according to the apprehensions of danger in one or the other province [...].

3.1.2 THE EMPIRE

From December 1507 to June 1508 Machiavelli was in Germany, sent on a mission to Emperor Maximilian I. After being to France twice, he could not but be struck by the weakness of the empire. Although Germany was rich and potentially very powerful, her resources could not be mobilized for imperial purposes due to a structural conflict between the free cities, the territorial lords, and the Emperor himself. Maximilian's peculiar personality only made things worse. In 1507, the Emperor called a diet to get the military and financial support of the empire for his descent into Italy. The 20,000 men he was promised at that time never materialized. The excerpt below explains why.

Report on the Affairs of Germany (1508)

[...] If the Emperor [Maximilian I] could have done one of two things, he would certainly have succeeded in his designs upon Italy, considering the condition in which she is at present: either he should have changed his temperament, or Germany should have supported him in good earnest. Examining now the first, they say that, considering his resources, and sup-posing that he knew how to avail himself of them, he would not be inferior to any other monarch of Christendom [...].

But the Emperor, with all his revenues, never has a penny; and what is worse, no one knows what becomes of them [...].

This is the very reason why his intended descent into Italy caused such alarm: for his necessities would have increased with his victories, and it is not reasonable to suppose that he would have stopped soon; and unless he had changed his ways, if all the leaves on all the trees in Italy had become ducats, they would not have sufficed him [...]. The Emperor's frequent needs of money are the consequences of his frequent irregularities; his frequent needs give rise to his frequent demands, which give rise to the frequent diets. And the little estimation in which he is held gives rise to his feeble resolutions and their still more feeble execution [...].

His people, being free and rich, are not influenced either by necessity or by affection, but serve him only by express orders of their cities, which bear the costs involved; so that if, at the end of thirty days, the money for their pay has not come, they leave at once, and neither prayers nor promises nor threats will make them to stay, if the money is wanting [...]. For these reasons the Emperor needs much more money than the King of Spain, or any other sovereign, whose people have different habits [...].

The power of Germany cannot be doubted by anyone, for she has abundant population, wealth, and armies [...]. What is still missing is that the free cities unite with the princes to favour the designs of the Emperor, or that they support the Emperor themselves, without the princes, which would suffice [...]. The cause of their lack of unity is to be found in the many different dispositions that exist in that country [...]: the Swiss are regarded as enemies by all Germany, the free cities by the princes, and the princes by the Emperor [...].

As the Emperor's greatest hostility is towards the princes, and not being able by himself to reduce them to obedience, he has availed himself of the support of the free cities; and for the same reasons he has for some time past established good relations with the Swiss, whose confidence he thought to have of late gained to some degree. So that, taking into consideration all these divisions, and adding thereto those which exist between one prince and another, and one city and another, it seems difficult to bring about that unity which the Emperor would need. But what has kept everybody hopeful, and made the affairs of the Emperor for some time past so promising, and his enterprises likely to succeed, was that there was not a prince in all Germany who could venture to oppose the Emperor's designs [...]. People deceive themselves in supposing that only war and sedition in Germany can constrain the Emperor, for he can be thwarted as effectually also by not supporting him. And those who would not dare to declare war against him do dare to refuse him their assistance, whilst those who would not dare to refuse him their support do dare not to fulfil their promises; and those who would not even dare doing this do dare yet to manage to delay their support until it would no longer be of use to the Emperor. All this offends the Emperor and upsets his plans [...].

And to explain still further as to the power and union of Germany, I would say that this power resides more in the cities than in the princes, for the princes are of two kinds, namely, temporal and spiritual. The temporal princes are reduced to a condition of great weakness, partly by their own action, each principality being divided between several princes, according to the custom of succession which they observe, and which requires such equal division; and partly because the Emperor, aided by the cities, has diminished their power, so that they have become useless as friends and little to be feared as enemies. As for the ecclesiastical princes, if their power has not been annihilated by hereditary divisions, the ambition of the cities favoured by the Emperor has reduced their authority very low; so that the Archbishop Electors and other similar dignitaries, can effect nothing in the big cities of their own dioceses. The consequence is that neither themselves nor their cities, being thus divided amongst themselves, can do anything to aid the Emperor's enterprises, even if they wished to do so. But let us come now to the free and imperial cities,[2] which are the very nerve of the country, and who possess riches and well-regulated organization. These are for many reasons very lukewarm in their disposition to aid the Emperor's projects; their chief aim is the preservation of their liberty, and not the increase of their dominions; and what they do not desire for themselves, they care not that others should acquire. Moreover, there being so many of them, and all accustomed to govern themselves, their support comes very slow, even if they are willing to grant it, and is not so useful as it should be [...]. The Venetians, owing to their commercial relations with the merchants of the German cities, have understood this better than anyone in Italy, and have therefore more effectually opposed the power of the empire. For if they had feared that power, they would not have ventured to oppose it; and even if they had, and had believed that it would have been possible for the whole empire to unite against them, they would never have attacked it [...]. The cities know that the conquest of Italy would not be for their benefit, but for that of the princes, who could come over to enjoy personally that country, which they could not do. And where the benefit is unequal, people are not willing to bear equal expenses [...].

---

[2] The free imperial cities, unlike the other free cities, had been granted a privileged constitutional and political status: no longer subordinate, even formally, to a territorial lord, they were under the direct authority of the Emperor.

3.2

Domestic Affairs and Foreign Affairs

3.2.1 LOCATION, GROWTH,
SECURITY—AND LAWS

In many cases, the decisive push towards the foundation of a new city comes from considerations related to sheer survival: powerful enemies, starvation, pestilence. Security concerns, this time specifically related to potential external enemies, suggest also the criterion according to which the selection of the location is made: a fertile place, from which the new city will grow and expand in order to defend herself. Wise legislators and good institutions, in turn, complete the picture by creating that 'necessity' that alone can induce human beings to behave.

Discourses I, 1

[...] All cities are founded either by natives of the country or by strangers. The first case occurs when the little security which the natives find in living dispersed, being impossible for each small group to resist isolated, either because of the location or because of their small number, the attacks of any enemy that might present himself; the fact that they have no time to unite for defence at his approach; or even if they do they would be forced to abandon the greater number of their retreats, which would quickly become a prize to the assailant—all this encourages the first inhabitants of a country to build cities for the purpose of escaping these dangers. They resolve, of their own accord, or by the advice of someone who had most authority amongst them, to live together in some place of their selection that might offer them greater conveniences and greater facility of defence. Of those, amongst many others, are Athens and Venice [...].[1]

---

[1] On Venice, cf. 2.2.6.

The second case is when a city is built by strangers; these may be either free men, or men who depend on others [...].

The founders of cities are free when they are people who, under the leadership of some prince, or by themselves, are obliged to flee their native country, due to pestilence, famine, or war, and seek a new home. These either inhabit the cities of the country of which they take possession, as Moses did; or they build new ones, as was done by Aeneas. In such a case we are able to appreciate the talents of the founder and the success of his work, which is more or less remarkable according as he, in founding the city, displays more or less wisdom and skill. His talents are recognized by the selection of the place where he has located the city and by the nature of the laws which he establishes in it. And as men act either from necessity or from choice, and as it has been observed that talents are greater where there is not much room for choice,[2] it is a matter of consideration whether it might not be better to select for the establishment of a city a sterile region, where the people, compelled by necessity to be industrious, and therefore less given to idleness, would be more united, and less exposed by the poverty of the country to occasions for discord; as was the case with Ragusa,[3] and several other cities that were built upon an ungrateful soil. Such a selection of site would doubtless be more useful and wise if men were content with what they possess, and did not desire to exercise command over others.[4]

Now, as men cannot make themselves secure except by being powerful, it is necessary to avoid a sterile country and select a most fertile region where the city, being able to expand thanks to the richness of the soil, will be able to repel all who might attack it and to crush all who might oppose the development of its power. As to the idleness which the fertility of the country might encourage, the laws should make the city subject to the necessities not provided by the region, as was done by those wise legislators who have inhabited very agreeable and fertile countries, such as are apt to make men idle and unfit for any talented activity. These, in order to offset the damages that pleasures and idleness would have caused, imposed upon the men who would be soldiers the rigours of a strict discipline, so that they became better warriors than those raised in harsh and sterile countries. Amongst these legislators we may cite those of the Kingdom of Egypt: despite the charms of the country, so strong was that necessity laid down by the laws that it formed excellent men; and if great antiquity had not buried their names in oblivion, we should see that they would deserve more praise than Alexander the Great and many others of more recent memory [...].

---

[2] The same theme is touched upon in *Discourses* I, 3; II, 12, and, in a military vein, III, 12 and 2.3.3 (*Art of War* VII). Cf. also 3.2.2.

[3] Present-day Dubrovnik, in Croatia.

[4] This is why states cannot refrain from expansion: cf. 3.2.2 and 4.1.4.

3.2.2 DOMESTIC DIVISIONS, FORMS OF GOVERNMENT, AND EXPANSION

Which is better, to be divided at home but powerful abroad, or to be united at home but weak abroad? If you are weak, not only will you be unable to expand (or to keep what you have conquered), but also to defend yourself; and if you are too powerful, not only will you have to cope with domestic divisions, but you will also invite the attack of those who are afraid of you. In this important piece, Machiavelli sheds further light on the complex interplay of domestic and international variables and shows the limits of even the best institutional arrangement.

Discourses I, 6

We have discussed above[5] the effects of the quarrels between the people and the senate. These same differences having continued to the time of the Gracchi,[6] when they became the cause of the loss of the Roman liberties, one might wish that Rome had done the great things she did, without bearing within her bosom such discords. It seems to me therefore important to examine whether it would have been possible to establish a government in Rome that could prevent all these troubles; and to do this well, we must necessarily turn to those republics that have maintained their liberties without such enmities and disturbances; we must examine what the form of their government was, and whether that could have been introduced in Rome. In Sparta we have an example amongst the ancients, and in Venice amongst the moderns [. . .].

Sparta had a king[7] and a senate, few in number, to govern her; Venice did not admit these distinctions, and gave the same name of gentlemen to all who were entitled to have a part in the administration of the government[8] [. . .].

The legislators of Rome had to do one of two things to assure to their republic the same quiet as that enjoyed by the two republics of which we have spoken; namely, either not to employ the lower classes in the armies, like the Venetians, or not to open the doors to foreigners, as had been the case in Sparta. But the Romans in both took just the opposite course, which gave to the people greater power, confidence in themselves, and infinite occasion for disturbances. But if the republic had been more tranquil, an inconvenience would have followed, namely that she would have been more feeble, because she would have been prevented from achieving that high degree of greatness

---

[5] *Discourses* I, 5.   [6] The last decades of the second century BC.
[7] In fact, Sparta had two kings.
[8] In the Venetian Republic, the supreme body, at least formally, was the Major Council, which included all the patricians.

which she attained; so that to have removed the sources of trouble from Rome would have been to remove the sources of expansion as well. And thus it is seen in all human affairs, upon careful examination, that you cannot avoid one inconvenience without incurring another.[9] If, therefore, you wish to make a people numerous and armed, so as to create a great empire, you make it such that you cannot then manage it as you like; and if you keep it either small or unarmed, so that you can manage it as you wish, it will become so feeble that you will fall a prey to whoever attacks you, or if you acquire other dominions you will not be able to hold them. And therefore in all our decisions we must consider well what presents the least inconveniences, and choose that as your best pick, for we shall never find any course entirely clean and free from objections.[10] Rome might, like Sparta, have created a king for life, and established a limited senate; but with her desire to become a great empire, she could not, like Sparta, limit the number of her citizens; and therefore a king for life and a limited senate would have been of no benefit to her so far as union[11] was concerned.

If anyone therefore wishes to establish a new republic, he will have to consider whether he wishes to have her expand in power and dominion like Rome, or whether he intends to confine her within narrow limits. In the first case, it will be necessary to organize her as Rome was, and submit to dissensions and troubles as best one may; for without a great number of men, and these well armed, no republic will ever be able to increase, or, if it will, to maintain itself. In the second case, he may organize her like Sparta and Venice; but as expansion is the poison of such republics, he must by every means in his power prevent her from making conquests, for such acquisitions by a feeble republic always prove their ruin, as happened to both Sparta and Venice; the first of which, having subjected to her rule nearly all Greece, exposed its feeble foundations at the slightest accident, for when the rebellion of Thebes occurred [...], the other cities of Greece also rose up and ruined Sparta completely.[12] In like manner, Venice, having obtained possession of a great part of Italy, and the most of it not by war, but by means of money and fraud, when occasion came for her to give proof of her strength, she lost everything in a single battle.[13] I think, then, that to found a republic which should endure a long time it would be best to organize her internally like Sparta, or to locate her, like Venice, in some strong place; and to make her so populated that no

---

[9] Cf. 4.4.1 and *Discourses* III, 37.

[10] Cf. 4.4.1 and *Discourses* III, 37. See also 5.3 and *Discourses* I, 38.

[11] The union of different peoples which had led to the growth of Rome in numbers and power.

[12] After defeating Athens in the Peloponnesian War (431–404 BC), Sparta was in turn defeated by Thebes in 371 BC, thereby losing her dominion over the Peloponnese and her hegemony over the whole of Greece. On Sparta, Athens, and their counterproductive expansionism cf. 4.4.2.

[13] Battle of Agnadello, 14 May 1509.

one could hope to overcome her readily, and yet on the other hand not so powerful as to make her neighbours afraid of her. In this way she might long enjoy her independence. For there are but two motives for making war against a republic: one, the desire to subjugate her; the other, the fear of being subjugated by her. The means which we have indicated remove, as it were, both these causes for war; for if the republic is difficult to conquer (as I presuppose if her defences are well organized), then it will seldom or never happen that anyone will venture upon the project of conquering her. If she remains quiet within her limits, and experience shows that she entertains no ambitious projects, the fear of her will never prompt anyone to attack her; and this would be even more certainly the case if her constitution and laws prohibited all aggrandizement.

And I undoubtedly think that if things could be kept in such a balance, this would be the best life for the citizens, and would insure to any state real tranquillity. But as all human things are in a perpetual movement, and can never remain still, they inevitably either rise or decline, and necessity induces you to many acts to which reason does not induce you;[14] so that, if a republic has been organized in such a way as to be apt to maintain herself without expanding and yet necessity forced her to do so, her foundations would give way and she would quickly be brought to ruin. On the other hand, if heaven favours her so as never to be involved in war, the continued tranquillity would make her a coward or politically divided, which together, or either of them separately, will be apt to prove her ruin. Seeing then the impossibility of keeping things balanced, and that a precise middle course cannot be maintained, it is proper in the organization of a republic to select the course that leads to more glory, and to constitute her so that, even if necessity should induce her to expand, she may yet be able to preserve her acquisitions. To return now to our first argument, I believe it therefore necessary rather to take the constitution of Rome as a model than that of any other republic, for I do not believe that a middle course between the two can be found,[15] and to tolerate the differences that will arise between the senate and the people as an unavoidable inconvenience in achieving greatness like that of Rome [...].

3.2.3 DOMESTIC DIVISIONS AND EXTERNAL ENEMIES

Florence was so badly divided that if she had come to ruined, this would not have come as a surprise. Yet she managed to survive and flourish. On the one hand, her divisions limited her greatness: her enemies (like Venice) were aware of her

[14] Cf. 4.1.4.
[15] Critical views on the 'middle course' are expressed also in *Discourses* I, 26, 30; II, 23; III, 2, 21.

domestic troubles and did their best to stir them up; on the other hand, each time Florence had to face a serious external threat (as the one posed by Castruccio), she successfully overcame her divisions. Just as the Romans did when they were attacked by the Veientes.

Florentine Histories, Introduction

[. . .] If the divisions of any republic were ever noteworthy, those of Florence certainly are most so, because the greater part of the other republics of which we have any knowledge limited themselves to one division, by which, according to chance, they either increased or ruined their city. But Florence, not content with one division, had many. In Rome, as everybody knows, after the expulsion of the kings, a division arose between the nobles and the people, and with that she maintained herself until her downfall.[16] So did Athens, and so all the republics that flourished in those times. But in Florence, the first division was amongst the nobles,[17] afterwards between the nobles and the middle class,[18] and finally between the middle class and the lower classes; and many times it happened that one of those parties, having achieved primacy, again divided in two. These divisions caused so many deaths; so many exiles, so much destruction of so many families, as never occurred in any other city of which we have any record. And truly no other circumstance so much illustrates the power of our city as that which resulted from these divisions, which would have been enough to destroy any other great and powerful republic. Ours, nevertheless, seemed always to be increasing in power [. . .]. And doubtless if Florence had had so much good fortune that, after having freed herself from the empire,[19] she could have adopted a form of government that would have kept her united, I know not what republic, modern or ancient, would have been her superior, such excellence in arms and industry would she in that case have achieved [. . .].

Florentine Histories V, 4

[. . .] After Cosimo de' Medici's return [from exile],[20] those who had brought about his restoration, as well as many citizens who had been wronged [by the

---

[16] Not the fall of the Roman Empire but the end of the republican age—a process that, to Machiavelli, began in the late second century BC.

[17] That is, between Guelph families and Ghibellin families.

[18] This is the fundamental cleavage that characterizes Florentine politics and society from the second half of the thirteenth century onwards.

[19] In the second half of the thirteenth century, when the Ghibellin party was defeated all across Italy.

[20] In 1434. On Cosimo, cf. 3.3.1.

adverse party], resolved to take advantage of the situation by recourse to any means. The Signoria[21] [...], not content with what had been done by their predecessors for the party [of Cosimo], prolonged and changed the place of banishment of many, and sent many other citizens into exile. And it was not so much the fact of belonging to the opposite party that proved dangerous to citizens, but their wealth, their relations, and their private enmities. If this wholesale proscription had been accompanied by bloodshed, it would have equalled those of Octavianus or Sulla. In fact, in some instances it was tainted with blood, for Antonio di Bernardo Guadagni was beheaded. Four other citizens [...], having gone beyond the limits of their banishment, ended up in Venice; and the Venetians, valuing the friendship of Cosimo more than their own honour, sent them to Florence as prisoners, where they were ignominiously executed. All this greatly increased the reputation of the party of Cosimo, and struck terror into his opponents, especially when they saw that so powerful a republic as Venice sacrificed its dignity to the Florentines, which it was believed that they had done, not so much to benefit Cosimo as for the purpose of stimulating party feeling in Florence to a still higher pitch, and by bloodshed to make the dissensions in our city still more dangerous. For the Venetians regarded the union of the Florentines as the only obstacle to their own primacy [...].

Florentine Histories II, 26

At this time[22] the lordship of Lucca and Pisa was taken from Uguccione, and Castruccio Castracani, a citizen of Lucca, was made lord of these cities in his stead; and being a brave and most courageous youth, and fortunate in his undertakings, he became in a short time chief of the Ghibellines in Tuscany. Because of this, the Florentines quieted their civil discords down and, for many years, they tried first to prevent the growth of Castruccio's power, and afterwards, when it increased beyond their expectations, they began to consider as to the best means of protecting themselves against it. And to enable the Signoria to deliberate with greater wisdom and execute their resolves with greater authority, they created a magistracy of twelve citizens, whom they called Buoni uomini,[23] without whose advice and concurrence the Signoria could not deliberate on anything of importance. In the midst of this the term of King Robert's lordship over Florence expired,[24] and the city, having thus

---

[21] Florence's ruling council.   [22] In 1316.
[23] 'Good Men', first established in 1321.
[24] Robert I of Anjou, King of Naples, to whom Florence—torn by factional war—gave herself from 1313 to 1321.

regained its independence, restored the former organization of the government, with the customary rectors and magistrates; and the great fear which
Castruccio inspired kept them united. After several attempts against the lords
of Lunigiana,[25] Castruccio assailed Prato; whereupon the Florentines, having
resolved to succour that place, closed their shops and marched there en masse,
being 20,000 foot soldiers and 1,500 mounted men. And by way of diminish-
ing the forces of Castruccio and increasing their own, the Florentine government published a proclamation to the effect that every banished Guelph who
came to the rescue of Prato should afterwards be reinstated in his country;
which caused 4,000 banished to flock to their standard. The bringing of so
great a force so promptly to Prato alarmed Castruccio, so that he retired
towards Lucca, unwilling to tempt fortune in a battle [. . .].

Discourses II, 25

The dissensions between the people and the nobility in the Roman republic
were so great[26] that the Veientes together with the Etruscans thought the
opportunity favourable for crushing out the power of Rome entirely [. . .]; but
their very attack restored union amongst the Romans, and caused the defeat of
the Veientes. These dissensions in republics are generally the result of idleness
and peace, whilst fear and war are productive of union. And therefore if the
Veientes had been wise, the more they had seen the Romans divided amongst
themselves, the more they would have kept war away from them, and should
have tried to crush their power with deceits to be practised at a time of peace.
The way to do this is to try and win the confidence of the citizens that are
divided amongst themselves, and to manoeuvre as an arbiter between them,
until they come to arms. As the parties come to arms, then sparingly to favour
the weaker side, so as to keep up the war and make them exhaust themselves,
and not to give them all occasion for fearing, by a display of your forces, that
you intend to subjugate them and make yourself their prince. And if this
policy is carried out skilfully, it will generally end in your obtaining the object
you aim at.

The city of Pistoia [. . .] did not come to the republic of Florence by any
other than the above means; for its people being divided amongst themselves,
the Florentines favoured first one party and then the other, without injuring in
fact either, and brought them to that point that, wearied of their disturbed
existence, they threw themselves spontaneously into the arms of Florence.[27]

---

[25] The area north of Lucca.
[26] At the time—in 480 BC—Rome was afflicted by serious domestic troubles due to the debate
on the agrarian reform.
[27] In 1329.

The city of Siena changed her government through the influence of the Florentines only when their favours were small and unimportant;[28] for when these favours have been large and of importance, they have made the Sienese unite in defence of the ruling government [...].

[28] In 1516 the Florentines gave some support to the Bishop of Grosseto (Raffaele Petrucci), who orchestrated a coup to replace Borghese Petrucci as lord of Siena.

3.3

Leaders and Strategies

3.3.1 COSIMO RULES OVER A DIVIDED CITY

Cosimo de' Medici (1389–1464), banker and de facto ruler of Florence for three decades, is one of the most representative figures of his time. Although he almost never held public office, he exerted a decisive influence on political and economic affairs thanks to his control of elections and the creation of new institutions whose direction was placed in the hand of his adherents. In his epitaph, Machiavelli insists on his moderation and prudence, his foresight, and the combination of virtù *and fortune that characterized his life. As a result, he was beloved and feared—just like the ideal prince should be.*

Florentine Histories VII, 5–6

5. [. . .] With the year 1464 Cosimo [de' Medici]'s illness became so aggravated as to cause his death. Both friends and enemies alike deplored this event; for those who did not love him because they belonged to a different party feared that after his decease they would be completely ruined and destroyed; for they had witnessed, even during his lifetime, the rapacity of those whose excesses had been somewhat restrained by their regard for him [. . .]. The regret at Cosimo's death was therefore very general. Of all citizens not of the profession of arms, Cosimo was the most illustrious and renowned, not only of Florence, but also of any other republic of which we have any record. For not only did he surpass all the others of his own time in influence and wealth, but also in liberality and sagacity; and amongst all the other qualities on account of which he became the first citizen of his country, was his exceeding munificence and generosity [. . .]. And although [. . .] he was the first citizen of Florence, yet he so tempered his magnificence with his prudence, that he never transcended the modesty that is proper to those who live in a climate of freedom. For in his conversation, in his servants, in his equipages, and in his whole mode of living, as also in selecting wives for his sons and grandsons, he was ever the same as any other modest citizen; for he knew that the constant

display of things that look extraordinary excites much more envy than the things that are indeed extraordinary but are concealed with modesty [...]. Nobody in his time equalled him in his understanding of princedoms and republics; whence it came that in a city so liable to change, and a population so variable, he was able to hold the government for thirty-one years. His extreme prudence and sagacity enabled him to foresee evil from afar, and whilst there was still time, either to arrest its growth, or to prepare for it in such manner that in case it should grow it might produce no mischief. Thus he not only triumphed over the ambition of his fellow citizens, but he overcame even that of many foreign princes so happily and with so much wisdom that whoever allied with him and his country remained equal or superior to his enemies; and whoever opposed him lost either his time and his money, or his state. The Venetians are a striking proof of this, for in union with Cosimo they proved always superior to [the] Duke [of Milan] Filippo [Maria Visconti]; and when separated from him they were beaten and defeated, first by Filippo and then by Francesco [Sforza]; and when they combined with King Alfonso [of Naples] against the Florentine republic, Cosimo, to his credit, so deprived Naples and Venice of money that they were constrained to accept such terms of peace as the Florentines chose to accord them. The many internal and external troubles, then, which Cosimo had to encounter, always terminated gloriously for him and disastrously for his enemies; and thus his power and influence in the city were increased by civil discords within, and the foreign wars added to his power and reputation [...]. And thus by his *virtù* and good fortune he destroyed all his enemies and exalted his friends.

6. [...] Thus his prudence, his wealth, his whole way of life, and his good fortune caused him to be feared and beloved[1] by the people of Florence, and to be in the most extraordinary degree esteemed, not only by the princes of Italy, but of all Europe [...].

3.3.2 DUKE VALENTINO ESTABLISHES A NEW STATE

Duke Valentino went through a spectacular rise and a precipitous fall. Thanks to the support of the King of France and the Pope, between December 1499 and January 1503, he imposed his rule over a territory stretching from Imola down to Perugia and Camerino. While accomplishing this, he did all a new prince should do, both at home and abroad, thus eliciting Machiavelli's admiration. Yet, he made a fatal mistake, that, combined with an 'extraordinary malignity of fortune', led to his ruin.

---

[1] Cf. 1.2.1 (*Prince* XVII).

Prince VII

[...] I should not know what better lesson I could give to a new prince, than to hold up to him the example of Duke Valentino's conduct. And if the measures which he adopted did not insure his final success, the fault was not his, for his failure was due to the extreme and extraordinary malignity of fortune. Pope Alexander VI, in his efforts to aggrandize his son, the Duke, encountered many difficulties, immediate and prospective. In the first place he saw that there was no chance of making him master of any state, unless a territory of the Church [...], and he knew that neither the Duke of Milan nor the Venetians would consent to that; for Faenza and Rimini were already at that time under the protection of the Venetians. In addition, he saw that the armies of Italy, especially those of which he could have availed himself, were in the hands of men who had cause to fear the power of the Pope and whom therefore he could not trust, namely the Orsini and the Colonna families, and their adherents. Thus it was necessary [for Pope Alexander] to disturb the existing order of things, and to disorganize the Italian states [...]. And this was easy for him to do; for he found the Venetians, influenced by other reasons,[2] favourable to the return of the French into Italy; which not only he did not oppose, but facilitated by dissolving the former marriage of King Louis XII.

The King thereupon entered Italy with the aid of the Venetians and the consent of Alexander; and no sooner was he in Milan than the Pope obtained troops from him to aid in the conquest of the Romagna [...]. Duke Valentino having thus acquired the Romagna, and having weakened the Colonna family, he both wished to hold that province and to push his possessions still further, but was prevented by two circumstances. The one was that his own troops seemed to him not to be reliable, and the other was the will of the King of France. That is to say, he feared that the Orsini troops, which he had made use of, might abandon him, and not only prevent him from acquiring more, but even take from him that which he had acquired; and that the King of France too might do the same [...]. The first thing he did was to weaken the Orsini and the Colonna in Rome, by winning over to himself all the gentlemen adherents of those houses, by taking them into his own pay as gentlemen followers, giving them liberal stipends and honouring them with commands and appointments according to their condition [...]. After that, having successfully dispersed the house of Colonna, he watched for an opportunity to crush the Orsini family, which soon presented itself, and of which he made the most [...].[3]

The chiefs thus destroyed, and their adherents converted into his friends, the Duke had laid quite good foundations for his power, having made himself

---

[2] The Venetians 'wanted to conquer half of Lombardy' (4.3.4).

[3] The text goes on with the account of the rebellion of the Duke's captains—including two members of the Orsini family—and of how he secured himself of them: cf. 1.1.2.

master of the whole of the Romagna and the duchy of Urbino, and above all
having attached the entire population of the Romagna to himself, by giving
them a foretaste of the new stability [which they were to enjoy under him].
And as this part of the Duke's proceedings is well worthy of notice, and may
serve as an example to others, I will dwell upon it more fully. Having
conquered the Romagna, he found that it had been ruled by impotent tyrants,[4]
who had devoted themselves more to plundering their subjects than to
governing them properly, and encouraging discord amongst them rather
than union; so that this province was infested by robberies, torn by quarrels,
and given over to every sort of lawlessness. He saw at once that, to restore
order amongst the inhabitants and obedience to the ruler, it was necessary to
establish a good government there. And for this purpose he appointed as
governor Ramiro Lorqua, a man of cruelty and of great energy, to whom he
gave plenary power. In a very short time Lorqua reduced the province to peace
and order, thereby gaining for himself and for the Duke the highest reputation.
After a while the Duke found such excessive exercise of authority no longer
necessary, for he feared that it might become odious. He therefore established
a civil tribunal in the heart of the province, under an excellent president, where
every city should have its own advocate. And realizing that the past rigour of
Ramiro had engendered some hatred against himself [...], he wished to show
to the people that, if any cruelties had been practised, they had not originated
with him, but had resulted altogether from the harsh nature of his minister.[5]
He therefore took occasion to have Ramiro's body, cut into two parts, exposed
in the market-place of Cesena one morning, with a block of wood and a bloody
cutlass left beside him. The cruelty of this spectacle caused the people to
remain satisfied and astonished at the same time [...].

The Duke [...] wishing now to proceed with his conquest, the only thing
remaining which he had to take into account was the King of France, who, he
knew, would not permit him to go on [...]. Therefore, he began to look for
new alliances, and to adopt a vacillating attitude towards the French when they
entered Italy to move towards the Kingdom of Naples for the purpose of
attacking the Spaniards, who were then engaged in the siege of Gaeta. His
intention was to place them in such a position that they would not be able to
harm him; and in this he would have succeeded easily if Pope Alexander had
lived.

Such was the course of Duke Valentino with regard to the immediate
present. As to the future, his main cause for apprehension was that the new
successor to the papal chair should not be friendly to him, and should attempt

---

[4] An 'impotent tyrant' is unable to enforce the law and despoils his subjects, thereby causing
insecurity and instability. The 'good government', instead, is 'potent' because it ensures the rule
of law, even by force, if necessary.

[5] As already noted (1.2.1, *Prince* XVII), a prince should never inspire hatred, but fear.

to take from him what Alexander had given to him. And this he thought of preventing in four different ways: one, by extirpating the families of those whom he had despoiled, so as to deprive the Pope of all pretext [of restoring them to their possessions]; secondly, by gaining over to himself all the gentlemen of Rome, in the ways mentioned above, so as to be able, through them, to keep the Pope in check; thirdly, by getting the College of Cardinals under his control as much as he could; and, fourthly, by acquiring so much power before the death of Alexander that he might by himself be able to resist the first attack [of his enemies]. Of these four things, he had accomplished three at the time of Alexander's death, and the last one he was about to accomplish; for of those whom he had despoiled he had killed as many as he could lay hands on, and but very few were able to save themselves; he had won over to himself the gentlemen of Rome; and had secured a large majority in the sacred college; and as to further acquisitions, he contemplated making himself master of Tuscany, having already possession of Perugia and Piombino, and having assumed a protectorate over Pisa. And as soon as he did not have to take the King of France into account—and he no longer did, being the French were about to be deprived of the Kingdom of Naples by the Spaniards, so that each of them would have to buy his friendship—he would have seized Pisa. After this, Lucca and Siena would have inevitably yielded to him, partly from jealousy of the Florentines and partly from fear, and Florence's fate would have been sealed. If he had succeeded in all this, as he could have in the very year of Alexander's death, he would have so increased his strength and reputation that he would have been able to sustain himself alone, without depending upon the fortune or power of anyone else, and relying solely upon his own power and excellence.

But Alexander died five years after the Duke had first unsheathed his sword. He left him with only the state of the Romagna firmly established, but all the others in the air, in between two very powerful hostile armies, and himself sick unto death [. . .]. That his foundations were well laid may be judged by the fact that the Romagna waited for him more than a month; and that, although half dead with sickness, yet he was perfectly safe in Rome; and that, although the Baglioni, Vitelli, and Orsini came to Rome at the time, yet they could not raise a movement against him [. . .]. And had the Duke been in health at the time of Alexander's death, everything would have gone well with him; for he said to me on the day when Julius II was made pope, that he had given thought to what could possibly occur in case of his father's death, and that he had provided for everything, except that he had never thought that at that moment he should himself be about to die [. . .].

Whoever, then, in a newly acquired state, finds it necessary to secure himself against his enemies, to gain friends, to conquer by force or by cunning, to make himself feared or beloved by the people, to be followed and revered by the soldiery, to destroy all who could or might injure him, to make existing institutions more effective by adopting new ways of governing, to be severe and yet agreeable, magnanimous and liberal, to disband a disloyal army and create a new one, to preserve the friendship of kings and princes, so that they have either to aid him with gratitude or to injure him with caution—such a one cannot find more recent examples than this man's actions.

The only thing we can blame him for was the election of Julius [II to the pontificate], which was a bad selection for him to make; for [...], though he was not able to make a pope to his own liking, yet he could have prevented anybody from becoming pope, and should have never consented to the election of any of those cardinals whom he had offended, or who, if elected, would have had reason to fear him; for men do injury through either fear or hatred [...]. And whoever thinks that amongst great personages recent benefits will cause old injuries to be forgotten, deceives himself [...].[6]

3.3.3 JULIUS II TEMPORIZES

Sent to Rome to denounce Venetian expansionism in the Romagna, Machiavelli witnesses the election of Julius II (October 1503) and his first weeks as a pope. What follows is the analysis of a rare moment of 'caution' of a leader whom Machiavelli always takes as an example of 'impetuosity'. Julius II is caught between opposing forces, has to cope with various tendencies, and is forced to wait for the right time to come.

I Mission to the Court of Rome

Roma, 11 November 1503

[...] Whoever examines the present state of things at Rome will find that all the important affairs of the day centre here. The first and most important of these is the affair of France and Spain;[7] the second is the business of the Romagna;[8] after that come those of the factions of the Roman barons,[9] and of Duke Valentino. The Pope finds himself in the midst of these broils, and although he was elected with a large majority and much to his reputation, yet as he has occupied the papal chair but for a short time, and having as yet neither troops nor money, and being under obligations to everybody for his

---

[6] Shortly after his election, Julius II deprived the Duke of his state and had him arrested.

[7] France and Spain were at war over the Kingdom of Naples.

[8] As we see below, the Venetians were making progress in the Romagna—a province then held by Duke Valentino but belonging to the Papal States.

[9] Above all, the Orsini and Colonna.

election since everybody has voluntarily contributed to it, he cannot as yet launch any undertaking at all; and therefore he is obliged to run with the hare and hunt with the hounds until the changes of time and things force him to declare himself, or until he is so firm in his seat that he may favour one or the other party, and engage in any enterprise he may please [...]. To begin with the most important affair, His Holiness passes for being favourably disposed towards the French by natural affection, yet in his dealings with Spain he bears himself in such a way that they have no reason to complain of him. Still, he does not go so far in this that France could take umbrage at it, and circum-stances cause both parties to excuse him. In the affair of the Romagna, the Venetians on the one hand are pressing the issue, and on the other hand you cry out; so that it is natural that this burns His Holiness, for he is a man of character, who desires that the Church shall increase and not diminish under his pontificate. And yet your lordships have seen above how he manages, and how on the one hand he accepts the excuses of the Venetians, feigning to believe that they are influenced in their conduct by their hatred of the Duke, and not by any desire to injure the Church, whilst on the other hand he manifests to your lordships his dissatisfaction [with the conduct of the Vene-tians], and takes the measures which in reality he is able to at present. As to the barons, it is easy for the Pope to manage them, as those who are here cannot really cause a political disorder: the Orsini are represented by the Archbishop of Florence[10] and by Giulio [Orsini], and the Colonna by their own cardinal[11] and certain individuals of no importance.

There only remains, then, Duke Valentino, for whom it is believed that His Holiness has a natural aversion; and yet he manages him for two reasons. The first, because he wishes to keep his word with him, of which it is claimed that the Pope is the most tenacious observer, and because of his obligations to him on account of his election, which he owes in great part to the Duke. The other is because, the Pope being still without troops, the Duke is better able than anyone else to offer resistance to the Venetians; and for that reason the Pope urges his departure, and has addressed briefs to your lordships, soliciting free passage and safe-conduct for the Duke, and also favours his cause in other ways [...].[12]

3.3.4 FERDINAND II RISES IN POWER AND PRESTIGE

Although Ferdinand II (ruler from 1479 to 1516) is described in a private letter as 'more crafty and fortunate than wise' (1.1.3), his portrait in the Prince *is rather flattering. His foreign policy is always conducted with an eye to domestic*

---

[10] Rinaldo Orsini.   [11] Giovanni Colonna.
[12] Not for long, as noticed above (fn. 6).

affairs, and his ways always combine the nature of the lion—the use of military force—with that of the fox—the 'cloak of religion'.

Prince XXI

Nothing makes a prince so much esteemed as great enterprises and exemplary deeds. An instance of this in our times is Ferdinand [II] of Aragon, the present King of Spain. He may be called, as it were, a new prince; for, from being a feeble king, he has, by his fame and glory, become the first sovereign of Christendom; and if we examine his actions we shall find them all most grand, and some of them extraordinary. In the beginning of his reign he attacked Granada,[13] and it was this undertaking that was the very foundation of his greatness. In the first place, he carried on this war while being at peace with all other states, and, without fear of opposition, he kept the nobles of Castile occupied with this enterprise. Since they were busy with the war, they did not think about rebellion, while he was acquiring reputation and control over them without their being aware of it. [In the second place,] the money of the Church and of the people enabled him to support his armies, and by that long war he succeeded in giving a stable foundation to his military establishment, which afterwards brought him so much honour. Besides this, to be able to engage in greater enterprises, he always availed himself of religion, and committed a pious cruelty[14] in clearing and driving the Marranos[15] out of his kingdom—no example can be more extraordinarily pitiable than this. Under the same cloak of religion he attacked Africa,[16] made a descent upon Italy,[17] and finally assailed France.[18] And thus he always planned and engaged in great deeds, which kept the minds of his subjects in a state of suspense and amazement, and occupied with their results. And these different enterprises followed so quickly one upon the other, that between one and the next he never gave his subjects a chance to make any attempt against himself at their leisure [...].

[13] The war to expel the Arabs from Granada (1481–92).

[14] Cruelty, although under the guise of religion.

[15] The Marranos were the Jews and the Arabs who had converted to Christianity.

[16] Ferdinand seized Oran in 1509, and Tripoli and Tunis in 1511.

[17] In 1500 Ferdinand signed a secret treaty with Louis XII for the partition of the Kingdom of Naples with France. Then he broke the treaty and drove the French out of Southern Italy in late 1503.

[18] By joining the Holy League in 1511.

3.4

Republics and Principalities

3.4.1 A REPUBLIC'S FOREIGN POLICY IS RECKLESS...

Although Machiavelli frequently expresses his admiration and preference for republican institutions, he cannot help noticing the shortcomings and the difficulties that afflict them. When it comes to foreign policy, one of the most serious problems is that the 'multitude' is easily deceived by arguments that look profitable and courageous even if they in fact entail severe risks. Significantly enough, the only barrier to this tendency is not an institution of sorts but an individual whom the 'multitude' trusts.

Discourses I, 53

After the capture of the city of the Veientes,[1] the Roman people became possessed of the idea that it would be advantageous for the city of Rome if one half of its inhabitants were to go and settle at Veii; arguing that, inasmuch as that city was rich in lands and houses and near to Rome, one half of the Roman citizens might thus enrich themselves without in any way altering, thanks to their proximity, the political life of Rome. This project seemed to the senate and the most sagacious men of Rome useless, and fraught with danger, so much so that they declared openly that they would rather suffer death than give their consent. When the subject came to be discussed, the people became so much excited against the senate that it would have led to violence and bloodshed, had not the senate sheltered itself behind some of the oldest and most esteemed citizens, the reverence for whom restrained the people from carrying their insolence further. Here we have to note two things; first, that the people often, deceived by an illusive good, desire their own ruin; and unless someone whom they trust makes them realize that what they think is good is

---

[1] In 395 BC. The conquest of Veii took place during the phase of consolidation of Rome's power in central Italy.

in fact bad and points out what is truly good, the republic will be exposed to infinite peril and damage. And if it happens that the people have no confidence in anyone (as sometimes will be the case when they have been deceived before by events or men), then it will inevitably lead to the ruin of the state [...].

If we consider now what is easy and what difficult to persuade a people to, we may make this distinction: either what you wish to persuade them to represents at first sight gain or loss, or it seems brave or cowardly. And if you propose to them anything that on the face of it seems profitable (though there really be a loss concealed under it) and courageous (though there really be the ruin of the republic concealed under it), the multitude will ever be easily persuaded to it. But if the measure proposed sounds cowardly or seems likely to cause loss, then it will always be difficult to persuade the people to it, even though safety and profit for the republic were concealed under it. All this is supported by numerous examples amongst the Romans as well as foreigners, and both in modern and in ancient times [...].

In the city of Athens in Greece, Nicias, one of the most wise and prudent of men, could not persuade the people that it would not be well for them to go and attack Sicily; and the Athenians resolved upon it, contrary to the advice of their wisest men, and the ruin of Athens was the consequence [...].[2] Ercole Bentivoglio, commander of the Florentine troops [...], after having defeated Bartolomeo d'Alviano at San Vincenzo,[3] went to lay siege to Pisa, which enterprise was resolved upon by the people in consequence of the boastful promises made by Ercole, although many wise citizens objected, but could not prevent it, being carried away by the general will of the people, who relied upon the commander's big talk.[4]

I say then that there is no easier way to ruin a republic where the people have power than to involve it in hazardous enterprises; for where the people have influence in the deliberations, they will always be ready to engage in such attempts, and no contrary opinion will prevent them [...].[5]

3.4.2 ... AND SLOW

A second shortcoming is that the multi-level decision-making process that is typical of republican institutions inevitably results in tardy decisions. In foreign

---

[2] Nicias's efforts to convince the Athenians not to launch the Sicilian expedition are described by Thucydides VI, 8–26.

[3] In August 1505.

[4] The Florentine army began the siege of Pisa on 6 September, only to withdraw a few days later.

[5] Cf. Florence's decision to attack Lucca, 4.3.2 (*Florentine Histories* IV, 18). Principalities do not score much better, however: 'And if they [the people] are misled in matters of valour or seeming expediency [...], so is a prince also many times misled by his own passions, which are much more numerous than those of the people' (*Discourses* I, 58).

*affairs, when prompt action is required, such a slowness may be detrimental to
state security. Unlike the previous problem, however, here the solution is not left
in the hands of some respected individual but in those of an ad hoc institution
upon which emergency powers are conferred.*

Discourses I, 34

[...] It is seen that the dictatorship, whenever created according to public law
and not for the purpose of exercising personal power, always proved beneficial
to Rome. It is the magistracies and powers that are created by extra-constitutional means which harm a republic, and not those that are appointed in the
regular way, as was the case in Rome [...].

The reasons for this are perfectly evident [...]: taking together the short
period for which he [the dictator] held the office, and the limited powers which
he possessed, and the fact that the Roman people were as yet uncorrupted, it
was impossible for him to exceed his powers and to harm the republic [...].

And truly, of all the institutions of Rome, this one deserves to be counted
amongst those to which she was most indebted for the greatness of her empire:
for without some such an institution, republics will with difficulty escape the
many extraordinary dangers that befall them. The customary proceedings of
republics are slow,[6] no council or magistrate being permitted to act independently on anything, but being in many instances obliged to act in concert one
with the other. Because much time is required to harmonize their several
opinions, the measures adopted by republics are most dangerous when they
deal with something that requires prompt action. And therefore all republics
should have some institution similar to the dictatorship. The republic of
Venice, which is excellent amongst modern ones, had reserved to a small
number of citizens the power of deciding by consensus all urgent matters[7]
without referring their decisions to a larger council. And when a republic lacks
some such system, either a strict observance of the established laws will lead
her to ruin, or, to save her from such danger, the laws will have to be
disregarded. And in a republic it should never be necessary to resort to
extra-constitutional measures; for although they may for the time be beneficial, yet the precedent is pernicious, for if the practice is once established of
disregarding the laws for good purposes, they will in a little while be disregarded under that pretext for evil purposes. Thus no republic will ever be
perfect if she has not by law provided for everything, having a remedy for
every emergency, and established rules for dealing with it. And therefore I will

---

[6] See also *Discourses* I, 59; II, 15; III, 6.
[7] The Council of Ten, first established in 1310.

say, in conclusion, that those republics which in time of danger cannot resort to a dictatorship, or some similar authority, will generally come to ruin when grave occasions occur [. . .].

Discourses II, 15

[. . .] It is well in all assemblies to come to the essential point, and not always to remain in a state of vagueness [. . .].

I have often known such indecision to interfere with proper public action, to the detriment and shame of our republic. And it will always happen that in doubtful cases, where boldness is required to make a decision, there will be this irresoluteness when weak men have to examine and resolve. Slow and dilatory deliberations are not less injurious than indecision, especially when you have to decide in favour of an ally; for tardiness helps no one, and generally injures yourself. Such deliberations arise either from lack of courage and of forces, or from the evil disposition of those who have to decide; being influenced by their own desire to ruin the state or to serve some personal interests, they do not allow any decisions to be made, but impede and thwart them in every way [. . .].

If the Florentines had taken notice of this [. . .], they would not have suffered so much trouble and injury from the French, when King Louis XII of France came into Italy to attack Ludovico [Sforza], Duke of Milan.[8] For when the King was negotiating his descent, he asked the Florentines for an agreement; and their ambassadors to the King agreed with him that Florence should remain neutral, and that the King after arriving in Italy should preserve their government and take them under his protection. And he gave the republic one month to ratify the agreement. But this ratification was protracted by those who most imprudently favoured the cause of Duke Ludovico, until the time when, the King being very close to victory, and the Florentines wishing therefore to ratify the agreement, ratification was declined, for the King realized that the Florentines had decided to be his allies not as a free choice but because they were forced by circumstances. This cost the Florentines a great deal of money,[9] and came near losing them their independence, as happened to them another time afterwards from a similar cause.[10] And this course was the more reprehensible as it was not even of

---

[8] In 1499.

[9] Florence was forced to pay Louis XII 25,000 florins and to provide him with troops.

[10] Although Florence's foreign policy had long been associated with France, the city remained neutral in the clash between Louis XII and the Holy League in 1511–12. The French defeat led to the fall of the republic and the restoration of the Medici.

service to Duke Ludovico, who, had he been victorious, would have shown even more resentment against the Florentines than King Louis did [. . .].

3.4.3 BOTH REPUBLICS AND PRINCIPALITIES RESORT TO FRAUD . . .

Just as a successful prince is half fox and half lion (cf. 1.2.1, Prince XVIII), states too, in their relations with one another, resort both to fraud and force as a matter of course. In fact, the former is necessary when the latter is not available yet, that is, in the initial phase of a state's rise. The need to resort to fraud, therefore, derives from the relation of forces among states; as such, it is independent of the nature of domestic institutions.

Discourses II, 13

I believe it to be most true that it seldom or never happens that men rise from low condition to high rank without employing either force or fraud,[11] unless that rank should be attained either by gift or inheritance. Nor do I believe that force alone will ever be found to suffice, whilst it will often be the case that cunning alone serves the purpose; as is clearly seen by whoever reads the life of Philip of Macedon,[12] or that of Agathocles the Sicilian,[13] and many others, who from the lowest or most moderate condition have achieved thrones and great dominions. Xenophon shows in his life of Cyrus[14] the necessity of deception to success: the first expedition of Cyrus against the King of Armenia is replete with fraud, and it was deceit alone, and not force, that enabled him to seize that kingdom.[15] And Xenophon draws no other conclusion from it than that a prince who wishes to achieve great things must learn to deceive [. . .]. Nor do I believe that there was ever a man who from obscure condition arrived at great power by merely employing open force without fraud; but there are many who have succeeded by fraud alone, as, for instance, Gian Galeazzo Visconti in taking the state and dominion of Lombardy from his uncle, Bernabò.[16]

---

[11] Cf. also *Prince* VII.

[12] Philip II, father of Alexander the Great, reigned from 359 to 336 BC.

[13] Agathocles was the tyrant of Syracuse from 316 to 289 BC, and, for a shorter period, King of Sicily.

[14] Cyrus II, the Great, ruled Persia from 559 to 530 BC.

[15] *Cyropaedia* II, 4 and III, 1.   [16] In 1385.

And that which princes are obliged to do in the beginning of their rise, republics are equally obliged to practise until they have become powerful enough so that force alone suffices them. And as Rome always employed every means, by chance or choice, to promote her aggrandizement, so she also did not hesitate to employ fraud. Nor could she have practised a greater fraud, at her beginnings, than by taking the course we have explained above[17] of making other peoples her allies, and under that title making them slaves, as she did with the Latins and other peoples surrounding her. For first she availed of their arms to subdue the neighbours, and thus to acquire the reputation of a powerful state; and after having subdued these, her power increased to that degree that she could defeat any enemy. The Latins never became aware that they were wholly slaves until they had witnessed two defeats of the Samnites,[18] and saw them obliged to accept the terms of peace dictated to them. As this victory greatly increased the reputation of the Romans with the more distant princes, who thus came to know the glory of Rome, but not her arms, so it excited envy and fear in those who saw and felt her arms, amongst whom were the Latins. And this jealousy and fear were so powerful that not only the Latins, but also the colonies which the Romans had established in Latium, together with the Campanians—whose defence the Romans had shortly before undertaken—formed an alliance against the Romans.[19] The Latins began the war in the way we have shown that most wars are begun, not by attacking the Romans, but by defending the Sidicians, against whom the Samnites were making war with the permission of the Romans. And that it is true that the Latins began the war because they had at last become aware of the Roman deceit is demonstrated by Livy, when at an assembly of the Latin people he puts the following words into the mouth of Annius Setinus, a Latin praetor: 'Now we can bear servitude under the specious name of a treaty among equals'. We see therefore that the Romans in the early beginning of their rise did not abstain even from fraud, which has ever been necessary for those to practise who from a modest condition wish to rise to the highest degree of power, and which is the less censurable the more it is concealed, as was that practised by the Romans.

3.4.4 ...AND END UP SUBJUGATING THOSE WHO INVOKE THEIR HELP

You should think twice before asking another state for military help and receiving foreign troops in your own territory: those who assist you will be

---

[17] Cf. 4.4.2.   [18] During the First Samnite War in 343 BC.
[19] The Latin War, 340–338 BC.

strongly tempted to take advantage of your dependence and weakness, and subjugate you. Here again, there is not much difference in behaviour between a republic and a principality.

Discourses II, 20

[...] I understand by auxiliary troops such as a prince or republic sends to your aid, but which are paid, and the commander of which is appointed by the prince or republic. Livy relates the following. The Romans had on two different occasions defeated the Samnites with the troops which had been sent from Rome to aid the Capuans; and having relieved these of the war of the Samnites, they returned to Rome, leaving, however, two legions in the country for the defence of the Capuans, who lacked any protection, so as to save their city from falling again a prey to the Samnites.[20] These legions, plunged in idleness, became so fond of it that, forgetful of their own country and of the respect due to the Senate, they conspired to make themselves masters of that country, which they had defended with their valour, deeming the inhabitants unworthy of possessing those goods that they were incapable of protecting. When this plot became known to the Romans, they suppressed and punished it [...].

Of all kinds of troops, auxiliaries are the most harmful, for the prince or republic that calls them to assistance has no authority whatever over them, as that remains entirely with him who sends them [...]. Such troops, when victorious, generally plunder as well him to whose assistance they were sent as the enemy against whom they have been employed; and this they do either from the perfidy of the prince who sends them, or from their own ambition. And although it was not the intention of the Romans to break the treaty and convention they had made with the Capuans, yet the facility of subjugating them seemed so great to the soldiers that it suggested the thought of taking the country and the independence from the Capuans.

We might cite many more examples, but this one suffices, together with that of the people of Rhegium, who lost their city and their lives by a legion which the Romans had sent there to garrison the place.[21] A prince or republic, then, should adopt any other course rather than bring auxiliaries into their state for its defence, especially when their reliance is wholly upon them; for any treaty or convention with the enemy, however hard the conditions, will be less hard to bear than relying upon auxiliaries. And if we read carefully the history of the past, and examine the course of present events, we shall find that for one who derived benefit from auxiliaries there are an endless number who have been

---

[20] During the First Samnite War in 343 BC.
[21] In 279 BC. In this case too, the Romans punished the rebel garrison (271 BC).

disappointed. And in truth no more favourable opportunity could be presented to an ambitious prince or republic for seizing a city or a province than to be asked to send troops there to assist in its defence. And therefore anyone who is so ambitious as to call in such aid—not only in his defence but in an attack upon others—seeks to acquire that which he will not be able to hold, and which will be easily taken from him by those who have acquired it for him. But the ambition of men is such that, to gratify a present desire, they think not of the evils which will in a short time result from it [...].

3.4.5 REPUBLICS ARE SOMEWHAT BETTER EQUIPPED TO ADAPT TO THE TIMES ...

As stated elsewhere too (Discourses I, 11 and 19–20), republics are superior to principalities because they can select the best individuals as rulers, whereas monarchies can only hope that fortune will always bring gifted men to the throne. At the same time, republics can change their mode of proceeding only by reforming their laws and institutions. This is a process in which they are willing to engage only under extreme circumstances: 'men accustomed to live after one fashion do not like to change, and the less so as they do not see the evil staring them in the face' (Discourses I, 18). As a result, republics too are vulnerable to decay in the long run.

Discourses III, 9

I have often reflected that the cause of the success or failure of men depends on a conformity between their mode of proceeding and the times.[22] We see one man proceed in his actions with impetuosity, another with prudence and caution; and as in both the one and the other case men are apt to exceed the proper limits, not being able always to observe the just middle course, they are apt to err in both.[23] But one errs less and will be more favoured by fortune when one happens to find a full correspondence between one's mode of conduct and the situation, as I said, for one always acts following one's nature. Everyone knows how Fabius Maximus[24] proceeded with his army with extreme caution and circumspection, and far from all impetuosity or

---

[22] See also 1.3.2 and 1.3.3 (*Prince* XXV).

[23] The right attitude, in short, would consist of a wise alternation of 'caution' and 'impetuosity', according to the circumstances. Yet this is not possible, for, as added below, 'we cannot resist what nature inclines us to do'. Cf. 1.3.2.

[24] Appointed Dictator in 217 BC during the Second Punic War.

Roman audacity. It was his good fortune that this mode of proceeding accorded perfectly with the circumstances. For Hannibal had arrived in Italy whilst still young and replete with fresh successes; he had already twice routed the Romans, so that the republic was, as it were, deprived of her best troops, and frightened. Rome could not therefore have been more favoured by fortune than to have a commander who by his extreme caution and temporizing tactic kept the enemy at bay. At the same time, Fabius could not have found circumstances more favourable for his character, to which fact he was indebted for his success and glory. And that this mode of proceeding was the result of his nature, and not a matter of choice, was shown by the fact that when Scipio wanted to take the same troops to Africa for the purpose of terminating the war, Fabius most earnestly opposed this, like a man incapable of breaking from his accustomed ways and habits. So that, had it depended on him, Hannibal would have remained in Italy, because Fabius failed to perceive that the times were changed and that one had to change the way of waging war too. Had Fabius been king of Rome, he could have easily lost the war, because he would have not known how to change his ways according to the change of circumstances. But he was born in a republic that produced citizens of various character and dispositions,[25] such as Fabius, who was excellent at the time when it was necessary to sustain the war, and Scipio, when it became possible to win it.

It is this which assures to a republic a longer life and more enduring success than a monarchy has; for the diversity of the genius of her citizens enables her better to accommodate herself to the changes of the times than can be done by a prince. For any man accustomed to a certain mode of proceeding will never change it [. . .], and consequently when time and circumstances change and no longer accord with his ways, he must of necessity succumb. Piero Soderini [. . .] was in all his actions governed by humanity and moderation. He and his country prospered so long as the times accorded with this mode of proceeding; but when afterwards circumstances arose that demanded that patience and humbleness be pushed aside, he could not do it, and his own and his country's ruin were the consequence.[26] Pope Julius II acted throughout the whole period of his pontificate with impetuosity and rush; and as the times and circumstances suited him well, he was successful in all his undertakings. But if the times had changed so that a different conduct would have been required, he would unquestionably have come to, for he would have changed neither his mode nor his principle of action. That we cannot thus change at will is due to two causes; the one is that we cannot resist what nature inclines us to do; and the other is the difficulty of persuading ourselves, after

---

[25] That is, 'impetuous' and 'cautious' citizens.
[26] Cf. 3.4.2, fn. 10. On the Gonfalonier's 'caution', see also *Discourses* III, 3 and 30.

having been accustomed to success by a certain mode of proceeding, that any other can succeed as well. This is why fortune varies for the same man, for she changes the circumstances and he does not change his mode of proceeding.[27] The ruin of states is caused in like manner because republics do not modify their institutions to suit the changes of the times [. . .]. Republics are slower in changing their mode of proceeding because it takes them longer to modify their institutions. In order for this to happen, a situation must occur that unsettles the whole state; and in this case, the change of proceeding of one man is not enough to reform the republic's institutions [. . .].

3.4.6 ... AND ARE SOMEWHAT MORE RELIABLE ALLIES

Both republics (like Athens) and principalities (like Egypt) tend to break alliances and show ingratitude when their security is at stake, or when 'fear dominates'. Both republics and principalities, however, may take risks in order to keep their promises if they have no-one to turn to. In a case like this, the slowness typical of republics (cf. 3.4.1) will make them less prompt than a prince to defect. Such a slowness, finally, becomes decisive when some immediate advantage—as opposed to sheer survival—is at issue: here republics are indeed more reliable than principalities.

Discourses I, 59

As it is a daily occurrence that princes or republics contract leagues or friendships with each other, or that in a like manner alliances and pacts are formed between a republic and a prince, it seems to me proper to examine whose faith is most constant and most to be relied upon, that of a republic or that of a prince. In examining the whole subject I believe that in many instances they are equal, but that in some others there is a difference. And I believe, moreover, that agreements which are the result of force will no more be observed by a prince than by a republic, and, where either the one or the other is apprehensive of losing their state, that to save it both will break their faith and show ingratitude to you.[28] Demetrius, called the Conqueror of Cities, had conferred infinite benefits upon the Athenians. It happened that, having been defeated by his enemies, he took refuge in Athens as a city that was friendly to him, and which he had laid under obligations; but the Athenians

---

[27] On these last considerations, including Julius II's profile, cf. 1.3.2 and 1.3.3.
[28] Cf. 1.2.1 (*Prince* XVIII) and 2.1.3.

refused to receive him, which gave Demetrius more pain than the loss of his men and the destruction of his army.[29] Pompey, after his defeat by Caesar in Thessaly, took refuge in Egypt with Ptolemy, whom on a former occasion he had reinstated in his kingdom, but was treacherously put to death by him.[30] Both these instances are attributable to the same reasons;[31] yet we see that the republic acted with more humanity and less cruelty than the prince. Wherever fear dominates, there we shall find equal want of faith in both.

And should either a prince or a republic risk ruin in order to keep faith, this may result from similar reasons.[32] For it may well happen that a prince is the ally of some other powerful prince, who for the moment may not be able to assist him, but who, the prince may hope, will be able to reinstate him in his possessions; or it may well happen that a prince, having declared himself too openly in favour of his powerful ally, may believe that he now can make no treaties with, nor can he be trusted by, his ally's enemies. Such was the kind of those princes of the Kingdom of Naples who adhered to the French party.[33] And with regard to republics, this occurred with Sagunto in Spain, which hazarded her own safety for the sake of adhering to the Roman party;[34] and with Florence when in the year 1512 she followed the fortune of the French.[35] Taking all things together now, I believe that in such cases which involve imminent peril there will be found somewhat more of loyalty in republics than in princes. For even if the republics were inspired by the same intentions and desires as the princes, yet the fact of their deliberations being slow will make them take more time in forming resolutions, and therefore they will break their faith less promptly than a prince.

Alliances are broken from considerations of some immediate advantage; and in this respect republics are much more careful in the observance of treaties than princes. It would be easy to cite instances where princes for the smallest advantage have broken their faith, and where the greatest advantages have failed to induce republics to disregard theirs; as in the case of the proposal of Themistocles to the Athenians,[36] when in a general assembly he told them that he had something to suggest that would be of greatest advantage to their

---

[29] The King of Macedon had liberated Athens from tyranny and restored democracy in the city in 307 BC. Yet, after his defeat at Ipsus in 301 BC, the Athenians declined to receive him.

[30] In 48 BC. However, Machiavelli mistakes Ptolemy XIII for Ptolemy XII: Pompey was killed by the former, but had benefited the latter.

[31] That is, the fear of being exposed to the revenge of Demetrius's and Pompey's enemies.

[32] That is, political reasons, as illustrated in the lines that follow.

[33] During the long struggle between France and Spain for the possession of the Kingdom of Naples (1495–1504), several barons sided with the King of France and stood by him until his final defeat since they had no hope of reconciliation with the Aragonese.

[34] Sagunto, a Roman ally, was destroyed by Hannibal in 219 BC.

[35] See 3.4.2, fn. 10.

[36] The episode, told by Plutarch (*Life of Themistocles* XX, 1–2), took place after the Greek naval victory against the Persians at Salamis (480 BC).

country; but that he could not disclose it publicly without depriving them of the opportunity of availing of it. The people of Athens therefore appointed Aristides to whom Themistocles might communicate his suggestion, upon which they would decide according to the judgment of Aristides. Themistocles thereupon showed him that the fleet of united Greece, relying upon the treaty still in force, was in such a location that they could easily make themselves masters of it or destroy it, which would make the Athenians arbiters of all Greece. Whereupon Aristides reported to the people that the proposed plan of Themistocles was most advantageous but most dishonest, and therefore the people absolutely rejected it; which would not have been done by Philip of Macedon,[37] nor the other princes, who have looked for, and gained, advantages, more by breaking faith than by any other means. I do not speak of the breaking of treaties because of some violation of the agreements by our ally, that being an ordinary matter; but I speak of the breaking of treaties from some extraordinary cause; and here I believe, from what has been said, that the people are firmer in their decisions than princes, and are therefore more to be trusted.

3.4.7 YET, REPUBLICS ARE MORE PREDISPOSED TO GROW AND EXPAND—AND ARE HARSHER MASTERS

While a republic tends to grow and expand, a tyranny leads to decay. Although a prince is not necessarily a tyrant, free institutions create a more dynamic and enterprising setting: where the 'general good' is promoted, population and wealth increase and citizens participate in public life. The same dynamism, however, leads to expansion at the expense of other states; in addition, it also makes republics a tougher kind of master than principalities.

Discourses II, 2

Nothing required so much effort on the part of the Romans to subdue the nations around them, as well as those of more distant countries, as the love of liberty which these peoples cherished in those days and which they defended with so much obstinacy, that nothing but exceeding military skills could ever have subjugated them. For we know from many instances to what danger they

---

[37] On Philip II, see 3.4.3.

exposed themselves to preserve or recover their liberty, and what vengeance they exacted on those who had deprived them of it. The reading of history teaches us also the injuries people suffer from servitude. And whilst in our own times there is only one country in which we can say that free cities exist,[38] in those ancient times all countries contained numerous peoples who were most free [...].

And it is easy to understand whence that attachment to free institutions arises in the people, for experience shows that cities never increased in dominion or wealth unless they were free.[39] And certainly it is amazing to think of the greatness which Athens attained within the space of a hundred years after having freed herself from the tyranny of Pisistratus;[40] and still more amazing is it to reflect upon the greatness which Rome achieved after she was rid of her kings.[41] The cause of this is manifest, for it is not individual interest, but the general good, that makes cities great. And certainly the general good is pursued nowhere but in republics, because they do all that is necessary for it, and although this might prove an injury to one or another individual, those who benefit from it are so numerous that they can carry the measure against the few that might be injured by it. But the very reverse happens where there is a prince:[42] as a general rule, what suits him offends the city, and what suits the city offends him. Thus, as soon as a republic is turned into a tyranny, the least evil that befalls that city is that it makes no further progress, nor does it grow either in power or wealth, but on the contrary it always declines. And if fate should have it that the tyrant is gifted and enterprising, and by his courage and valour extends his dominions, it will never be for the benefit of the city, but only for his own; for he will never bestow honours and office upon the good and brave citizens over whom he tyrannizes, because he does not wish to have to suspect and fear them [...].

All the cities and countries that are free in all respects make the utmost progress. Population is greater there because marriages are more free and more appealing to the citizens; for people will gladly have children when they know that they can support them, not fearing to be deprived of their patrimony, and where they know that their children, not only are born free and not slaves, but can arrive at the highest dignities of the state thanks to their own talents. In free countries we also see wealth increase on a larger scale, both that which results from agriculture and that which is produced by craft and trade activities; for everybody gladly multiplies those things, and seeks to acquire

---

[38] That is, Germany: cf. 3.1.2.

[39] That republics are more effective expanders than principalities is also noted in *Discourses* I, 58.

[40] In 527 BC.

[41] At the end of the sixth century.

[42] In this case, a tyrant—as it becomes immediately clear.

those goods, the possession of which one can tranquilly enjoy. Thence men vie with each other to increase both private and public goods, which consequently increase in an extraordinary manner.

But the contrary of all this takes place in countries that are subject to another; and the more rigorous their subjection, the more will they be deprived of the prosperity to which they had previously been accustomed. And the hardest of all servitudes is to be subject to a republic, for two reasons: first, because it is more enduring, and there is no hope of escaping from it; and secondly, because a republic aims to enervate and weaken all other bodies so as to increase its own. This is not the case with a prince who holds another country in subjection, unless indeed he should be a barbarous devastator of countries and a destroyer of all human communities, such as the princes of the Orient. But if his ways are humane and civilized, he will treat all cities that are subject to him as he treats his own city, and will leave them in the enjoyment of all their arts and industries and next to all their ancient institutions. So that if they cannot grow the same as if they were free, they will at least not come to ruin whilst in bondage [...].

Part IV

Foreign Policy and International Politics

4.1

Preferences, Opportunities, and Constraints

4.1.1 WHEN WILL ONE ACT?

Maximilian I was the first Holy Roman Emperor not to be crowned by the Pope. Although he often thought of descending into Italy, his projects never material-ized. In the relatively calm spring of 1506, the rumour of his expedition prompts Machiavelli to assess the likelihood of such an event. Although Maximilian did try to force his way to Rome (cf. 3.1.2), as Machiavelli anticipates, the letter below is important above all for its analytical outlook: what one will do is a function not only of one's intentions, but also of the opportunities and the constraints that are to be found in any given situation—in this case, the attitude and the strength of those who can be expected to support the Emperor or to thwart his designs.

Letter to Giovanni Ridolfi, 12 June 1506

[...] When one sets out to judge if anybody is going to do a thing, it is necessary first to see if he wishes to do it, then what assistance he may have, and what hindrance in doing it. Whether the Emperor wishes to go into Italy or not, all reasons are in favour of his desiring to do so. The first is that he may reasonably desire to crown himself for his own glory, and to pass on that dignity to his son. The other is to avenge himself for the injuries received from the Italians and reacquire the honour he lost in his expedition into Tuscany.[1] It is believed, then, that he wishes to come. Now, in order to see who is able to hold back or aid him, it is necessary to consider whom he has at home and who his neighbours are. We do not know much, here, about the attitude of the German princes. However, he is believed to be more powerful than in the past, since he has overcome the Count Palatine[2] and laid taxes on

---

[1] In 1496 Maximilian had intervened against the Florentines in the war for Pisa, but had been repelled.

[2] Philip of Wittelsbach, who had been defeated in the Landshut War of Succession in 1505.

the cities and the lords for their shares of the cost of his expedition to Italy. His neighbours are the Archduke,[3] the King of France, and the King of England.[4] The powers of Italy, where he intends to come, are the Pope, the Venetians, the King of Spain, the Florentines, and others of little weight.

If the news is true, it appears that the Archduke, the King of Spain, and the King of England are in accord. And if they are in accord, it follows that they are in agreement with the Emperor, since the Archduke is his son and the two of them have everything in common in this business. As to the Pope, though he treats with the King of France to get soldiers from him, it is apparent that he is more favourable to the affairs of the Emperor. And that is reasonable: the fortune of the King of France is weary, especially in Italy because of what has happened here; that of the Emperor is fresh. This Pope is probably intending to do with the Emperor what Alexander [VI] did with the King of France.[5] Of the little states of Italy there is no need to say anything if the others are in agreement. There remains, then, to object to his expedition, among the greater powers, the French and the Venetians, who should together oppose his coming; but both of them will tread very carefully, for they do not trust one another. And it must be considered that they can oppose the Emperor with force and craft; they will not fail to use every kind of craft and effort to upset his plan, as France is seen to be doing, according to the news. But it is likely that craft will not be enough, and that if they have to come to force, they will not be willing to do it. It is hardly credible that the King of France will decide to make war on the Emperor against the wishes of England, the Archduke, and Spain. Nor can it be believed that the Venetians, since they would have to make war in their own country, would wish to do it, for they would always be afraid that the French at a critical moment would abandon them. Hence it is probable that since their craft will not avail to keep him back, they will plan on letting him come, and everybody will try to take care of his own interests. If they have to come to blows with him, they will do it when he has come into Italy, as the Duke of Milan and the Venetians did to King Charles [...].[6]

4.1.2 REVISIONIST POWERS AND INTERNATIONAL STABILITY

The French, allied with the Venetians (Treaty of Blois, March 1513), have tried to take Milan and have been defeated by the Swiss in June. In addition, they have to face the League of Malines (April 1513), consisting of the King of Spain,

---

[3] Philip of Habsburg.   [4] Henry VII.
[5] As Charles VIII invaded Italy in 1494–95, Alexander VI reached an agreement with him.
[6] The League of Venice of 1495.

the King of England, the Emperor, and the Pope. During the summer, Vettori
and Machiavelli debate the terms of a possible peace (cf. 2.1.4). To Machiavelli,
any settlement will inevitably produce revisionist powers. But if the latter are
constrained in such a way that they cannot take any significant initiative,
stability may nevertheless follow.

Letter to Francesco Vettori, 10 August 1513

[...] If one wants to find out if a peace settlement is stable or secure, one has among other things to figure out who is dissatisfied with that settlement, and what can grow out of such dissatisfaction. According to your peace plan, the King of England,[7] the King of France, and the Emperor would be dissatisfied, because none of them would have achieved his goals. According to my peace plan, the King of England, the Swiss, and the Emperor would be dissatisfied for the same reason. The dissatisfaction entailed by your peace can easily lead to the ruin of Italy and Spain: as soon as the peace treaty is signed, although the King of France has agreed to it and the King of England has not rejected it, both of these kings will change their aim and mind. Whereas the former intended to enter Italy again and the latter desired to tame France, they will take revenge against Italy and Spain. And reason suggests that they will reach yet another agreement which will allow them to do just about anything they want at no risk, provided the King of France is willing to break cover; for the next day the Emperor, supported by France and England, will jump over Castile,[8] move to Italy at will, have the King of France enter Italy again; so that these three combined can stir up and ruin everything in a very short time. Neither the Spanish and Swiss armies nor the Pope's money is enough to contain such a tide, for these three would have too much money and too many troops. It is only reasonable that the King of Spain is aware of these dangers and that he wants to avoid them at all costs, because under such a peace settlement the King of France has no reason whatsoever to be favourably predisposed toward him and a great opportunity to harm him; and the King of France is not likely at all to waste such a chance [...]. But under my peace settlement, the dissatisfied parties would be the King of England, the Emperor, and the Swiss, and they could not, either together or alone, easily harm the other allies, because France would be a barrier on both sides of the Alps. With the support of the others, France would mount such an opposition that the allies would be safe and the enemies, realizing those difficulties, would not undertake any campaign.

---

[7] Henry VIII.

[8] After Isabella of Castile's death in 1504, her husband Ferdinand II of Aragon had become regent of Castile on behalf of his grandson Charles. Emperor Maximilian was Charles's other grandfather. This could have provided a pretext for an imperial intervention in Castile, for in 1513 the Iberian kingdoms were not formally united yet.

And there would be no reason why the allies should fear each other [...], because each would have achieved his aim, and their enemies would be so powerful and dangerous as to keep them chained together [...].

4.1.3 GOALS CHANGE AND NECESSITY OVERRULES INTENTIONS

Between the last decades of the fifteenth century and the beginning of the sixteenth century, the Swiss infantry played a paramount role in the European wars and contributed to the demise of heavy cavalry, so typical of medieval warfare. In the Italian wars, the Swiss were often decisive. Their military organization, coupled with their 'republican' institutions, elicited Machiavelli's admiration (and concern), and induced him to express the views below. Although his belief in Swiss invincibility would soon be shaken (the Battle of Marignano in 1515 will show all the limits of the Swiss infantry against the effective French artillery), these two excerpts are important because they argue that means, independently of initial intentions, shape behaviour; that one does not need a master plan to become a hegemonic power; that success transforms original preferences; and that one can end up doing, by 'necessity', something one would have never thought of doing.

Letter to Francesco Vettori, 10 August 1513

[...] Your peace plan[9] entails yet another severe danger for Italy, that is, every time one leaves a weak Duke in Milan, Lombardy will not belong to that Duke but to the Swiss [...]. I do not share your view that the Swiss are not going to move because they would be afraid of France, because they would have to face the rest of Italy combined, and because they would be content with raking the country and then leaving. To begin with, the King of France, as I said above, will desire revenge, and having been harmed by all of Italy, will take pleasure in seeing Italy ruined [...]. As for the union of the other Italians, you make me laugh: first, because there will never be any union that will do any good; and even if the leaders were united, this would not be enough, for the available armies are not worth a single penny [...]; second, because the peoples are cut off from their leaders. As soon as the Swiss make a move [...] everyone will scramble to become their ally. As for their being content with raking and leaving [...], I beg you to think seriously of how human things—such as the

---

[9] See 4.1.2.

opinion that men have of themselves—and how earthly things—above all states—develop and grow. And if you do, you will see that at first men are satisfied with being able to defend themselves and not being dominated by others;[10] from here, then, they move on to attacking others and seeking to dominate others. At first, the Swiss were content with defending themselves from the Dukes of Austria,[11] which increased their own reputation at home; afterwards, they were content with defending themselves from Duke Charles,[12] which extended their fame abroad; afterwards, they were content with getting their pay from others, so that they could keep their youth ready for war and acquire glory. This has further consolidated their reputation, has made them bolder because they have come to observe and to know more provinces and peoples, and has instilled in their minds an ambitious spirit and the will to engage in military enterprises of their own. And Pellegrino Lorini once told me that when the Swiss came to Pisa with Beaumont they would often discuss the extraordinary quality of their military organization, how it was similar to that of the Romans, and the reason why they might not do, one day, what the Romans had done; they boasted that they had given to the King of France all of his victories up until then, and wondered why they might not fight for themselves in the future. Now this opportunity has arrived, and they have seized it; and they have entered Lombardy under the pretext of restoring the Duke and have made themselves rulers.[13] As soon as they have the chance, they will become the absolute masters of Lombardy, annihilating the Duke's line and all that state nobility; at the next opportunity, they will overrun all of Italy, to the same effect. Therefore, I conclude that raking and leaving will not be enough for them; quite the contrary, they are to be most remarkably feared [. . .].

Letter to Francesco Vettori, 26 August 1513

[. . .] I believe you completely deceive yourself in the case of the Swiss, and about whether they are to be feared much or little. I feel sure they are very much to be feared. And Casavecchia and many of my friends [. . .] know how low my estimate of the Venetians has always been, even at the height of their power. It has always seemed to me a much greater miracle that they should have acquired that dominion and that they should hold it than that they should lose it [. . .]. What always influenced me was their mode of proceeding, for they get on without generals or soldiers of their own. Now the reasons that prevented me from fearing them make me fear the Swiss. I do not know what

---

[10] Cf. 1.2.2 (*Discourses* I, 37) and 4.1.4. See also *Discourses* I, 46—the very title of that chapter.
[11] *Discourses* II, 19. Some cantons rebelled against the Habsburgs as early as the end of the thirteenth century. The struggle for independence went on until the end of the fifteenth century.
[12] Charles the Bold, Duke of Burgundy. He was defeated by the Swiss twice in 1476.
[13] June 1512.

Aristotle says about confederated republics,[14] but I consider well what reasonably can be, what is, and what has been. I remember reading that the Etruscans held all Italy to the Alps, until they were driven from Lombardy by the Gauls.[15] If the Aetolians and the Achaeans[16] did not make much progress, it can be charged to their times rather than to themselves, for they had always felt the pressure of a very powerful King of Macedon, who did not let them get out of their nest, and later they had the Romans. Hence it was more the force of the others than their own form of government that did not allow them to increase their territory. The Swiss do not wish to gain new subjects now because they do not see that it is to their advantage. They say that now, because they do not see it now, but as I said to you before, things go on little by little, and men are often forced by necessity to do what they did not intend to. The habit of popular governments is to go slowly. If we consider the situation, they already have as tributaries in Italy the Duke of Milan and the Pope. They have made these tributes part of their income, and do not wish to do without them. If sometime a payment is missing, they will look on the failure as rebellion and have recourse to their spears. Then when they have won, they will plan to make themselves sure of their tribute. To do this they will impose more obligations on those they have conquered, and so, little by little, the process will be completed.

Do not rely at all on those armies which you say can one day have some effect in Italy, for this is impossible; first, because of those armies themselves, for there would be several leaders and they would not be united, and it does not seem possible to give them a leader who can keep them united; second, because of the Swiss [...]. Only armies like them can resist them [...].

I do not believe, indeed, that they will form an empire as the Romans did, but I do believe that they can become masters of Italy because of their nearness and our bad methods and despicable habits [...].

4.1.4 ON MOLESTING AND BEING MOLESTED

Even if a state entertains no desire of expansion, the pressure of international competition will push it in that direction; being attacked by others, it will find it necessary to attack others. As such, conflict among states is inevitable. Yet, expansionism is detrimental if it is not conducted with appropriate means.

---

[14] Aristotle had been mentioned by Vettori in his letter of 20 August 1513—yet he has nothing to say on the subject. Thus Machiavelli is right in dismissing his friend's groundless reference. For the type of expansion in which 'confederated republics' usually engage, see 4.4.2.

[15] Between the beginning of the sixth century and the middle of the fourth century BC.

[16] Both peoples organized themselves in confederations, or leagues, between the beginning of the third century BC and the Roman conquest of Greece in 146 BC.

Discourses II, 19

[...] As I have said when discussing the difference between a state organized for conquest and one organized only for its own preservation,[17] it is impossible for a republic to remain in the quiet enjoyment of her liberty and its limited territory; for even if she does not molest others, others will molest her, and from being thus molested will spring the desire and necessity of conquests. And even if she had no foe abroad, she would find him at home,[18] for such seems to be the inevitable fate of all large cities. The fact that the free cities of Germany have been able to exist in this fashion for a length of time, is owing to certain conditions prevailing in that country, such as are not found elsewhere, and without which they could not live free and safe [...].

[The free cities of Germany] can live in the tranquil enjoyment of their small domain because they have no chance to increase it, due to imperial authority; and they can live united within their walls because they have an enemy near who would quickly avail himself of any internal dissension to seize and occupy them.[19] But if Germany were differently constituted, they would be forced to seek to aggrandize themselves, and would have to abandon their quiet life. As the same conditions do not exist anywhere else, one cannot adopt the same system as these free imperial cities, but must seek to extend one's power by confederations, or to extend it like the Romans.[20] And whoever attempts any other mode will quickly come to ruin, for in a thousand ways, and for many reasons, acquisitions of territory prove injurious.

For one may well extend one's territory without increasing one's military power, but the acquisition of dominion without power inevitably brings with it ruin. You acquire no power if you impoverish yourself by war, even though you be victorious, or if your conquests cost you more than they are worth. This the Venetians did, and the Florentines, who were much weaker when they held, the one Lombardy,[21] and the other Tuscany,[22] than they were when the one was satisfied with the dominion of the sea, and the other with her six miles of territory. All of which resulted from their desire of aggrandizement without the knowledge of the proper means. And they deserve the more blame, as they have less excuse, having before their eyes the method practised by the Romans, which they might have followed, whilst the Romans, having no precedents to guide them, had to develop the system exclusively by their own sagacity [...].

---

[17] Cf. 3.2.2.   [18] Possibly a reference to the idleness denounced in 3.3.2.
[19] That is, the Emperor.   [20] Cf. 4.4.2.
[21] More precisely, present-day Eastern Venetia and Western Lombardy; such expansion took place in the first half of the fifteenth century.
[22] The rise of Florence to the rank of regional power can be traced back to the first half of the fourteenth century.

4.2

Dealing with Threats

4.2.1 BALANCING AGAINST A GREAT POWER IS NOT EASY AT ALL

Although security and stability rest upon a more or less even distribution of power and fear (cf. 2.1.4), balancing power is more easily said than done. To begin with, such a policy must be timely: states can resort to force against a great power only in the initial phase of its rise, because when it has grown too strong the use of force is likely to be counterproductive. In addition, when coalitions are involved, a single player can always exploit the inevitable divisions among the allies, thus making their effort vain.

Discourses I, 33

As the Roman republic grew in reputation, power, and dominion, her neighbours, who at first had not thought of how great a danger this new republic might prove to them, began (too late, however) to see their error; and wishing to remedy their first neglect, they united full forty tribes in a league against Rome. Hereupon the Romans resorted, amongst other measures which they were accustomed to employ in urgent dangers, to the creation of a dictator;[1] that is to say, they gave the power to one man, who, without consulting anyone else, could determine upon any course, and could have his decisions carried into effect without any appeal. This measure, which on that occasion proved useful in overcoming the imminent perils, was equally most useful to them in all the critical events that threatened the republic during her rise in power. Upon this subject we must remark, first, that when any evil arises within a republic, or threatens it from without, that is to say, from an intrinsic or extrinsic cause, and has become so great as to fill everyone with apprehension, the more certain remedy by far is to temporize with it, rather than to attempt

---

[1] The Romans established the extraordinary magistracy of Dictator in 501 BC as they were fighting against the Latins. Cf. 3.4.2.

to extirpate it; for almost invariably he who attempts to crush it will rather increase its force, and will accelerate the harm apprehended from it [...].

The neighbours of Rome [...] found that it would have been safer, after Rome had grown so much in power, to try and placate her and keep her within her limits by peaceful means than by warlike measures to make her think of new institutions and new defences. For their league had no other effect than to unite the people of Rome more closely, and to make them bolder, and to cause them to adopt new institutions that enabled them to increase their power in a briefer time [...].

Discourses III, 11

[...] Whenever many powerful individuals join forces against another powerful individual, the presumption of success must always be in favour of the one who is alone and less powerful than of those who are many, however superior in power they may be. For independent of the infinity of circumstances of which an individual can take advantage better than a combination of many, he will always have the opportunity, with a little address, to create divisions among the many, and thus to transform a strong body into a feeble one [...].

In the year 1483 all Italy leagued together against the Venetians; who, being on the verge of defeat and no longer able to field an army, succeeded in corrupting Ludovico Sforza, governor of Milan, and concluded a treaty with him by which they not only recovered all the cities they had lost, but actually seized a portion of the principality of Ferrara. And thus, although they had been losers in war, yet they proved to be gainers in peace.[2] A few years ago a general league was formed against France;[3] yet, before the termination of the war the King of Spain broke from the league, and made terms with France,[4] so that the other confederates were soon afterwards constrained also to come to terms with her. We must therefore always believe that when many combine to make war upon one, the latter will triumph over the combination, provided he has force enough to resist the first attacks and gain time by dragging the war out. But if he could not do this, he would be exposed to a thousand dangers, as was the case with the Venetians in 1508.[5] If at that time they could have temporized with the French army and gained over some of those who had combined against them, they would have escaped the disasters by which they were overwhelmed. But being without a strong and well organized army that could temporarily hold the French in check, and thus having no time to detach any one power from the league, they were crushed.[6] In fact, we saw

[2] For further details, see 4.4.6.   [3] The Holy League of 1511. Cf. 2.1.1.
[4] On 1 April 1513. On this truce, see 1.3.3.   [5] The League of Cambrai.
[6] Battle of Agnadello, May 1509.

that the Pope, after having recovered what belonged to him, became their friend;[7] and so did the King of Spain; and both of these powers would gladly have saved for the Venetians their possessions in Lombardy, if they could have done it, so as to prevent the King of France from becoming so powerful in Italy.[8] The Venetians, by sacrificing a part, might have saved the rest; this would have been a most wise course for them to pursue, provided they had done so when they could seem not to be forced to it by necessity, that is before the outbreak of the war; but after the war was actually begun, such a course would have been disgraceful, and probably of little advantage.[9] Before the war only a few of the citizens of Venice could discern the danger, still fewer perceived the remedy, and none advised it [...]. Any one prince will find a remedy, when assailed by many enemies, provided he has wisdom to adopt means that are suitable to divide them.

4.2.2 HAVING ACHIEVED SECURITY, STATES AIM AT MORE

In Part III the point was made that state behaviour reflects above all the opportunities and the constraints that characterize any given situation at any given time. As long as a state is kept under pressure by some impending threat, security will be its immediate goal. But the removal of that threat almost automatically predisposes the same state to wish something more than mere security, as these short stories below nicely illustrate.

Florentine Histories V, 9–10

9. It did not need so many words to persuade the Duke [of Milan, Filippo Maria Visconti] to make war against the Florentines, for he was disposed to it by an hereditary hatred[10] and a blind ambition that urged him to it; all the more so, as he was impelled by the new offence of the alliance with the Genoese [...].[11] The Duke, at the persuasion of the Florentine exiles, ordered Niccolò

---

[7] Faenza and Rimini, seized by the Venetians in 1503. Julius II made peace with Venice in February 1510.

[8] Venice had to hand over to France the territory contained between the rivers Adda and Mincio, including a few cities conquered in the fifteenth century.

[9] Because the allies would have realized that Venice was simply trying to divide them.

[10] For the long tradition of hostility between Milan and Florence, see also 4.4.5.

[11] Genoa had rebelled against Visconti's rule in 1435. The following year she adhered to an anti-Milanese alliance with Florence and Venice.

Piccinino to attack the eastern Riviera, and to push the war vigorously into the Genoese territory on the frontier of Pisa [...]. Niccolò thereupon attacked and took Sarzana, and after having done considerable damage, he marched upon Lucca [October 1436]; and for the purpose of scaring the Florentines more, he started the report that he was going down to the Kingdom of Naples to assist the King of Aragon. Upon the occurrence of these events, Pope Eugene left Florence and went to Bologna, where he negotiated a new arrangement between the Duke and the league [...]. Although the Pontiff exerted himself very much in this matter, yet it was all in vain; for the Duke would not make any terms until he should first have recovered Genoa, whilst the league wanted Genoa to remain entirely free; and thus each party, mistrusting peace, prepared for war.

10. When, therefore, Niccolò Piccinino came to Lucca, the Florentines became apprehensive about some new initiative of his, and ordered Neri di Gino [Capponi], with the cavalry, into the Pisan territory; and they obtained the Pope's consent that Count Francesco [Sforza] should unite with him;[12] and they established themselves with their army at Santa Gonda.[13] Piccinino, who was at Lucca, demanded free passage to go on to Naples; and upon its being refused, he threatened to take it by force. The two armies were nearly equal in numbers and in the ability of their respective commanders, and therefore neither of them wished to expose themselves to the hazards of fortune, being, moreover, restrained by the cold season (being in the month of December); and thus they remained many days without either making any movement to attack the other. Niccolò Piccinino, however, was the first to move, it having been represented to him that, if he were to make a night attack upon Vico Pisano,[14] he would easily take it. Niccolò made the attempt, but failed to take Vico; whereupon he wasted the surrounding country, and plundered and burned Borgo San Giovanni alla Vena.[15] This attempt [...] encouraged Niccolò to advance further; and having ascertained that Count Francesco and Neri di Gino had not moved, he attacked Santa Maria in Castello and Filettole,[16] and took them both. With all this, the Florentine troops still did not move, not because Count Francesco was afraid, but because the magistrates of Florence had not yet definitely resolved upon war, out of reverence for the Pope, who was still treating for peace. Niccolò, mistaking the prudence of the Florentines for fear, felt encouraged to still more fresh attempts, and resolved to attack Barga[17] with all his forces. This new attack made the Florentines put

---

[12] Sforza was at that time at the service of the Pope.
[13] About 15 miles north-west of Florence.
[14] About 15 miles east of Pisa.
[15] In the surroundings of Vico Pisano.
[16] Both places are roughly between Pisa and Lucca.
[17] About 20 miles north of Lucca.

aside all considerations, and decide not only to succour Barga, but also to attack the territory of Lucca. Francesco, therefore, having gone to encounter Niccolò, engaged him in battle and defeated him [February 1437]; and having almost dispersed his army, he raised the siege of Barga. The Venetians, meanwhile, considering that Filippo Visconti had broken the peace, sent their general, Gian Francesco Gonzaga, to the Ghiaradadda,[18] where he ravaged the Duke's territory to the degree that Filippo found it necessary to recall Niccolò Piccinino from Tuscany. This recall of Piccinino, together with the victory which Count Francesco had gained over him, encouraged the Florentines to make an attempt upon Lucca, with the hope of taking it.[19] In this attempt they were neither restrained by fear, nor any other consideration, seeing that Duke Filippo, the only power they had to fear, was attacked by the Venetians, and that the Lucchese, having received the enemies of Florence within their territory, and permitted them from there to attack her, had thereby deprived themselves of all right to complain.

Florentine Histories V, 17–22

17. Peace having now been restored between the people of Lucca and the Florentines, and between the Duke of Milan [Filippo Maria Visconti] and Count Francesco Sforza [March–April 1438], it was thought that the wars of Italy, and especially those that had so long plagued Lombardy and Tuscany, would now cease [...]. But matters went differently; for neither the Duke nor the Venetians would rest. Arms were therefore again resumed, and Lombardy and Tuscany were once more overrun by warring armies.[20] The proud spirit of Duke Filippo could not tolerate that the Venetians should possess Bergamo and Brescia; and he was all the more greatly annoyed at seeing them in arms and constantly plundering and disturbing many parts of his territory. He thought that he would be able not only to keep the Venetians in check, but also to recover his possessions whenever they should be abandoned by the Pope, the Florentines, and Count Francesco. Thus, Filippo resolved to take the Romagna from the Pope; judging that, once he held that country, the Pope would not be able to molest him, and the Florentines, seeing the fire so near, would either not move from fear of him, or if they would, they could not readily attack him. The Duke was aware also of the indignation which the Florentines felt against the Venetians on account of their disappointment in

---

[18] The territory contained between the rivers Adda and Serio.

[19] The Florentines had tried to seize Lucca in 1429 as well: cf. 4.3.2.

[20] This is the second war that Venice and Florence fought against Milan (1438–41). For the first one, see 4.4.5.

regard to Lucca,[21] and judged that, for this reason, they would be less disposed to take up arms on their behalf [...].

18. Niccolò [Piccinino], having thus taken the Romagna [...], went into Lombardy, where [...] he attacked the territory of Brescia, of which he made himself master in a few days, and then laid siege to the city itself [October 1438] [...]. The Venetians [...], being filled with pride and believing themselves able to resist the Duke's forces alone, disdained to ask help of anyone, and carried on the war single-handed [...].

19. [As] the war in Lombardy continued, the Venetians lost daily more cities, and the fleets which they had placed upon the rivers had been taken by the ducal forces. The whole country of Verona and Brescia was occupied, and the two cities were so closely pressed that according to general opinion they could resist but a little while longer. The Marquis of Mantua [Gian Francesco Gonzaga], who had for many years been general of the forces of the republic, had quite unexpectedly left their service and gone over to the Duke of Milan. So that fear compelled them during the progress of the war to do that which their pride would not allow them to do in the beginning. For satisfied now that their only remedy was the friendship of the Florentines and of Count Francesco Sforza, the Venetians began to solicit it, although with shame and full of doubts; for they feared to receive from the Florentines the same answer which they had given to them at the time of the attempt of the Florentines upon Lucca [...]. But they found the Florentines more ready to comply than they had hoped for, or than they would have deserved for their former conduct, so much more were the Florentines influenced by their hatred of their ancient enemy, the Duke of Milan, than by resentment at the conduct of their old and habitual friends [...].

20. [...] Neri di Gino Capponi having been deputed to treat with the Count [...], the Signoria deemed it proper that he should also proceed to Venice in order to make this benefit the more acceptable to the government of that city, and at the same time to arrange with them for the safety of the route and the passage of the river [Po] by the Count [...].

21. [...] Neri, having been introduced to the senate, spoke the following words: '[...] We were and are still certain that we might have remained neutral in this war, much to the gratitude of Duke Filippo, and with little risk to ourselves. For even if by your ruin he had made himself master of Lombardy, there were enough allies left to us in Italy to prevent our despairing of our safety [...]. We also knew what heavy expenses and imminent dangers we should have avoided by avoiding this war, how many imminent dangers we would have escaped, and how, since we are leaving our country undefended, this war might be transferred from Lombardy into Tuscany. But all these

[21] Cf. 2.2.4.

concerns have been counterbalanced by the ancient affection which we cherish for your state [...]. My government, judging that before anything else Verona and Brescia should be relieved, and supposing that this could not be done without the Count, sent me first to persuade him to pass over into Lombardy, and to carry on the war wherever directed [...]. I come, therefore, to offer to you Count Francesco, with seven thousand cavalry and two thousand infantry, ready to meet the enemy anywhere [...].' Neri's address was listened to by the senate as though he had been an oracle; and they were so excited by it that they did not wait for the Doge to reply, as is customary; but, rising to their feet, the greater part of the senators, with uplifted hands, called out to thank the Florentines for this affectionate service [...], promising at the same time that it should never be cancelled from their hearts or those of their descendants, and that Florence and Venice should ever be considered as just one homeland.

22. When this excitement had subsided they discussed the route which Count Francesco should take, so that [...] all necessary things might be provided [...]. And so soon as it was made known to the Count, he started with the utmost promptness [...]. The arrival of Count Sforza in Lombardy [June 1439] filled all Venice and all her dominions with high hopes; and where at first the Venetians had despaired of their safety, they now began to indulge in hopes of new acquisitions [...].

4.2.3 DECIDING TO RESIST

As we have just seen (cf. 4.2.2), Florence, liberated from the threat of Milan, has decided to try and take Lucca. What follows is the speech given by some Lucchese leader to incite the people to resist. The anonymous speaker shows, among other things, that the reasons the Florentines might invoke to justify their aggression are nothing but pretexts. The 'necessity' invoked at the beginning of the speech thus refers to a basic political law, according to which the inequality in terms of power between the two cities predisposes the stronger to seize the weaker, independently of what the latter has done or might do to deserve such a treatment. Attacking a weaker state is perfectly understandable: had Lucca been stronger, she would have done the same to Florence.

Florentine Histories V, 11

[...] The only thing [the Lucchese] feared was the fickleness of the lower classes, who, tired of the siege, might think more of their own dangers than of the liberty of others, and might thus force them to some disgraceful and injurious terms of capitulation. With the view, therefore, of stimulating them to the most energetic defence, they called the people together in the square, and one of the oldest and wisest citizens addressed them as follows: 'You know well that what is done from necessity merits neither praise nor censure. If, therefore, you accuse us of having provoked this war with the Florentines by having received the Duke [of Milan, Filippo Maria Visconti]'s troops in our territory, and allowed them thence to attack the Florentines, you will commit a very great error. You know well the ancient enmity of the people of Florence towards you, which has its origin not in injuries done them by you, nor in any fear they have of you, but rather from your weakness and their ambition; for the one gives them the hope of being able to subjugate you, and the other urges them on to do it. Nor must you believe that any service you could render them would remove that desire from their mind, any more than that any offence you might give them could still more excite their desire to injure you. They think of nothing but to rob you of your liberty, and you should think of nothing but to defend it; and whatever may be done by either party to further these objectives may cause us regret, but should not surprise us. Certainly we are much grieved that they should attack us, that they seize our places, burn our houses, and lay waste our country; but which of us is foolish enough to be surprised at it? For, if we could, we would do the same to them, or even worse. They pretend that they have begun this war against us because we received Niccolò [Piccinino]; but had we not done so, they would have found some other pretext, and if thus the evil had been deferred, it would probably have been the greater [...].[22] Moreover, we could not have refused to receive the troops of the Duke of Milan; and having come as they did, it was not in our power to prevent them from attacking the Florentines. You know well that, without the support of some powerful ally, we could not save our city, and there is none that could aid us more effectually and more in good faith than Duke Filippo. It was he who restored us our liberty;[23] it is reasonable, therefore, that he should maintain it for us; and he has always been a most determined enemy to our perpetual enemies. If, then, we had irritated the Duke for the sake of not offending the Florentines, we should have lost a friend, and made our enemy stronger and readier to attack us. So that it is better for us to have incurred this war while preserving the friendship of the Duke, than for the sake of peace to have exposed ourselves to his enmity. We have the right, therefore, to hope that he will help us out of the danger to which he has subjected us, provided that we do not yield to despair [...]. We have besides good reason for believing that the Venetians will hesitate to offend us, as it is not to their interest that the power of Florence should increase. On the former occasion when the Florentines attacked us, they

---

[22] Cf. 4.3.4.

[23] In 1430 the Lucchese got rid of their tyrant; on that occasion, Visconti backed them and prevented Florence from taking advantage of the situation.

were more free from embarrassments and had more hope of assistance, and were of themselves stronger; whilst we were in all respects weaker.[24] For then we defended a tyrant, but now we are defending ourselves; then the glory of the defence accrued to others, now it is ours; then our assailants were united, now they are divided amongst themselves, having filled all Italy with their banished citizens. But even if we had not all these encouragements, an ultimate necessity commands us to the most determined resistance. Every enemy is reasonably to be feared, for they all aim at their own glory and your destruction; but above all others we should fear the Florentines, for neither submission nor tribute nor the mastery over our city would satisfy them. They want our very persons and substance, so as to glut their cruelty with our blood and their avarice with our possessions; and therefore are they to be feared in every way by each one of you. Be not troubled, therefore, at seeing your fields wasted, your villages burnt, and your places seized by them; for if we save this city, we shall of necessity save all the rest. But if we lose Lucca, then it would be of little avail for us to save all the other things. If we maintain our liberty, the enemy will find it difficult to hold the rest, which we will keep in vain if our liberty is lost. To arms, then, fellow-citizens! And when you combat, think that the reward of your victory will be not only the safety of your country, but that of your homes and of your children.' These last words were received by the people with the utmost enthusiasm, and with one voice they pledged themselves to die rather than to yield or to entertain the thought of any arrangement that would in the least stain their liberty; and then they set to work to make all necessary preparations for the defence of the city.

---

[24] When the Florentines attacked Lucca in 1429, the city was diplomatically isolated.

4.3

Engaging in Expansion

4.3.1 THE ROMAN EXAMPLE

In 4.2.1 we dealt with the defensive policies of a great power under attack. We now see what a great power can do when it takes the offensive. If it can rely on good institutions, a solid army, and wise leaders, it will find it relatively easy to subjugate its rivals. As it openly fights and defeats one of its enemies, it can deceive others into submission; still others are too far away to feel immediately threatened, or are simply too scared to intervene. When they all realize their mistake, it is too late. In addition, the support of regional powers greatly facilitates expansion.

Discourses II, 1

Many, amongst them that most authoritative writer Plutarch, have held the opinion that the people of Rome were more indebted in the acquisition of their empire to the favours of fortune than to their own *virtù* [...]. It seems that Livy accepts that opinion, for he rarely makes a Roman speak of *virtù* without coupling fortune with it. Now I do not share that opinion at all, and do not believe that it can be sustained; for if no other republic has ever been known to make such conquests, this is because none other was so well organized for that purpose as Rome. It was the valour and organization of her armies that achieved those conquests, but it was the wisdom of her conduct and the nature of her institutions, as established by her first legislator, that enabled her to preserve these acquisitions [...]. The Romans never had two important wars to sustain at the same time; but it rather appears that as one war broke out the other ended, or that as one war ended the other broke out.

This is readily seen by examining the succession of their wars [...], in which we cannot fail to recognize a combination of fortune with the greatest *virtù* and prudence. And if we examine the cause of that good fortune[1] we shall

---

[1] That is, not having fought two great wars simultaneously.

readily find it; for it is most certain that when a prince or a people attain that degree of reputation that all the neighbouring princes and peoples intrinsically fear to attack him and are afraid of him, none of them will ever venture to do it except under the force of necessity; so that it will be, as it were, at the option of that powerful prince or people to make war upon such neighbours as may seem advantageous, whilst adroitly keeping the others quiet. And this he can easily do, partly by the respect they have for his power, and partly because they are deceived by the means employed to keep them quiet. And the other powers that are more distant and have no immediate intercourse with him, will look upon this as a matter too remote for them, something not to be concerned about, and will continue in this error until the fire spreads to their door; at this point, they will have no means for extinguishing it except their own forces, which will no longer suffice, the rising power having grown too strong. I will say nothing of how the Samnites remained indifferent spectators when they saw the Volscians and Aequeans defeated by the Romans;[2] and not to be too prolix I will start with the Carthaginians, who had already acquired great power and reputation when the Romans were fighting with the Samnites and the Etruscans;[3] for they were masters of all Africa,[4] they held Sardinia and Sicily, and had already a foothold in Spain. Their own power, and the fact that they were remote from the confines of Rome, did not make them think about attacking the Romans, or succouring the Samnites and Etruscans; in fact—as one is apt to do with regard to a growing power[5]—they acted to the advantage of Rome, forming an alliance with her and looking for her friendship.[6] Nor did they become aware of the error they had committed until after the Romans, having subjugated all the peoples situated between them and the Carthaginians, began to fight for the dominion of both Sicily and Spain. The same thing happened to the Gauls as to the Carthaginians, and also to King Philip of Macedon[7] and to Antiochus.[8] Each one of these believed that, whilst the Romans were occupied with the other, they would be overcome, and that then it would be time enough either by peace or war to secure themselves against the Romans. So that I believe that the good fortune which followed the Romans in this regard[9] would equally attend all those princes who acted as the Romans did, and displayed the same *virtù*.

It would be proper and interesting here to show the course which the Romans adopted when they entered the territory of an enemy, if we had not

---

[2] In 347 BC. The First Samnite War broke out in 343 BC.
[3] Between the middle of the fourth century BC and the first two decades of the third century BC.
[4] North Africa, of course.
[5] One more reason why balancing power is so problematic.
[6] A first treaty between Rome and Carthage was signed in 509 BC; a second one in 348 BC.
[7] 200–196 BC.
[8] 193–189 BC.   [9] Again, not having fought two wars simultaneously.

already explained this at length in our treatise *The Prince*[10] [...]. I will only say in a few words that they always endeavoured to have some friend in these new countries who could aid them by opening the way for them to enter, or serve as a means for retaining their possession. Thus we see that by the aid of the Capuans they entered Samnium,[11] and through the Camertini they got into Tuscany;[12] the Mamertini helped them into Sicily,[13] the Saguntines into Spain,[14] Masinissa into Africa,[15] the Aetolians into Greece,[16] Eumenes and other kings into Asia,[17] the Massilians and Eduans into Gaul.[18] And thus they never lacked similar support to facilitate their enterprises, both in the acquisition and preservation of new provinces.

4.3.2 A WAR OF AGGRESSION

Florence decides for a war of sheer aggression against Lucca. Although the attempt has been promoted by a few individuals, the Florentines as a whole take up this opportunity enthusiastically. The antilogy that follows captures the terms of most debates on a war like this: to Rinaldo degli Albizzi, seizing Lucca would be both just and expedient, to Niccolò da Uzzano unjust, costly and possibly harmful.

Florentine Histories IV, 18–20

18. [...] Niccolò Fortebraccio [...] had been for a considerable time in the service of the city of Florence during the wars with [the] Duke [of Milan] Filippo [Maria Visconti].[19] Upon the declaration of peace he was discharged by

---

[10] Chapter III.

[11] The Campanians asked the Romans for help against the Samnites; this led to the First Samnite War in 343 BC.

[12] In 310 BC Rome was backed by the Camertini in the war against the Etruscans.

[13] Threatened by Carthage, the Mamertini placed themselves under the protection of Rome, whose intervention in Sicily paved the way for the First Punic War in 264 BC.

[14] An ally of Rome, Sagunto was taken by Hannibal in 219 BC; the Romans took it back five years later and shortly afterwards began their conquest of the Iberian peninsula.

[15] In the final phase of the Second Punic War (218–202 BC), the African king allied himself with the Romans and contributed to Carthage's defeat.

[16] The Aetolians supported the Romans during the First Macedonian War (214–205 BC).

[17] In 193 BC, the King of Pergamon signed an alliance with the Romans against Antiochus III, King of the Syrian Empire.

[18] Around 150 BC the Romans intervened to help the Massilians against the Ligures, and about 30 years later to help the Eduans against the Allobroges.

[19] That is, from 1423 to 1428. Cf. 4.4.5.

the Florentines [. . .]. Rinaldo degli Albizzi[20] persuaded Niccolò to attack Lucca under some pretext, pointing out to Niccolò that if he did so, he, Rinaldo, would make the Florentines openly declare war against Lucca, and that then Niccolò would be made commander of their forces [. . .]. [Thus Niccolò] with 300 mounted men and 300 infantry, seized, in November 1429, the Lucchese castles of Ruoti and Compito, and then descended into the plain, where he took a large amount of booty. When this became known in Florence people of all sorts gathered in groups throughout the city, the greater part of which wanted war to be waged against Lucca. Of the principal citizens who were in favour of this were the adherents of the Medici with whom Rinaldo had sided, being influenced either by the belief that it would be advantageous for the republic, or perhaps by the ambitious hope that he would have the merit of victory. Those who were opposed to it were Niccolò da Uzzano[21] and his party. It would almost seem incredible that in the same city there should be such a diversity of opinion as to the undertaking of this war; for those very citizens and the same people who, after ten years of peace, had blamed the war undertaken against Duke Filippo in defence of the independence of the republic, now, after the heavy expenditures and affliction in which that war involved the city, eagerly demanded that a war should be undertaken against Lucca to suffocate somebody else's independence. And, on the other hand, those who had been in favour of the former war now strenuously opposed this one. So wildly do opinions change with time, and so ready are the multitude to seize upon the goods of others than to defend their own, and so greatly are men more influenced by the hope of gain than by the fear of loss; for the latter, unless very near, is not felt; and the former, being still remote, is believed in. And thus the people of Florence were filled with hopes by the conquests already made and yet expected to be made by Fortebraccio, and by the letters written by their rectors from near Lucca. For the governors of Pescia and Vico were writing that, if permission were given them to receive those castles that were willing to surrender to them, the whole Lucchese territory would very quickly be acquired [. . .]. The Signoria assemble[d] the Council, at which 498 citizens came together, before whom the question was discussed by the principal men of Florence.

19. Amongst the first to speak in favour of the attempt against Lucca was [. . .] Rinaldo. He pointed out the advantages that would result from the acquisition, and all the reasons why the enterprise was likely to succeed, Lucca being left an easy prey to them by the Venetians and Duke Filippo.[22]

---

[20] Extremely influential, especially in the 1420s, Rinaldo was the most formidable political adversary of Cosimo de' Medici.

[21] Yet another important man, who held the most relevant public positions from the 1390s onwards.

[22] The peace treaty of 1428 did not mention Lucca at all—the city was diplomatically isolated.

Nor could the Pope intervene, being occupied with the affairs of the Kingdom of Naples.[23] He furthermore showed the facility with which the city could be taken, being enslaved by one of her own citizens,[24] and having lost her natural vigour and ancient zeal in defence of her liberties;[25] so that the city would be given up to them, either by the people for the sake of ridding themselves of their tyrant, or by the tyrant from fear of the people. He recited the injuries done them by the lord of Lucca, his ill-will against the Florentine republic, and how dangerous he would prove if ever they should again be involved in war with either the Pope or the Duke; and concluded by saying that no enterprise ever engaged in by the Florentines had been more easy, more expedient, or more just. Against this opinion Niccolò da Uzzano argued that the city of Florence had never attempted a more unjust nor more hazardous enterprise, and from which greater injury would result. And, first, because it was a Guelph city which it was proposed to attack, and one that had ever been friendly to the Florentine people, and had many times, at her own peril, received in her bosom the Guelphs who were not permitted to remain in their own country; and that never, within the story of our city, had Lucca, when free, injured Florence; and that if those who had enslaved her—as formerly Castruccio and now Paolo Guinigi—had done so, the guilt could not be imputed to her, but to her tyrant. And if Florence could make war against the tyrant without doing so against the Lucchese, it would displease him less; but as that was impossible, he could not consent that a friendly city should be despoiled of her liberty and her property. But as people nowadays took little account of what was just or unjust, he would not now touch upon that point, but would only look to the question of expediency for their own city. He believed that only those things should be called expedient which could not readily be productive of injury; but he did not know how anyone could call an undertaking expedient in which the damage was certain and the benefit doubtful. The certain damage was the cost it would entail, which would be found so great that it should alarm a city that for a long while had enjoyed the repose of peace, and much more so one that was wearied by a serious and protracted war, as was the case with Florence. The benefit that could possibly result from it would be the conquest of Lucca, which he confessed would be a great one; but that it was proper to consider the uncertainty in which that was involved, which in his judgment was so great that he regarded the conquest impossible. And that they must not believe that the Venetians and Duke Filippo would rest satisfied with such an acquisition on their part; for the former only made pretence of consent to avoid appearing ungrateful, having but a short time before they added so largely to their dominions

---

[23] Although Pope Martin V had conceded the investiture of the Kingdom of Naples to Louis of Anjou, Queen Joan II designated Alfonso V of Aragon as her successor.

[24] Paolo Guinigi had become tyrant of Lucca in 1400.

[25] Cf. *Prince* V and 3.4.7.

by means of Florentine money.[26] And Duke Filippo would be glad to see them involve themselves in new wars and expenditures, so that, when wearied and exhausted in all respects, he might the more safely assail them anew; and that whilst they were engaged in this undertaking, and full of high hopes of victory, the Duke would not lack means of aiding the Lucchese, either covertly, with money, or by disbanding some of his troops, and letting them go to their assistance as soldiers of fortune. He therefore advised them to abstain from the attempt, and to live on such terms with the tyrant of Lucca as would cause him to increase the number of his enemies as much as possible within the city; for there would be no more convenient way of subjugating Lucca than to let her live under the rule of her tyrant, and to have her weakened and exhausted by him. For if the matter were managed prudently, things would soon come to that point in Lucca that, the tyrant not being able to hold her, the city, being incapable of governing herself, would of necessity fall into their hands.[27] Since he realized, however, that most Florentines were willing to make war and that his words were not listened to, this he would predict to them, that [...] instead of taking Lucca, they would deliver her from her tyrant, and convert her from a friendly, feeble, and enslaved city into a free and hostile city, which in time would prove an obstacle to the greatness of their own republic.

20. After the speeches in favour of and against the enterprise, a secret vote was taken, according to custom; and of the whole number present only ninety-eight were against it [...].

4.3.3 TAKING A CITY BY FORCE MAY BE COUNTERPRODUCTIVE

Volterra, despite her considerable degree of autonomy, has rebelled against Flor-entine rule (April 1472). As she sends ambassadors to Florence in order to discuss the terms of a possible settlement, the Florentines debate what they should do with her. Here again we find two opposite views that can be seen as paradigmatic of the difficult decision that imperial powers have to make when facing the rebellion of their subjects: unconditional surrender vs. negotiated settlement.

Florentine Histories VII, 30

After this first outrage [the people of Volterra] resolved before anything else to send ambassadors to Florence, who were to give the Signoria to understand that if they would maintain the ancient privileges of Volterra, they would in

---

[26] Cf. 4.4.5.   [27] Cf. 3.2.3.

return continue their ancient allegiance. The reply to be made to this was discussed at great length. Tommaso Soderini[28] advised that the Volterrans should be received in any way they were disposed to return; it seemed to him most inopportune to light a conflagration so near them that the flames of it would set their own house on fire, for he feared the character of the Pope and the power of the King of Naples, had no confidence in the alliance of the Venetians, nor in that of the Duke of Milan [...], and remembered the old proverb, that a lean peace is better than a fat victory. On the other hand, Lorenzo de' Medici, thinking the opportunity favourable for displaying the value of his counsel and prudence, and being mainly urged to it by those who were jealous of the authority of Tommaso, maintained that the arrogance of the Volterrans ought to be punished by force of arms; and affirmed that if they were not corrected in some exemplary manner, others would not hesitate to act in a similar manner at the slightest occasion, regardless of all respect for or fear of the Florentine authority. This course was thus resolved upon, and the answer given to the Volterrans was that they could not ask for the continuation of those privileges which they themselves had destroyed, and that therefore they must submit to the decision of the Signoria or expect war. The ambassadors having returned with this answer, the Volterrans prepared for defence; they fortified their town, and called upon all the Italian princes for assistance. But only a few paid any attention to their call, and none but the Sienese and the lord of Piombino gave them any hope of succour.[29] The Florentines, on the other hand, deeming that the most important means to victory was the celerity of the enterprise, assembled 10,000 infantry and 2,000 horsemen, who [...] entered the Volterran territory and easily occupied the whole of it. They then laid siege to the town [...]. The Volterrans had hired about a thousand soldiers for their defence, who, seeing the bold attack made by the Florentines, lost confidence in their own ability to resist, and were as slow in their defence as they were prompt in daily injuring the inhabitants of Volterra. The unfortunate citizens, being thus attacked by their enemies from without, and oppressed by their friends within, despaired of their safety and began to think of making terms. And seeing no better way, they unconditionally surrendered to the commissaries, who at once had the gates opened, and admitted the larger part of the Florentine troops; then went to the palace where the priors were assembled and ordered them to return to their homes. On their way there, one of the priors was in derision stripped by one of the soldiers; and so much more ready are men for evil than for good[30] that this

---

[28] Although portrayed in this episode as an adversary of Lorenzo, Tommaso was always a loyal supporter of the Medici.
[29] Piombino and Siena were the two Tuscan cities that, at that time, had reason to fear Florentine expansionism.
[30] Cf. 1.2.1 (*Prince* XVII, XVIII), *Prince* XXIII, *Discourses* I, 3, 9, 37; III, 23.

beginning led to the destruction of the city, which was sacked and pillaged an entire day. Neither women nor sacred places were spared; and the soldiers, both those who had so badly defended her and those who had assailed her, despoiled the city of her substance. The news of this victory was received with great joy by the Florentines; and as this undertaking had originated entirely with Lorenzo, his reputation quickly rose to the highest point. Thus, one of his closest friends taunted Tommaso Soderini for the advice which he had given, saying to him, 'What say you now since Volterra has been conquered?'; to which Tommaso replied, 'To me the place seems rather lost than won; for if you had received Volterra back by agreement, that city would have proved a source of profit and of security to you; but having to hold it by force, it will prove a source of weakness and anxiety to you in time of trouble, and of injury and expense in time of peace'.

4.3.4 LOUIS XII'S MISTAKES

In this well-known chapter of the Prince, *Machiavelli critically assesses the policies adopted by Louis XII in Italy. He points out that the French king has made a number of mistakes, most of which involve clumsy miscalculations, in terms of power, of the implications that his decisions have entailed. Hence, the memorable exchange between Machiavelli and the Cardinal of Rouen, in the last paragraph.*

Prince III

[...] King Louis [XII] was called into Italy by the ambition of the Venetians, who wanted to conquer half of Lombardy thanks to his coming.[31] I will not blame the King for his decision; for, wishing to gain a foothold in Italy, and having no allies there [...] he was obliged to avail himself of such friends as he could find; and his decision would have turned out well, but for an error which he committed in his subsequent conduct. The King, then, having conquered Lombardy, quickly recovered that reputation which Charles [VIII] had lost.[32] Genoa yielded; the Florentines became his friends; the Marquis of Mantua, the Duke of Ferrara, the Bentivoglio, the lady of Forlì, the lords of Faenza, Pesaro, Rimini, Camerino, and Piombino, the Lucchese, the Pisans, and

---

[31] September 1499. According to the terms of the alliance, Venice would take Cremona and the Ghiaradadda.

[32] In 1495.

the Sienese,[33] all came to meet him with offers of friendship. The Venetians might then have recognized the rashness of their course, when, for the sake of gaining two cities in Lombardy, they made King Louis master of two thirds of Italy.[34]

Let us see now how easily the King might have maintained his influence in Italy if he had observed the rules given above. Had he secured and protected all these friends of his, who were numerous but feeble—some fearing the Church, and some the Venetians, and therefore all forced to adhere to him—he might easily have secured himself against anyone who continued to be strong in Italy. But no sooner was he in Milan than he did the very opposite, by giving aid to Pope Alexander VI to enable him to seize the Romagna.[35] Nor did he realize that in doing this he was weakening himself, by alienating his friends and those who had thrown themselves into his arms; and that he had made the Church great by adding so much temporal to its spiritual power, which gave it already so much authority. Having committed this first error, he was obliged to follow it up; so that for the purpose of putting an end to the ambition of Pope Alexander VI, and preventing his becoming master of Tuscany, he was obliged to come into Italy.[36]

Not content with having made the Church great, and with having alienated his own friends, King Louis, in his eagerness to possess the Kingdom of Naples, shared it with the King of Spain;[37] so that where he had been the sole arbiter of Italy, he established an equal there, to whom the ambitious men of that country and those dissatisfied with him might have a ready recourse. And whilst he could have left a King in Naples who would have been his tributary, he dispossessed him, for the sake of replacing him by another who was powerful enough in turn to drive him out.[38] The desire of conquest is certainly most natural and common, and whenever men do it who can, they will be praised or at least not blamed; but when they cannot, and yet try to do it anyhow, here is their mistake and the reason why they will be blamed. If, then, the King of France was powerful enough by himself to successfully attack the Kingdom of Naples, then he was right to do so; but if he was not, then he

---

[33] Francesco IV Gonzaga, Ercole I Este, Giovanni Bentivoglio (lord of Bologna), Caterina Sforza Riario, Astorre III Manfredi, Giovanni Sforza, Pandolfo Malatesta, Giulio Cesare Varano, Jacopo IV Appiani, respectively.

[34] An exaggeration in light of the territory under direct French control. However, as we have just seen, Louis XII could also rely on a number of minor states (including Florence, significantly omitted by Machiavelli) that had rushed to offer him their services.

[35] Cf. 3.3.2.

[36] In 1502, Duke Valentino was getting ready to attack the Florentine territory, but was stopped by the French veto. However, Louis XII descended into Italy again not because of this but to prepare an expedition against the Kingdom of Naples.

[37] Treaty of Granada (November 1500).

[38] Defeated on the River Garigliano in December 1503, the French were forced to leave Southern Italy.

should not have divided it with the King of Spain. And if the partition of Lombardy with the Venetians was excusable because it enabled him to gain a foothold in Italy, that of Naples [with the Spaniards] deserves censure, as it cannot be excused on the ground of such necessity.

Louis had then committed these five errors: he had destroyed the weak; he had increased the power of one already powerful in Italy;[39] he had established a most powerful foreigner there; he had not gone to reside there himself; nor had he planted any colonies there. These errors might still not have injured him during his lifetime had he not committed a sixth one in depriving the Venetians of their possessions.[40] For if Louis had not increased the power of the Church, nor established the Spaniards in Italy, it would have been quite reasonable and necessary to weaken Venice; but having made those earlier decisions, he ought never to have consented to her ruin. For so long as Venice was powerful, she would always have kept the others from any attempt upon Lombardy, both because she would never have permitted this unless it should have led to her becoming mistress of it, and because the others would not have taken it from France for the sake of giving it to Venice; nor would they have had the courage to attack the French and the Venetians combined.

And should it be said that King Louis gave up the Romagna to Pope Alexander VI, and divided the Kingdom of Naples with the King of Spain for the sake of avoiding a war,[41] then I reply [...] that no one should ever submit to an evil for the sake of avoiding a war, for war is not avoided, but is only deferred to one's own disadvantage. And should it be argued that the King felt bound by the pledge which he had given to the Pope to conquer the Romagna for him in consideration of his dissolving the King's marriage, and of his bestowing the cardinal's hat upon the Archbishop of Rouen,[42] then I meet that argument with what I shall say further on concerning the pledges of princes, and the manner in which they should keep them.[43]

King Louis then lost Lombardy by not having conformed to any one of the rules that have been observed by others, who, having conquered provinces, wanted to keep them [...]. I conversed on this subject with the Cardinal of Rouen whilst at Nantes, when Valentino—the popular name for Cesare Borgia, son of Pope Alexander VI—was making himself master of the Romagna. On that occasion the Cardinal said to me that the Italians did not

---

[39] That is, Pope Alexander VI.

[40] In 1508, Louis XII adhered to the anti-Venetian League of Cambrai.

[41] Louis XII feared that Spain and the Pope might ally with the Emperor. His deal with Spain, therefore, might have been seen as an attempt to prevent that coalition from materializing.

[42] In 1498 Pope Alexander had dissolved Louis' marriage. This permitted the French king to marry Anne of Brittany, thereby securing his new wife's duchy for the Crown. In the same year, the Archbishop of Rouen, George d'Amboise, an extremely influential man in French politics, was made cardinal.

[43] Cf. 1.2.1.

understand the art of war. To which I replied that the French did not understand politics; for if they had, they would not have allowed the Church to attain such greatness. For experience proves that the greatness of the Church and that of Spain in Italy were brought about by France, and that her own ruin was brought about by them. From this we draw a general rule, which never or rarely fails, that he who causes another to become powerful thereby works his own ruin; because he has contributed to the power of the other either by his own ability or force, and both of these are mistrusted by the one who has grown powerful.

4.4

Neutrality and Alliances

4.4.1 WHY NEUTRALITY IS TO BE AVOIDED

Machiavelli's dislike for the 'middle course' finds one of its most famous expressions in the condemnation of neutrality. Taking sides is always recommended, because if you do not, you will end up as the enemy of both the conqueror and the vanquished, each of whom will have good reasons to injure you. But fear is not the only rationale for avoiding neutrality: in some cases, alliances bring about solid gains too—as will be seen also in the next excerpt.

Prince XXI

[...] If two of your neighbouring potentates should come to blows, they are either of such character that, when either of them has won, you will have cause to fear the conqueror, or not. Either way, it will always be better for you to declare yourself openly and make fair war; for if you fail to do so, in the first case you will always fall prey to the victor, to the delight and satisfaction of the defeated party, and you will have neither claim nor anything else for protection or assistance. For the conqueror will want no doubtful friends who do not stand by him in time of trial; and the vanquished will not help you because you have not been willing, with arms in hand, to take the chance of his fortunes. When Antiochus came into Greece, having been invited by the Aetolians to drive out the Romans, he sent ambassadors to the Achaeans, who were friends of the Romans, to induce them to remain neutral; whilst the Romans, on the other hand, urged them to take up arms on their behalf. The matter came up for deliberation in the council of the Achaeans, and the ambassador of Antiochus endeavoured to persuade them to remain neutral; to which, the Roman legate replied: 'For as to what they say is best, that you should not take any part in the war, nothing, on the contrary, is so inconsistent with your interests: disregarded and discredited, you will be the prize of the conqueror'.[1] And it will always be the case that he who is not your friend will claim neutrality at your hands, whilst your friend will ask your armed intervention in his favour. Irresolute princes, for the sake of avoiding immediate danger, adopt most frequently the course of neutrality, and most frequently come to ruin in consequence. But when a prince declares himself boldly in favour of one party, and that party proves victorious, even though the victor be powerful, and you are at his discretion, yet is he bound to you in obligation and affection has developed; and men are never so base as to oppress you with such flagrant ingratitude.[2] Moreover, victories are never so complete as to dispense the victor from all regards, above all for justice. But when the party whom you have supported loses, then he will receive you in his state, and, when able, will assist you; and you will have become the sharer of a fortune which may rise again.

In the second case, when the contending parties are such that you need not fear the victor, taking sides is all the more wise, for you bring about the defeat of one with the help of another who should save him, if he were prudent; for if he wins, he remains at your discretion, and it is impossible for him not to win if you aid him. And here it should be noted that a prince ought carefully to avoid making common cause with anyone more powerful than himself for the purpose of attacking another power, unless he should be compelled to do so by necessity [...]. For if [the more powerful ally] is victorious, then you are at his mercy; and princes should avoid placing themselves in such a position as much as possible. The Venetians allied themselves with France against the Duke of Milan, an alliance which they could easily have avoided, and which proved their ruin.[3] But when it is unavoidable, as was the case with the Florentines when Spain and the Pope united their forces to attack Lombardy,[4] then a prince ought to take sides, for the reasons above given. Nor should any state suppose it can ever make safe decisions; on the contrary, it should realize that every decision it makes is uncertain; for such is the order of things that one inconvenience cannot be avoided except at the risk of being exposed to another.[5] But prudence consists of knowing how to discriminate amongst these inconveniences, and of accepting the least evil for good [...].

---

[1] Livy XXXV, 49 (trans. by E. T. Sage). Cf. 3.4.2 (*Discourses* II, 15).

[2] Such a statement contradicts the bleak views on human nature expressed in 1.2.1; however, it is immediately followed by a much more pragmatic consideration.

[3] In 1499. Cf. 4.3.4.

[4] The Holy League of 1511. Louis XII tried hard to convince Florence to stand by him, to no avail: cf. 5.2.

[5] Cf. 3.2.2 and *Discourses* III, 37.

4.4.2 ALLIANCES AND THE RISE OF ROME

Alliances can be a highly effective method of aggrandizement, under certain conditions. A great power that leads its junior partners to one conquest after another will subjugate not only the states against which the alliance has been created but its very allies too. The competitive dimension of international politics is thus pushed to its logical extreme: conflict permeates even inter-allied relations. In addition, the excerpt points out that those who deliberately limit their own expansion sooner or later will be threatened by those who do not: this was the case with the Etruscans.

Discourses II, 4

Whoever has studied ancient history will have found that republics had three methods of aggrandizement. One of these was that adopted by the Etruscans, namely, to form a confederation of several republics, neither of which has any eminence over the other in rank or authority and, in the process of expansion, to associate other cities to the confederation, in a similar manner to that practised by the Swiss nowadays, and as was done anciently in Greece by the Achaeans and the Aetolians [...]. Before the establishment of the Roman dominion, the Etruscans were very powerful in Italy, both by land and by sea [...]. They subjected to their authority the entire country stretching from the Tiber to the foot of the Alps, comprising the main body of Italy [...]. The Etruscans then lived in that equality, and employed for their aggrandizement the first method mentioned above [...].

The second method is to make allies of other states, reserving to yourself, however, the position of command, the seat of dominion, and the glory of the enterprises. This was the method adopted by the Romans. The third method is to make the conquered people immediately subjects, and not allies, as practised by the Spartans and Athenians. Of these three methods the latter is perfectly useless, as was proved by these two republics who perished from no other cause than having made conquests which they could not maintain. For to undertake the government of conquered cities by violence, especially when they have been accustomed to the enjoyment of liberty, is a difficult and troublesome task.[6] Unless you can rely on your own forces and are powerfully armed, you will never secure their obedience nor be able to govern them. And to enable you to be thus powerful it becomes necessary to have allies and to increase the population of your own city; and as neither Sparta nor Athens did either of these things, their method proved useless.[7] Rome, on the contrary,

---

[6] Cf. *Prince* V.   [7] Cf. 3.2.2.

followed the second method, and did both things, and consequently rose to such extraordinary power; and as she was the only state that adhered to this system, so she was also the only one that attained such great power. Having created for herself many allies throughout Italy, she granted to them in many respects equal conditions, always, however, reserving to herself the seat of dominion and the position of command; so that they, without being themselves aware of it, ended up devoting their own efforts and blood to their own subjugation. For the Romans began to lead their armies beyond the limits of Italy, to reduce other kingdoms to provinces, to make subjects of those who, having been accustomed to live under kings, were indifferent to becoming subjects of another; and from having Roman governors, and having been conquered by Roman arms, they recognized no superior to the Romans. Because of all this, the associates of Rome in Italy found themselves all at once surrounded by Roman subjects, and at the same time pressed by a powerful city like Rome; and when they became aware of the trap into which they had been led, it was too late to remedy the evil, so great was the authority Rome had acquired by the acquisition of foreign provinces, and so great was the strength she harboured in her bosom, being the most heavily populated and most powerfully armed. And although her allies conspired together to revenge the wrongs inflicted upon them by Rome, yet they were quickly subdued, and their condition made even worse; for from allies they became subjects too. This mode of proceeding, as has been said, was practised only by the Romans; and a republic desirous of aggrandizement should adopt no other plan, for experience has proved that there is none better or more sure [...].

The first method of which we have spoken, that of forming confederations like those of the Etruscans, Achaeans, and Aetolians, or the Swiss of the present day, is next best after that practised by the Romans, for if it does not admit of extensive conquests, it has at least two other advantages: the one, not to become easily dragged into war, and the other, that whatever conquests are made are easily preserved. The reason why expansion cannot be extensive is that a confederation of republics is divided and is structured around several seats of power. This makes it difficult for its members to engage in consultation and to make decisions. It also makes them less desirous to expand. The communities that are to share in this dominion are numerous; as such, they do not value conquests as much as a single republic that expects to enjoy the exclusive benefit of them herself.[8] Furthermore, they are governed by a federal council, which naturally causes their resolutions to be more tardy than those that emanate from a single city. Experience has also shown that this system has an established limit (which in no instance has been transgressed): such

---

[8] Cf. similar observations about the German free cities in 3.1.2.

confederations are composed of twelve or fourteen cities at most,[9] and they do not try to extend beyond that. Having acquired so much power as to believe they can defend themselves against anybody, they seek no further extension of their dominion—either because the necessity to be more powerful does not force them to, or because they see no advantage in further conquests for the reasons given above. For in such a case they would have to do one of two things: either to continue adding other cities to their confederation, which would then become so numerous as to create confusion, or they would have to make the conquered people subjects. And as they see the difficulties of gaining subjects, as well as the little advantage that would result from keeping them, they attach no value to it.[10] When, therefore, these confederations have become sufficiently strong by their number, so that they consider themselves secure, they are apt to do two things: one, to take smaller states under their protection, and thus to obtain money from them which they can easily divide amongst themselves; and the other is to engage in the military service and pay of one prince or another, as the Swiss do nowadays, and as we read in history was done by those mentioned above[11] [...].

All this proves, therefore, the excellence of the system adopted by the Romans, which is the more to be admired as they had no previous example to guide them, and which has not been followed by any other state since Rome [...]. If it has seemed too difficult to imitate the example of the Romans, certainly that of the ancient Tuscans should not be deemed so, especially by the Tuscans of the present day. For although they failed, for the reasons mentioned, to create a dominion similar to the Roman one, they still managed to acquire all the power in Italy that their mode of proceeding allowed them to. Such power was secure for a long time, with much glory of dominion and of arms, and the highest praise for their manners and religion. It was first brought down by the Gauls, and afterwards crushed by the Romans. It was so completely annihilated that, although two thousand years ago it was very great, now there is scarcely any memory of it [...].

4.4.3 NO WAY OUT

The goal of retaking Pisa (cf. 1.1.1) with the support of the French affects Florence's foreign policy for years to come. As such, Florentine dependence on

---

[9] These numbers have a historical foundation: the Etruscan confederation was composed of twelve cities; the Swiss confederation (established in 1513) of thirteen cantons.

[10] In a similar vein, writing about the Swiss, 4.1.3 (Letter to Francesco Vettori, 26 August 1513).

[11] The Achaeans and the Aetolians—but not the Etruscans.

France continues to increase as the city finds herself increasingly isolated among the other Italian states. In the spring of 1500, Louis XII intends to move against the Kingdom of Naples with the financial support of Florence: the city will pay for part of the French forces (the Swiss and the Gascons), with the understanding that they will first take Pisa on Florence's behalf. Everything goes wrong, though. The Swiss and the Gascons mutiny, and the Pisans seize an important stronghold. Florence, at this point, refuses to pay for the Swiss, who, on their way back home, threaten to pillage the French-occupied duchy of Milan. Louis XII has to pull out the money from his own pocket to prevent devastation. He blames the Florentines for the mutiny, and now he wants his money back. Machiavelli is sent to him in order to explain that the Pisa fiasco has not been Florence's fault. To no avail: the King and his ministers do not hesitate to make sinister threats to force the city to give in. The Florentines eventually capitulate when Duke Valentino, in October, begins to exert pressure on their eastern borders. Since the Duke is supported by the French, the French alliance is all the more necessary to keep him from injuring Florence.

I Mission to France

Melun, 8 September 1500

[. . .] In our previous two letters [we pointed out that] His Majesty of France was much irritated against your lordships because of your inability to resume the war against Pisa, and that thus he was prevented from retrieving the honour of his arms at your expense; and then that he had been obliged to spend his own money to pay the Swiss, and the artillery, and the Gascons, all of which, according to His Majesty, should have been paid by you. This is the sum and substance of all that has to be settled here; and unless these points are satisfactorily arranged, it will be impossible to attempt any new negotiations, or, even if begun, to conclude them satisfactorily [. . .]. To the above two causes of discontent on the part of His Majesty a third must be added, which is no less important than the others; and this is the suspicion which His Majesty has conceived that you are willing to change policy.[12] This doubt has been excited in His Majesty's mind by the Pisa business, and makes him think that you may consider yourselves as having been badly served in that affair; and that it was in consequence of this that your ambassadors left, so to say, *ex abrupto*, and that nothing is heard of the coming of any new ones. Your enemies here make him doubt even more and make him attach more importance to such suspicions than what their nature would otherwise merit. And above all others have the Italians been active in this; for they may be said to

---

[12] That is, an alliance with the Emperor, as mentioned at the end of this dispatch.

labour without restraint to put you in disgrace with His Majesty, and to compass your ruin [...]. And yet matters remain in suspense for the present, for no reason but to ascertain your intentions, which, according to our judgment, should have for their first result the determination to pay the sum which the King claims to have expended for your account; and next to send ambassadors here whose departure from Florence should be immediately notified to this court. And the sooner they leave, the sooner shall we be able to begin negotiations touching your lordships' interests [...]. Upon receiving your lordships' letters of the 14th and 30th of last month, we presented ourselves at court [...] to inform His Majesty about what you had written on Librafatta[13] [...]. And by way of disposing His Majesty more favourably towards us, and inducing him to give us a more benevolent hearing, we thought it well to begin our address with mentioning the coming of your ambassadors [...]. After that we told His Majesty of the loss of Librafatta; and to save our credit as much as possible, we said that, although your lordships had been deprived of your men-at-arms from having relied upon His Majesty's troops, and that since their withdrawal you had not had the time to reorganize your forces, yet the Pisans never could have taken Librafatta without the treachery of the castellan in charge of it, and the aid and support of the Lucchese, who in that affair, as in all other instances, had manifested their bad disposition and evil-mindedness towards us; [... we added] that His Majesty could by a single blow make them sensible of the mistake they have made, and at the same time relieve somehow our republic from the wretched situation in which it is placed by the restitution of Pietrasanta. And here we pointed out to His Majesty the good that would result from it, in such terms as the time and the nature of the audience admitted, recommending to him at the same time our republic, and assuring him of your constant good faith, and of the malignity of those who were not ashamed boldly to accuse your lordships of having sent ambassadors to the Emperor [...].

His Majesty graciously replied that if your ambassadors were ready to leave Florence he would be greatly pleased, for he should then know that your lordships feel the same towards him now as you have always done in the past, and as you say you desire to do in the future. But that he should still be more convinced on the subject when he should see that he was not to suffer any loss, by having to pay what, according to the stipulations of the convention, should be paid by you. In speaking of this blessed money which he has paid to the Swiss and others for your account, after the raising of the siege of Pisa, His Majesty made use of expressions that should be seriously weighed, coming as they do from the mouth of so powerful a person; for he said, 'If your lordships

---

[13] This stronghold, located between Pisa and Lucca, was instrumental in controlling the Serchio Valley.

were to refuse to pay this money, I should consider that they are no friends of mine, and should recompense myself anyway' [. . .].

Blois, 11 October 1500

[. . . The Cardinal of Rouen] spoke for more than half an hour, beginning with complaints of your obstinacy before the first treaty was concluded with His Majesty of France; and how badly your lordships afterwards observed the stipulations of that treaty; and how tardy you had always been in all matters; and blaming us in a measure for the money spent in the recovery of Milan, after the revolt of that city.[14] After that he came to the new treaty made with Piero Soderini at Milan, and to the army that had been directed against Pisa; and how, from his affection for you, His Majesty's arms had suffered dishonour in that affair; and how you had backed out of every commitment ever since, although you had shown yourselves very brave in refusing to pay one farthing of the money for the Swiss and the artillery, etc., leaving it all to be paid by His Majesty. And finally he concluded by saying, that he was willing to forget all the other things, but that it was indispensable for your lordships to decide upon refunding that money to His Majesty; that there was not a day but that the Lucchese, the Genoese, and the Pisans came about His Majesty's ears with offers of large sums of money, without agreement or obligations of any kind; at which His Majesty could not but be astonished, seeing on the one hand their good disposition, and noting on the other hand your obstinacy, first in refusing to pay despite your obligations, and your delay now in putting off to do anything under pretence of waiting for the new ambassadors. 'But I tell you', said he, 'from the affection which I have for your republic, although of course not equal to that which I have for the King, that these ambassadors of yours can neither negotiate, nor will they be listened to upon any point, unless payment is first made of the amount due [. . .]; write therefore at once to your government, for we want a response at once; nor do we wish to, nor can, remain any longer in suspense upon this point; and let them understand that, whether they choose to be friends or enemies, in any event they will have to pay. But if you remain our friends, as you will if you are wise, His Majesty will pass Christmas at Lyons, and Easter at Milan. He has sent up to two thousand lances[15] into Italy, and added over six thousand infantry to those who were already there; and we shall see whether Pisa will resist him, and whether those who oppose him are stronger than he is. His friends will know then that he is King, and that his promises are carried out' [. . .].

---

[14] Driven out of Milan by Louis XII in 1499, Duke Ludovico Sforza made a comeback in February 1500 as the Milanese rebelled against French rule. In April, however, he was defeated again and taken prisoner by Louis.

[15] The 'lance' was the basic tactical unit consisting of at least three men: one man-at-arms, one lighter horseman, one page. Mounted archers could then be added in varying numbers.

Your lordships will judge whether it would have been possible for me to have made a reply to such a proposition, even in case our assets could have made them patient enough to listen to me [...].

Nantes, 4 November 1500

[...] I determined [...] to speak to the King and the Cardinal of Rouen about your lordships' apprehensions on account of the rumours that have reached you from many quarters as to the evil disposition of the army of Duke Valentino towards your lordships; and how seriously this matter disturbs you, being without any organized force of men-at-arms; and how you rely altogether upon His Majesty, whom you entreat to be pleased to aid you with such means as he might deem necessary; and that on your part you would not fail to do everything in your power to save your liberty; and that if your enemies sought to injure you with the help of the Orsini and the Vitelli, you would seek to defend yourselves with the help of the Colonna troops. His Majesty, being at the moment very much occupied, made no reply except that I should speak to the Cardinal of Rouen about it. I therefore went immediately to see His Eminence, and spoke to him in the same sense as I had done to His Majesty, adding such further remarks in favour of your cause as the time permitted. He replied that he did not believe that the Pope would attempt to engage in any enterprise in Italy without first conferring with His Majesty on the subject; and as he had not done so, he did not think the Pope would make any such attempt. But should he yet consult His Majesty, or attempt such an attack independently, then in the first case His Majesty would not give his consent, and in the latter he would lend you his assistance, provided you maintained friendly relations with him. And then he began to complain of the delay in the coming of your ambassadors, etc. And as to the part of the Colonna, he reflected a moment, and then said, 'Preserve the friendship of the King, and then you will not need that help; but if you lose his good graces, that help will not suffice you' [...].

4.4.4 THE RISKS OF ASYMMETRICAL ALLIANCES

For the general context of this mission, see 1.1.2. In anticipating further overtures that he will make after liquidating the rebels, Duke Valentino hints at an amicable arrangement, in fact an alliance, with Florence. Machiavelli—just like the Florentine government later—is quite reluctant: the gap in military power between the two parties is simply too wide, and Florence would risk finding herself in the Duke's hands. As we know (cf. 4.4.1 and 4.4.2), one should never enter an offensive alliance with a stronger partner.

II Mission to Duke Valentino

Imola, 8 November 1502

[. . .] I must communicate to your lordships a conversation I had with that friend of mine, who, as I have mentioned to you, told me within the past few days that it was not well for you to remain on general terms with the Duke [Valentino], and that it would be an easy matter for you to form an alliance with him, having both the same aims and the same enemies. That individual, having appointed an interview with me yesterday evening, said to me: 'Secretary, I have on a former occasion intimated to you that for your government to remain on mere general good terms with the Duke is of little advantage to him, and still less to you; for this reason, that the Duke, seeing that all remains vague with regard to your government, will form an alliance with others. I wish to talk this over with you at length this evening. Although I speak only for myself, yet I have good grounds for what I am about to say to you. The Duke knows very well that the Pope may die any day,[16] and that, if he desires to preserve the territories which he has, it behoves him to think of basing his power upon some other foundation before the death of the Pope. His first reliance is upon the King of France, the next upon his own armed forces; and you see that he has already brought together nearly five hundred men-at-arms, and as many light cavalry, which will be operational within a few days. But as he foresees that in time these two foundations might not suffice him, he thinks of making friends with his neighbours and those who of necessity must defend him, if they wish to defend themselves, such as the Florentines, the Bolognese, Mantua, and Ferrara [. . .]. To remain on mere general terms would be a greater disadvantage for your government than for the Duke; for he having the good will of the King and of the aforementioned princes, whilst your lords having no other support than that of the King, they will find that they have more need of the Duke than the Duke of them. I do not by any means wish to say that the Duke is not disposed to render them any service; but should it happen that they really have need of him, and he being under no obligations to them, he would be free to aid them or not, as might seem good to him. Now were you to ask me what they ought to do, and that I should specify some particulars, I would reply, that you for your part have two sores, which, if you do not heal them, will enfeeble you and perhaps cause your death. The one is Pisa, and the other is Vitellozzo [Vitelli].[17] If now you were to recover the former, and if the latter were crushed, would not that be a great advantage for

---

[16] It might be worth reminding the reader that Duke Valentino was the son of Pope Alexander VI.

[17] Vitellozzo and his brother Paolo were at the service of Florence as condottieri in the war against Pisa. Suspected of treason, Paolo was beheaded by the Florentine government in 1499. Vitellozzo—now in the service of Duke Valentino—spent the rest of his life trying to take revenge on Florence for his brother's death.

your republic? And so far as the Duke is concerned, I tell you that His Excellency would be satisfied with the honour of having his former engagement renewed by your government, which he would value more than money or anything else; so that if you were to find means for bringing this about, everything would be settled. And if you were to tell me with regard to Vitellozzo, "The Duke has made a compact with him and the Orsini", I should reply that their ratification of it has not yet been received, and that the Duke would give the best town he possesses that ratification should not come or that such a compact had never been talked about. Still, if the ratification should come, I would say, "Where there are men there are means";[18] and it is better to come to an understanding, even an oral one, provided it is based upon expediency, than to a pact, even a written one, which one does not intend to keep. You must understand, furthermore, that it is necessary for the Duke to save some of the Orsini; for in case of the Pope's death it is important for him to have some friends in Rome. But he cannot bear to hear the name of Vitellozzo as much as mentioned; for he regards him as a venomous serpent, and as a firebrand for Tuscany and for all Italy, who has done and continues to do all he can to prevent the Orsini from ratifying the treaty. I desire, therefore, that you should write to the Gonfalonier, or to the Ten, what I have said to you. Remind them also of another thing—which comes altogether from me— namely, that it might easily happen that the King of France should direct your government to maintain the engagement of the Duke, and to place their troops at his service, which they would in that case be obliged to do without receiving any credit for it. And therefore remind your government that when a service has to be rendered, it is better to perform it of one's own free will, and so as to have it appreciated rather than otherwise' [...].

I replied briefly, and only to those points that seemed specially to require it. In the first instance, I told him that the Duke had acted wisely in arming himself and in securing allies; and secondly, I confessed to him that it was our earliest desire to recover Pisa, and to secure ourselves against Vitellozzo, although we did not regard him as of much account. Thirdly, as for the engagement of the Duke, I said [...] that he, in light of the dominion he holds, was not to be compared to the other princes, who had nothing but their carriages; in fact, the Duke must be looked upon as a new power in Italy, with which it was better to conclude a friendship and alliance rather than an engagement. And [I added that] as alliances between princes are maintained only by arms, inasmuch as the power of arms alone could enforce their observance,[19] your lordships would not be able to see what security they could have for their part when three fourths or three fifths of their troops

---

[18] Literal translation of a proverb, whose meaning is that among human beings it is always possible to make a deal, even if this entails breaking another arrangement previously made.
[19] Cf. 2.1.1, fn. 6.

were under the control of the Duke. But I wanted him to know that I did not say this because I doubted the trustworthiness of the Duke, but because I knew your lordships to be prudent men; that it was the duty of governments to be circumspect, and never to expose themselves by their acts to be deceived [...].

4.4.5 ALLIED MISGIVINGS

The excerpts below further highlight the ambiguities of alliances. In the first case, Florence enters the Milanese alliance only to keep an eye on the Duke of Milan and to have, later on, a justification for war against him. In the second case, although Venice and Florence cooperate successfully against Milan, their collaboration is short-lived because the Florentines are resentful of their own ally's success.

Florentine Histories IV, 3–5, 13, 15

3. [...] Filippo [Maria] Visconti [Duke of Milan] [...], who [...] had become master of all Lombardy,[20] believing himself capable of undertaking any enterprise, greatly desired to recover the mastery over Genoa [...]. But he was doubtful whether success would be certain in this or any other enterprise, unless he first concluded a new treaty with the Florentines, and to have it made publicly known; for he thought that the credit he would gain thereby would suffice to enable him to accomplish his desires. He therefore sent ambassadors to Florence to obtain such a treaty. Many citizens advised that it should not be made, as, without any new treaty, they ought to continue the peace with Filippo, which had been maintained for so many years; for they knew the great advantage which such a treaty would afford to Filippo, and of how little benefit it would be to their city. Many others thought it best to make such a treaty, and by virtue of it to impose conditions upon Filippo, the transgression of which would make his evil intentions manifest to everybody; and that then, in case he broke the peace, they might with the greater justice make war against him. And thus, after the matter had been much debated, a treaty of peace was concluded [in 1420], in which Filippo pledged himself in no way to interfere with anything on the Florentine side of the rivers Magra and Panaro.[21]

4. As soon as this treaty was made, Filippo seized Brescia, and soon after he took Genoa, contrary to the expectations of those Florentines who had advised the making of the treaty; for they had believed that Brescia would be protected

---

[20] In 1412, after his brother's death, Filippo united all the Visconti territories under his rule.
[21] The treaty thus established two spheres of influence: Genoa and Lombardy to Milan, Tuscany (and possibly the Romagna) to Florence.

by the Venetians, and that Genoa would be able to defend herself. And inasmuch as in the terms which Filippo had made with the Doge of Genoa, he had left him Sarzana, and other places situated on this side of the Magra, on condition that he should not part with them except to the Genoese, it was considered that Filippo had violated his treaty with Florence. He had, moreover, concluded a treaty with the Legate of Bologna. These things caused great uneasiness to our citizens, who, apprehensive of further troubles, began to think of further remedies [...]. The Ten were appointed, troops were levied, and fresh taxes imposed, which, bearing much heavier upon the lower classes than upon the wealthy citizens, filled the city with complaints [...].

5. [...] But what alarmed everybody, and was the main cause for declaring war, was the attempt which Duke Filippo made upon Forlì[22] [...]. When this fact became known at Florence, together with the news of the arrival of troops at Bologna, it facilitated the determination to declare war. Still there was great opposition to it, and Giovanni de' Medici publicly counselled against it, pointing out that, however certain the Duke's evil intentions were, yet it would be better to wait until he should make an attack than to move against him at once; for in the latter case the war would be justified in the opinion of the other Italian princes on the part of the Duke as well as on our own part; and that then we could not claim their assistance with the same energy as we might do if we allowed the Duke to manifest his ambitious projects; and that, finally, people defend what belongs to them with more courage and determination than what belongs to others. To this it was replied that one should not await the enemy at home, but that it was better to go to meet him, and that fortune favoured the assailants more than the defendants;[23] and that it was less injurious, even if more costly in money, to carry the war into the enemy's country, than to have it in one's own. This opinion prevailed, and it was resolved that the Ten should take all means for recovering the city of Forlì from the hands of the Duke [...].

13. [After various vicissitudes] the Florentines [...] frightened by this event[24] and alarmed by their frequent defeats, concluded that they were not able to carry on this war alone; and therefore sent ambassadors to the Venetians to pray them, whilst it was still easy for them to do so, to oppose the greatness of one man, who, if they allowed him to increase in power, would be as dangerous for them as he was for the Florentines [...]. And [the Venetians] concluded a league with them, by which both parties obligated themselves to carry on the war at joint expense; and that the conquests in Lombardy should belong to the Venetians, and those in the Romagna and

[22] Forlì placed itself in Visconti's hands in 1423.   [23] Cf. 1.3.3.
[24] The sudden defection of their commander, Niccolò Piccinino, who went into the service of Duke Filippo in November 1425.

Tuscany to the Florentines; and Carmagnola was appointed the commander-in-chief of the forces of the league [...].

15. [...] Having [Carmagnola] come to battle with the Duke's forces, he routed them at Maclodio [October 1427]. After this defeat Filippo entered into new negotiations for a treaty, which were acceded to by the Venetians and Florentines; by the latter, from being suspicious of the Venetians, for it seemed to them that they had spent enough to make others powerful; and by the former, because they had observed that Carmagnola after the defeat of the Duke had become less active, so that they thought that they could no longer trust him. Peace was therefore concluded in 1428; according to the terms of which the Florentines were to receive back the places lost in the Romagna, and the Venetians retained Brescia, besides which the Duke gave them Bergamo with its territory. Florence spent in this war the sum of three and a half million ducats; and whilst the Venetians increased in power and possessions, the Florentines in poverty and divisions [...].

4.4.6 COALITIONS ARE UNRELIABLE ...

In keeping with their expansionist policy, the Venetians move towards Ferrara in 1482. They are opposed by a triple alliance consisting of Naples, Florence, and Milan. Military operations go well for the allies at the beginning. Then, as is frequently the case when many fight against one, the latter is able to exploit the differences among the former (cf. 4.2.1), so that the victory that was within reach eventually evaporates.

Florentine Histories VIII, 24–6

24. This was the state of things in the Romagna and in Rome, when the Venetians took Ficarolo [June 1482] and passed the River Po with their forces [...]; they were becoming daily more hopeful of getting possession of Ferrara. The King of Naples [Ferdinand I] and the Florentines, on the other hand, were making every effort to induce the Pope to come around to their view, and [...] threatened him with the convocation of the council which had already been proclaimed by the Emperor to be held at Basle [...].[25] The Pontiff, actuated partly by fear and also because he saw that the aggrandizement of Venice would be the ruin of the Church and of Italy, turned to make terms with the

---

[25] The Emperor, in fact, had proclaimed no council. That was simply the idea of a prelate—Andrea Zamometi—who, wishing to embarrass Pope Sistus IV, intended to reopen the Council of Basle (1431–49).

league, and sent his nuncios to Naples, where a new league was concluded for five years between the Pope, the King of Naples, the Duke of Milan [Ludovico Sforza],[26] and the Florentines; leaving it open to the Venetians also to join it if they so desired [December 1482]. This being accomplished, the Pope sent word to the Venetians to desist from their war upon Ferrara, which the Venetians refused, but rather increased their efforts for the continuance of the war; and having routed the troops of the Duke of Milan and of the Marquis[27] at Argenta, they approached so near to Ferrara that they established their camp in the very park of the Marquis himself.

25. The league therefore thought that there was no time to be lost in sending powerful assistance to the Marquis; and accordingly they ordered the Duke of Calabria to proceed to Ferrara with his own troops and those of the Pope. The Florentines likewise sent all their forces there; and the better to organize the campaign, the league held a diet at Cremona [. . .]. Convinced that there would be no more effectual way of succouring Ferrara than by a powerful diversion, they wanted Ludovico Sforza to make open war against the Venetians moving from the territory of the duchy of Milan. This he refused to do, fearing to involve himself in a war which it might be impossible for him to stop when so he had wished [. . .]. The first thing to do, in the opinion of the league, was to attack the flotilla which the Venetians had on the River Po; and having attacked it near Bondeno, they defeated it, destroying over two hundred vessels [. . .]. Seeing all Italy combined against them, the Venetians, by way of magnifying their reputation, had engaged the services of the Duke of Lorraine,[28] with 200 mounted men; and after the disaster to their fleet, they sent him with a part of their army to keep the enemy at bay, and ordered Roberto da San Severino to cross the River Adda with the remainder of their forces, and to proceed to Milan, there to raise the cry of the Duke and the lady Bona, his mother.[29] In this way they hoped to stir up a revolution in Milan, believing that Ludovico Sforza and his government were odious to the people of that city. This attack [. . .] in the end resulted very differently from the expectations of the Venetians, for it caused Ludovico now to consent to do what at first he had refused. Therefore, having left to the Marquis of Ferrara 4,000 horsemen and 2,000 infantry for the defence of his own possessions, the Duke of Calabria, with 12,000 horsemen and 5,000 infantry, entered the territory of Bergamo, and thence that of Brescia, and after that the Veronese, and devastated almost the entire country belonging to those three cities. The Venetians were utterly unable to prevent this; in fact, it was with the utmost difficulty that Roberto succeeded in saving the cities themselves. On the other hand, the

---

[26] In fact, Ludovico Sforza was the regent of the duchy (see fn. 29 below).

[27] Ercole I.   [28] René of Anjou.

[29] When Galeazzo Maria Sforza died in 1476, his son Gian Galeazzo was only seven years old. His uncle, Ludovico Sforza, successfully disputed the regency of the duchy with his mother Bona.

Marquis of Ferrara had also recovered the greater part of his territory [...]. And thus during the whole summer of 1483 the results of the war were favourable for the league.

26. Winter having passed without any active hostilities, the armies again took the field with the opening of spring [1484]. The league had united all their forces for the purpose of more promptly crushing the Venetians; and if the war had been maintained as in the preceding year, they would easily have taken from the Venetians all the territory they held in Lombardy, for their forces were reduced to 6,000 horsemen and 5,000 infantry, whilst the league had 13,000 horsemen and 6,000 infantry [...]. But as it often happens where there are many of equal authority, differences arise between them that give the victory to the enemy. After the death of Federigo Gonzaga, Marquis of Mantua, who by his influence and authority had held the Duke of Calabria and Ludovico Sforza to their engagements, differences began to arise between them, which soon ripened into jealousies. Gian Galeazzo [Sforza], Duke of Milan, was now of suitable age to take the government into his own hands; and having married the daughter of the Duke of Calabria, the latter thought that his son-in-law, and not Ludovico Sforza, ought to govern the state. But Ludovico, aware of the Duke's desire, was resolved to prevent his carrying it into effect. As soon as Ludovico's suspicion became known to the Venetians, they seized upon the opportunity as a favourable one to enable them, according to their wont, to recover by peace what they had lost by war; and terms having been secretly negotiated between them and Ludovico, they concluded a peace in August 1484. When this came to the knowledge of the other members of the league, it caused them the greatest dissatisfaction, mainly because they saw that they would have to restore to the Venetians the places they had taken from them, and to leave in their hands Rovigo and the Polesine, which the Venetians had taken from the Marquis of Ferrara, and give them back all those prerogatives over the city of Ferrara as they formerly had. Each member of the league seemed to think that they had at great expense made a war, the conduct of which had been creditable to them, but its termination ignominious; for the places they had taken they would have to restore, whilst those they had lost they were not to recover. They had nevertheless to accept the peace, for they were weary of the expense of the war, and were unwilling, on account of the defections and ambition of others, to risk their own fortune any longer.

4.4.7 ... AND LITIGIOUS

Florence was not a member of the League of Cambrai; as such, she did not participate in the general war against Venice in 1509. At the same time, however, she agreed to finance the war effort of France, Spain, and the Emperor.

After the Venetian defeat at Agnadello in May, the Florentine government sends
Machiavelli to the Emperor to pay homage and give him an account of the
money it has promised. Having thus travelled first to Mantua, then to Verona,
Machiavelli is a first-hand witness to the hesitations of the French and the
impotence of the imperial forces, as well as their joint mistreatment of the local
population. All this will prevent the allies from exploiting their great victory and
help Venice to recover many of the lost cities.

Mission to Mantua on Business with the Emperor

Verona, 29 November 1509

[...] Since my last dispatch some two hundred men-at-arms arrived here, part
French and part Italian [...]. The Emperor and the grand master [...],[30]
when they meet, will have to decide as to the manner in which this war is to be
waged. I have made every effort to find out whether the King of France claims
any compensation, or is about to receive any, from the Emperor for carrying
on this war, or whether he will really do it without compensation, deeming it
sufficient gain to keep the enemy at a distance from his frontiers, and thus
deprive the peoples which are not very loyal of the opportunity to rebel. But
I have not yet been able to obtain any information upon this point satisfactory
to myself, for I do not believe that there is anyone here that knows anything
about it; and those with whom I have talked on the subject are reluctant to
speak out, and say that the Emperor Maximilian will not give the King of
France a single battlement in all the territory that belongs to him; and that the
King of France ought to be satisfied to have the territories of the Emperor as a
shield to his own, and to allow the Emperor to be trampled underfoot first [by
the Venetians]; and that the King of France is obliged to undertake this
defence, inasmuch as he thereby defends his own state more advantageously
and more securely in keeping the enemy at a distance than by waiting until he
is on his frontiers. They seem to think that France is obliged to take this
course. It remains now to be seen how the King himself will view the matter.
All I can say to your lordships is that this country cannot remain in the present
condition; for the longer these sovereigns protract this war, the more ardent
will the desire of these peoples become to return under the dominion of their
original masters; for the inhabitants of the cities are devoured by the troops
quartered in their houses, whilst those who live in the countryside are plundered and killed. The Venetians, who are aware of all this, act in exactly the
opposite way, causing everything to be respected both within and without the
cities, to a degree that is almost incredible on the part of such an armed

---

[30] Charles d'Amboise, Grand Master of France and governor of Milan.

multitude; thus, if these two sovereigns keep each other in check, and do not make a short and vigorous war, this may give rise to events that will cause these cities to return to their former allegiance more readily than they broke from it [...].

Verona, 1 December 1509

[...] Some three thousand German infantry came here today; they are said to be a part of the garrison of Vicenza [...]. The bishop,[31] desiring to relieve the city, at the request of the inhabitants, and believing himself that there were troops enough here to warrant their going out into the country to be quartered in some of the neighbouring castles, whence they could press the enemy and at the same time alleviate the city, requested yesterday the French troops that are here to do so; but they replied that they would not leave the city to advance without orders from the grand master. As chance would have it, news came at the same time that the Emperor had sent Ludovico Gonzaga to the grand master with a similar request, and that the latter had made a similar reply; namely, that without fresh orders from the King he would not make his troops go beyond Verona. Thus the imperials began to talk very disparagingly about the French, saying that the Emperor would make terms with the Venetians, and drive the French out of Italy. Consequently, the whole of last night the French troops remained under arms and on horseback in the city. And some of the gentlemen here were greatly afraid that the French would return this morning to Peschiera, and that on the day after the Venetians would come back here. And yet today all seems to be arranged, but how it was done I know not. The French captains have had a long consultation with the bishop, but the result of it is not yet made public. But we see as it were from a distance that here are two sovereigns, one of which has the ability to make war, but is not willing, whilst the other is willing but lacks the ability;[32] and the one who is able trifles away his time. Would to God that the latter knew what he is doing, for if he reflected to what point the desperation of the inhabitants here goes, he should feel that he cannot be prompt enough in removing from their sight the army [...], nor would he give thought to anything else. And if one continues by the present proceedings to keep up the desperation of the people of this country, and to keep alive the Venetians, then, as I have before remarked, it may at any moment give rise to events that will make Kings and popes, as well as ourselves, repent that we have not done our duty at the right time [...].

---

[31] Georg von Neideck, Bishop of Trento and governor of Verona.
[32] The former is Louis XII, the latter Maximilian I.

Part V

History and Analysis

5.1

The Italian State System, 1444–1454

This long excerpt deals with the Italian state system in the decade leading to the Peace of Lodi of 1454—a general settlement that will put an end to some thirty years of wars and that will persist until 1494. Individuals—kings and popes, but above all Francesco Sforza, a formidable condottiero looking for a state of his own—and collective actors—such as the Venetians and the Florentines—engage in all sorts of opportunistic behaviour, whose main aims are to injure one's enemies and to increase one's own power: promises cannot be trusted, alliances are full of poison, sudden volte-faces are a matter of course. The five main Italian states—Naples, Florence, Milan, Venice, and the State of the Church— thus engage in never-ending quarrels and wars, always keeping an eye on each other and preventing one another from growing too powerful.

FLORENTINE HISTORIES VI, 11–14, 17–27, 31–2

11. After the death of Niccolò Piccinino and the peace of the Marca [of Ancona] [September 1444], [the] Duke [of Milan] Filippo [Maria Visconti], being in search of a commander for his troops, secretly negotiated with Ciarpellone, one of the best captains of Count Francesco Sforza. An engagement having been agreed upon, Ciarpellone asked Count Sforza for leave to go to Milan, for the purpose of taking possession of some castles that had been given to him in the late wars. The Count, mistrusting the real motive of this journey, and with the view of preventing the Duke from availing himself of Ciarpellone in any way contrary to his designs, first had Ciarpellone imprisoned, and soon after put to death, alleging that he had discovered his plotting treason against him. Duke Filippo was much displeased and angered by this, whilst the Venetians and Florentines were gratified by it, for they much feared a union between the Duke and the Count. The Duke's resentment thus gave occasion for fresh wars in the Marca. Sigismondo [Pandolfo] Malatesta, lord of Rimini, and son-in-law to the Count, hoped on this account to obtain the lordship of Pesaro; but after occupying this town, Count Sforza bestowed it upon his

brother, Alessandro, which greatly irritated Sigismondo. This feeling was increased still more when he saw that his enemy, Federico di Montefeltro, had become lord of Urbino thanks to the support of the Count. All this caused Sigismondo to throw himself into the ranks of Duke Filippo, and to solicit the Pope [Eugene IV] and the King of Naples [Alfonso I] to make war upon Count Sforza. Count Sforza, for the purpose of making Sigismondo himself taste the first fruits of the war which he wished for, resolved to forestall him, and suddenly attacked him. In consequence of this the Romagna and the Marca were quickly involved in confusion; for Duke Filippo, the King of Naples, and the Pope sent powerful aid to Sigismondo, whilst the Florentines and Venetians provided Count Sforza with money, if not with men. Filippo, not content with making war upon Sforza in the Romagna only, attempted also to take Cremona and Pontremoli from him; but Pontremoli was defended by the Florentines, and Cremona by the Venetians. Thus the war was also renewed in Lombardy, where, after general engagements in the Cremonese territory, Francesco Piccinino, general of the Duke's forces, was defeated at Casale[1] by Micheletto and the Venetian troops. This victory allowed the Venetians to dare to hope that they could drive Duke Filippo from his states. They sent a commissary to Cremona, and attacked the Ghiaradadda, and took the whole of it excepting Crema. Afterwards they crossed the River Adda, and scoured the country up to the very gates of Milan; as a consequence, the Duke had recourse to King Alfonso, begging him for assistance, and pointing out to him the danger to which the Kingdom of Naples would be exposed if the Venetians should become masters of Lombardy. Alfonso promised to send him troops, which, however, could not pass into Lombardy except with great difficulty, unless with Count Sforza's consent.

12. Duke Filippo thereupon entreated Count Sforza—his father-in-law, now old and blind—not to abandon him. The Count was offended with him for having made war against him; on the other hand, he did not like the aggrandizement of the Venetians, and besides began to lack funds, which the league provided, but sparingly. For the Florentines had no longer that fear of Duke Filippo which had made them look for an alliance with Count Sforza, and the Venetians desired his ruin, believing him to be the only man that could take Lombardy from them. Nevertheless, whilst Duke Filippo sought to draw the Count into his pay, and offered him the command of all his troops provided he would leave the Venetians and restore the Marca to the Pope, the Venetians also sent messengers to him promising him Milan if they should take it, and the command in perpetuity of their forces, provided he continued the war in the Marca and prevented Alfonso from sending assistance into Lombardy. These promises of the Venetians were large and tempting, and they

---

[1] About 35 miles north-west of Cremona.

had rendered important services to the Count in having gone to war to save Cremona for him; in addition, the injuries received at the hands of the Duke were still fresh, and his promises were insignificant and not to be relied upon. With all this, Count Sforza was in doubt as to which side he should take; for on the one hand he was influenced by his obligations to the league, his pledged faith,[2] the recent benefits received, and the promises for the future. On the other hand were the entreaties of his father-in-law, and, above all, his fear that there was some secret poison concealed under the great promises of the Venetians. For he judged that, in case the Venetians had won the war, he would be at their discretion, both as regards their promises and his own states, a position to which no prudent prince would expose himself except out of necessity. These difficulties in coming to a determination were removed by the ambition of the Venetians, who, from some secret agreement which they had reached with the Cremonese,[3] were hopeful of taking Cremona, and sent, under some pretext, their troops into the neighbourhood of that city. But the plot was discovered by those who guarded Cremona for Count Sforza, and the plan of the Venetians proved of no avail, for they did not take the city and lost the Count, who now, putting aside his hesitations, joined the Duke of Milan.

13. In the meantime, Pope Eugene had died and Nicholas V had been chosen his successor. Count Sforza was already with his whole army at Cotignola[4] for the purpose of passing into Lombardy, when news came to him, on the last day of August 1447, of the death of Duke Filippo Visconti. This intelligence filled Count Sforza with consternation, for his troops did not seem to him in condition to proceed on account of their pay being in arrears; he feared the Venetians, whose army had taken the field and who were now his enemies, as he had so lately left them and gone over to the Duke; he feared King Alfonso, who was his inveterate enemy, and he had nothing to hope from the Pope or the Florentines, the latter being allies of the Venetians, and the former hostile to him on account of his having seized the lands of the Church.[5] With all this he resolved to face fortune, and to govern himself according to circumstances; for often one comes to see, in action, political designs that, in inaction, would remain hidden forever. He took much hope from the belief that, if the Milanese wished to defend themselves against the ambition of the Venetians, they could not look to anyone but himself for armed assistance. Thus, having made up his mind, he entered the Bolognese territory and [...] sent to Milan to offer his services. After the death of Duke Filippo a portion of the Milanese desired to live as a republic, and a portion under a prince; and of those who wanted a prince, some wanted Count Sforza and others King

---

[2] As a condottiero at the service of Venice.
[3] With the leaders of the local Guelph party.
[4] About 15 miles west of Ravenna.
[5] In the Marca of Ancona, according to the terms of the 1444 peace.

Alfonso. Therefore, being those who wanted a republic more united, they prevailed, and organized a government in their fashion, which, however, was not obeyed by many of the other cities of the duchy, who wanted to enjoy their independence the same as Milan; and though they did not aspire to independence were yet unwilling to submit to the rule of Milan. Thus, Lodi and Piacenza gave themselves to the Venetians, and Pavia and Parma declared themselves independent. When Count Sforza heard of all those uncertainties he went to Cremona, where it was agreed between the Milanese ambassadors and his ambassadors that he should be the general of the Milanese on the same terms and conditions as had been agreed upon between him and Duke Filippo before his death; and further, that Sforza should have Brescia, and in case of the capture of Verona he was to have that city in place of Brescia, which he was then to give up.

14. After the assumption of the pontificate, and before the death of the Duke, Pope Nicholas sought to restore peace amongst the Italian princes; and for this purpose he endeavoured, together with the ambassadors whom the Florentines had sent to congratulate him on his accession, to have a diet convened at Ferrara, for the negotiation of either a long truce or a lasting peace [...]. The negotiations lasted several days, and after much debating it was resolved to have either a truce for five years or a definite peace, whichever might be approved of by Duke Filippo. But when the ducal envoys returned to Milan to obtain his decision, they found the Duke dead. The Milanese wished, nevertheless, to conclude the agreement; but the Venetians were not willing, as they cherished the hope of becoming masters of Milan, particularly as they found that immediately after the Duke's death Lodi and Piacenza had voluntarily placed themselves under their dominion. They expected, either by treaties or by force, to strip Milan of all her possessions, and then to press her so hard that she would surrender to them before anyone could come to her assistance; and they became the more confident of succeeding in this as they saw that the Florentines were getting involved in war with King Alfonso.

17. [...] Count Francesco Sforza, having become general of the Milanese forces, before everything else, won the friendship of Francesco Piccinino, who was in the pay of the Milanese, so as to secure his support in his undertakings, or at least to make him less determined in thwarting them. He then took the field with his army; and the people of Pavia, believing themselves unable to resist him, and unwilling, on the other hand, to come under the rule of Milan, offered to give themselves to him on condition that he should not subject them to the government of Milan. Sforza greatly desired possession of this city, which he thought would be a wonderful first step towards achieving his goals. And it was neither fear nor shame at breaking his faith that restrained him, for great men deem it a shame to lose, not to gain by fraud;[6] but he apprehended

---

[6] Cf. 1.2.1 (*Prince* XVIII), and 4.2.3.

that, if he took Pavia, this would so irritate the Milanese as to cause them to transfer their allegiance to the Venetians; and, if he did not take it, he feared the involvement of the Duke of Savoy,[7] to whom many citizens wished to give the city. In either case, it seemed to him that he would lose the dominion of Lombardy. After much reflection, however, he concluded that there was less danger in taking Pavia, than in allowing it to be taken by someone else; and therefore he resolved to accept the offer of the people of Pavia, trusting to be able afterwards to soothe the Milanese. To whom he explained how dangerous it would have been to their cause had he declined Pavia, for then she would have given herself to the Venetians or to the Duke of Savoy, and in either case they would have lost their independence; and that they ought to be better satisfied to have him for a neighbour as a friend than somebody powerful, as either of the others, and hostile to them. The Milanese were much perplexed by this matter, which seemed to them to disclose Sforza's ambition, and the end at which he aimed. But they deemed it best not to make their suspicions known, as they did not know where else to turn, if they alienated the Count from them, except to the Venetians, whose pride, and the onerous conditions they were likely to impose, they feared. They resolved, therefore, not to break with Count Sforza, but for the present to avail of his aid in meeting the impending difficulties, hoping that, when they should be relieved of these, they would be able to relieve themselves of the Count too [...].

18. With the first return of spring [1448], both the Venetian and the Milanese armies took the field. The Milanese were desirous of taking Lodi, and then to make peace with the Venetians; for the expenses of the war had been onerous to them, and they seriously suspected their general. So that they became exceedingly anxious for peace, to enable them to enjoy some repose, and to make themselves secure against Count Sforza. They resolved, therefore, to have their army attempt the capture of Caravaggio, hoping that when that castle is taken Lodi would surrender. Sforza obeyed the wishes of the Milanese, although his own intention was to cross the Adda, and to attack the territory of Brescia. Having, therefore, laid siege to Caravaggio, he fortified himself with ditches and other works, so that, if the Venetians should attempt to compel him to raise the siege, they would have to attack him at great disadvantage [...]. This caused the Venetians the greatest uneasiness, for they regarded the loss of Caravaggio as ruinous to their whole enterprise [...]. They resolved, therefore, to attack the Count anyhow [...]. [The Venetian troops], after desperate efforts to pass the entrenchments, were not only repulsed, but put to flight, and were so completely routed that from their army of over twelve thousand horses, not one thousand were saved, and all the baggage and camp equipage was captured. Never had the Venetians before experienced a more complete and terrible defeat [September 1448] [...].

---

[7] Ludovico I.

19. After this victory, the Count marched with his victorious army into the territory of Brescia and took possession of the whole of it, and then pitched his camp within two miles of the city. The Venetians, on the other hand, having experienced defeat, and apprehending, as indeed it happened, that Brescia would be the first to be attacked, had supplied it as quickly and as well as they could with a garrison; and then they set to work with all diligence to collect more troops and to gather the fragments of their army, and called upon the Florentines for assistance, according to the terms of their alliance. The Florentines, being now relieved of the war with King Alfonso,[8] sent them 1,000 infantry and 2,000 horsemen, which accession of force gave the Venetians time to agree terms. It was almost the fate of the republic of Venice at that time to fail in war and to be successful in negotiations; so that what they lost in war was restored to them by peace many fold. The Venetians knew of the mistrust which the Milanese had of Count Sforza, that the Count aimed not at being their general but their lord, and that they could at will make peace with either party, the one desiring it from ambition and the other from fear. And they elected to make it with Count Sforza, and offered him their assistance in taking Milan. They believed that the Milanese, on finding themselves duped by Sforza, would from resentment subject themselves to any other authority than his, and that, being brought to the condition that they could neither defend themselves nor place any confidence in the Count, they would be obliged, not knowing where else to go, to come to terms with Venice, however disadvantageous for them this might be. Having resolved upon this course they sounded the Count's disposition, and found him greatly inclined to peace, being determined that the victory of Caravaggio should prove to his own advantage, and not to that of the Milanese. A treaty was therefore concluded between them [October 1448], according to which the Venetians obligated themselves to pay the Count the sum of 13,000 florins per month, until he should have effected the acquisition of Milan, and moreover to furnish him during the war 4,000 horsemen and 2,000 infantry. Sforza, on the other hand, bound himself to restore to the Venetians the places, prisoners, and whatever else he might have taken from them during that war, and to remain satisfied with only those places which Duke Filippo held at the time of his death.

20. When the news of this treaty became known to the Milanese, they were more afflicted by it than they had been rejoiced at the victory of Caravaggio [...]. They sent ambassadors to him [the Count] to see with what face and words he would attempt to carry out his villainy; and having appeared before Sforza, one of them addressed him as follows: '[...] Knowing now, although too late, your cruelty, ambition, and pride, we come not for the purpose of obtaining anything, nor in the belief that we should obtain it even were we to ask for it; but to recall to your memory the benefits you have received at the

---

[8] After an inconclusive campaign, Alfonso had just left Tuscany.

hands of the people of Milan, and to show you with what ingratitude you have rewarded them [...]. For you must remember only too well what your condition was after the death of Duke Filippo [...]. What more could we give or promise you? And what more could you at that time not only have had but even have desired, not only from us but from anyone else? [...] We cannot be accused of any other fault than that of having confided too much in one whom we should have trusted but little; for your past life and your ambition, which no state or station could ever satisfy, ought to have served us as a warning [...]. And though your own ambition may blind you, yet the whole world, witness to your iniquity, will make you open your eyes. God himself will open them for you, if it be true that perjuries, violated faith, and treason be hateful to him, unless he should continue forever as, in the pursuit of some occult good, he seems to have been until now, to be the friend of the evil-doers. Do not therefore anticipate a certain victory [...]; we are resolved to yield our liberty only with our lives; and even should we not be able to defend it, we would prefer to surrender it to any other prince rather than to you. And if from the excess of our sins we should, contrary to our will, fall into your hands, rest assured that a reign begun by you in fraud and infamy will end with you or your children in shame and ruin.'9

21. Count Sforza [...] replied that he was content to ascribe the grave offence of their imprudent words to their angry feelings, to which he would reply point by point if he were before anyone who could be a judge of their differences; for then it would appear that he had not injured the Milanese, but had merely taken precautions that they should not injure him. For they well knew their own conduct after the victory of Caravaggio, when, instead of rewarding him with Brescia or Verona, they sought to make peace with the Venetians, so that he would have been left with nothing but the rancours of the war, whilst they would have had the fruits of victory, the gratitude for the peace, and the advantages derived from war. They could not therefore complain of his having concluded that peace which they themselves had been the first to try to make [...]. The ambassadors having left, the Count prepared to attack the Milanese, and they in turn to defend themselves [...] until they should have succeeded at least in detaching the Venetians from Count Sforza, persuaded that these would not remain his faithful allies long. Sforza, on the other hand, being fully cognizant of all this, deeming that the treaty obligations were not a sufficient guarantee, judged that it would be wise to bind the Venetians to him by interest. And therefore in assigning to each their respective share of the enterprise he agreed that the Venetians should assail Crema, whilst he with his own troops would attack the other parts of that territory.

---

9 The speech is a product, by and large, of Machiavelli's imagination. The last sentence hints at the fall of the Sforza family that took place when Louis XII descended into Italy in 1499–1500.

This meal put before the Venetians caused them to adhere to their alliance with Count Sforza sufficiently long to enable him to take possession of the whole territory of the Milanese and to force them to lock themselves up in the city in such a way that they could not obtain any supplies. So that, despairing of any other help, they sent messengers to the Venetians [July 1449] to beg them to have compassion upon their condition, and in accordance with the custom of republics, to support them in the defence of their liberties, and not a tyrant whom, after he should have succeeded in making himself master of their city, they would be unable to contain at will. Nor was it likely, they added, that Sforza would remain satisfied with the conditions of the treaty, but would want to have the ancient limits of the state recognized.[10] The Venetians had not yet made themselves masters of Crema, and desiring to do so before changing sides, they replied publicly to the Milanese envoys that according to their treaty with the Count they could not come to their assistance; privately, however, they had such conversations with them that they, feeling encouraged, were induced to give the Milanese government every hope of help from Venice.

22. Sforza was already so close upon Milan with his troops that they were fighting in the suburbs [September 1449], when the Venetians, having now taken Crema, thought the time had come for their alliance with the Milanese, with whom they concluded a treaty, one of the first conditions of which was that they were to aid them in the defence of their liberties. This treaty made, they ordered such of their troops as were with the Count to leave his camp and retire into the Venetian territory. They also signified to the Count that they had made peace with the Milanese, and gave him twenty days to accept it also. Sforza was not surprised at this action of the Venetians, which he had expected for a long time and feared it could take place any day. Nevertheless, when it actually happened, he could not but regret it, experiencing the same annoyance which the Milanese felt when he deserted them. He asked for two days time to give his answer to the Venetian ambassadors; and throughout that time he resolved to pretend he was interested in negotiating with them, and not to desist from his enterprise. Therefore he declared publicly that he was willing to accept the peace, and sent ambassadors of his own to Venice with ample powers to ratify it; but privately he instructed them under no circumstances to do so, but to delay its conclusion by various objections and cavilling. And by way of making the Venetians believe the more that he was in earnest, he made a truce with the Milanese for one month, withdrew from the city and distributed his troops in quarters in the surrounding places which he had taken. This course was the cause of his success and the ruin of the

---

[10] That is, Brescia, Bergamo, and the Ghiaradadda, all of which the treaty between Sforza and the Venetians had assigned to the latter.

Milanese; for the Venetians, confident of peace, became dilatory in making the necessary provisions for the war, and the Milanese, seeing the truce concluded and the enemy withdrawn, and having secured the alliance of the Venetians, fully believed that Sforza intended to give up the enterprise. This belief proved ruinous to them in two ways; one, because they neglected to make the necessary dispositions for their defence; and the other, because, it being seedtime, they planted the whole country not occupied by the enemy with grain, thus enabling Sforza the more easily to starve them [. . .].

23. In this war in Lombardy the Florentines had not declared themselves in favour of either side, nor had they given any support to Count Sforza, either when he defended the Milanese or afterwards; for not standing in need of it, the Count had not asked for it. The only thing the Florentines had done was after the defeat at Caravaggio to send assistance to the Venetians in virtue of the obligations of the alliance. But Sforza, being now isolated, and not knowing where to look for help, was obliged to ask for help from the Florentines in the most pressing manner. He addressed himself publicly to the government and privately to his friends, and especially to Cosimo de' Medici, with whom he had always kept up an uninterrupted friendship, and who had in all his enterprises counselled him faithfully and aided him liberally. Nor did Cosimo forsake him now in his great strait, but aided him largely in his private capacity and urged him to persevere in his present enterprise. Cosimo endeavoured also to make the city aid Sforza, in which, however, there was a difficulty. Neri di Gino Capponi was at this period very influential in Florence; he thought it would not be advantageous for Florence that Sforza should succeed in making himself master of Milan, and believed it to be more for the benefit of all Italy that the Count should ratify the peace rather than continue the war. In the first place, he feared that the indignation of the Milanese against Sforza would induce them to give themselves entirely to the Venetians, which would be ruinous to all; and next, it seemed to him that, even if the Count should succeed in taking Milan, the union of such large forces and such extensive possessions under one man would be most formidable, and that if Sforza had been dangerous as a Count, as a Duke he would be most dangerous. He argued, therefore, that it would be better for the republic of Florence, and for all Italy, that Sforza should not increase his military power, and that Lombardy should be divided into two republics, which should never be allowed to combine for any attack upon others, whilst each by itself would be too feeble to attempt it. And to effect this Neri saw no better means than not to furnish aid to the Count, but strictly to maintain the old alliance with the Venetians. The friends of Cosimo did not accept this argument; for they believed that Neri had reasoned thus, not because he deemed it for the good of the republic, but because he did not wish Sforza, who was the friend of Cosimo, to become Duke of Milan, which in the opinion of Neri would strengthen the influence of Cosimo. On the other hand, Cosimo pointed out

that aiding the Count would prove most beneficial to the republic, as well as to the whole of Italy. It was not reasonable to suppose that the Milanese would be able to maintain their independence, because the character of the citizens generally, their mode of life, and the deeply rooted factions in that city, were in all respects most unfavourable to a republican form of government. Thus, it was inevitable either that Sforza should become Duke of Milan, or that the Milanese should throw themselves into the arms of the Venetians. And in that case, Cosimo thought that none would be so foolish as to doubt which would be better as a neighbour for Florence, either a powerful friend, or a most powerful enemy. Nor could he believe that there was any reason to apprehend that the Milanese, from their enmity to the Count, would yield themselves to the Venetians; for the Count had a large group of supporters in Milan, whilst the Venetians had not; so that whenever the Milanese should no longer be able to defend their liberty, they would always be more apt to subject themselves to Count Sforza than to the Venetians. This diversity of opinion kept Florence for some time in suspense; and finally it was resolved to send ambassadors to Count Sforza to arrange a treaty with him, with instructions to conclude it promptly in case they found him strong and confident of victory; otherwise, to delay its conclusion on some pretext or other.

24. The ambassadors had hardly reached Reggio, when they learned that Sforza had taken Milan; for upon the expiration of the truce the Count closed in upon the city with his forces [...]. The Venetians meantime sent an ambassador to Milan to exhort the inhabitants to a vigorous defence, and to promise them large and speedy succour [...]. When the season became milder, the Venetian forces, under command of [Sigismondo] Pandolfo Malatesta, established themselves above the River Adda, where they debated whether they should attack the Count, and try the fortune of battle in aid of the Milanese. Pandolfo advised against the attempt, well knowing the Count's valour and that of his army, and believing that it would be safer to conquer him without fighting, because the Count was harassed from want of provisions and forage. He therefore counselled the holding of that position, as they would thereby encourage the Milanese to hope for succour, and prevent their surrendering to the Count out of despair. This plan was approved by the Venetians, partly because they considered it a safe one, and partly also because they had the hope that by keeping the Milanese in this necessitous condition, they would be forced to place themselves under their government; for they had persuaded themselves that the Milanese would never give themselves to the Count because of the injuries they had received at his hands. The Milanese were meantime reduced to the utmost misery; and as that city habitually abounded in poor, many of these died in the streets from starvation [...]. The multitude is always slow in being moved to open rebellion, but, once so disposed, the slightest accident will start it to violence. Two men of low

condition were conversing near Porta Nuova about the calamities of the city and their own misery, and as to what means there were for their safety; a few others began to join them, so that it very soon became a numerous group. This gave rise to a report in Milan that the people at Porta Nuova were in arms against the magistrates. Upon this all the multitude, who was only awaiting an opportunity, seized its arms, chose for its captain Gaspare da Vimercate, and marched to where the magistrates were assembled [...]. Having thus in a manner become masters of the city, they consulted amongst themselves as to what should be done to escape from all those troubles and finally obtain some peace. All agreed that, inasmuch as they were not able to preserve their liberty, it was best to take refuge under some prince who was competent to defend them. Some were for calling in the King Alfonso, some wanted the Duke of Savoy, and some the King of France, but no one mentioned the name of Sforza, so strong was still the feeling against him. But as the people could not agree upon any other, Gaspare da Vimercate was the first to suggest the name of Count Sforza, showing them eloquently that, if they wanted to get rid of the war, there was no other way but to call him; for the people of Milan had need of a certain and immediate peace, and not of the distant hope of future succour [...]. Gaspare was listened to with extraordinary attention, and after he had finished speaking, all cried out that Count Sforza should be called in, and they deputed Gaspare for that purpose. He went by command of the people to seek the Count, and made known to him the joyful and happy news, which Sforza accepted most gladly. He entered Milan as prince on 26 February 1450, and was received with the greatest and most wonderful rejoicings by the very men who but a short time before had loaded him with imprecations.

25. When this news became known to the government of Florence, they instructed their ambassadors, who were on the way to Sforza, instead of negotiating a treaty with the Count, to congratulate the Duke upon his success. These ambassadors were received with the greatest distinction by the Duke and bountifully honoured, for he well knew that he could not in all Italy have more faithful or stronger allies against the power of the Venetians than the Florentines. For being relieved now of the fear of the house of Visconti, it was plain for all to see that they would have to contend against the forces of the Aragonese and the Venetians. The Aragonese, kings of Naples, were their enemies on account of the friendship which the Florentine people had always borne to the house of France; and the Venetians were aware that their ancient fear of the Visconti had been transferred to themselves, and knowing with how much zeal the Florentines had machinated against the Visconti, they feared similar machinations now themselves, and therefore sought their ruin. Such were the considerations that induced the new Duke so readily to form an alliance with the Florentines; whilst the Venetians and King Alfonso united against their common enemies, obligating themselves mutually to put their

armies into the field simultaneously.[11] King Alfonso was to attack the Florentines, and the Venetians the Duke, who, having but recently risen to power,
was believed by them unable to resist them, either by his own forces or by the
aid of others. But as the alliance between the Florentines and the Venetians
was still in force, and King Alfonso, after the war of Piombino,[12] had made
peace with the Florentines, it did not seem well to them to break the peace
unless they could first with some pretext justify the war. And therefore they
both sent ambassadors to Florence to explain that their alliance had not been
made for the purpose of attacking anyone, but only for the defence of their
respective states. In addition, the Venetian ambassador complained that the
Florentines had allowed Alessandro, the Duke's brother, to pass with troops
through Lunigiana into Lombardy; and moreover that they had been the
mediators and advisers of the treaty made between the Duke and the Marquis
of Mantua;[13] all of which acts, he affirmed, were adverse to the interests of
their state and to the terms of the alliance existing between them; and
therefore he reminded them amicably that he who offends wrongfully gives
cause to the other party to be rightfully offended, and that he who breaks the
peace must expect war. The Signoria commissioned Cosimo [de' Medici] to
reply, who in a lengthy and judicious speech went over all the benefits
conferred by his city upon the Venetian republic; he pointed out what
extensive possessions they had gained by means of the money, troops, and
counsel of the Florentines,[14] and reminded them that, since the friendship had
originated with the Florentines, so they would never be the cause of enmity.
And having ever been lovers of peace, they were well pleased with the alliance
made between the Venetians and King Alfonso, insofar as its object was peace,
and not war. In truth, he wondered much at the complaints made, and that so
great a republic should make so much account of such a slight and trivial cause
[. . .]. Therefore he feared that these complaints concealed some ill disposition
towards Florence, and added that if this should prove the case, it would readily
be seen by everyone, that the friendship of the Florentines was as advantageous as their enmity harmful.

26. For the present the matter passed lightly over, and the ambassadors
retired seemingly satisfied. But the alliance of the Venetians with the King of
Naples, and their proceedings, caused the Duke and the Florentines to fear a
renewal of the war, rather than to hope for a lasting peace. The Florentines,

[11] Venice and Naples reached a preliminary deal in July 1450; the following spring, then, they
signed an alliance to which the Emperor and the Duke of Savoy adhered as well.

[12] The Tuscan campaign referred to in section 19 above. Peace was signed in June 1450.

[13] In November 1450, Ludovico III Gonzaga had entered service under the Duke of Milan.

[14] This is the main reason why Florence was not pleased with her former ally: in twenty-five
years of wars, Venice had taken Bergamo, Brescia, and Ravenna, while Florence had not been
able to lay hands even on Lucca.

therefore, formed an alliance with the Duke,[15] and meanwhile the hostile disposition of the Venetians began to manifest itself, for they allied themselves with the Sienese, and expelled all the Florentines and their subjects from their city and territory. King Alfonso very soon after did the same thing, wholly regardless of the peace concluded the preceding year, and without any just grounds or even pretext for such action. The Venetians also sought to obtain possession of Bologna [...]. These events and demonstrations firmly convinced the Florentines that war was near at hand. They therefore made their usual preparations for defence, appointed the Council of Ten, engaged new captains, and sent envoys to Rome, Naples, Venice, Milan, and Siena, to ask help of their friends, ascertain the suspects, win over the doubtful, and to discover the designs of the enemy. From the Pope they received nothing but vague words, protestations of good will, and counsels of peace; from the King of Naples, vain excuses for having expelled the Florentines, and the offer of a safe conduct to whoever might ask for it. Although he sought in every way to conceal his designs about a new war, yet the ambassadors became convinced of his unfriendly disposition, and discovered many of his hostile preparations against their republic. The alliance with the Duke of Milan was strengthened by fresh mutual obligations; through the Duke's mediation an alliance was concluded with the Genoese, and all the old differences as to reprisals and other complaints were adjusted, although the Venetians sought in every possible way to disturb this settlement, and even appealed to the Byzantine Emperor to expel the Florentines from his dominions. Such was the bitterness of feeling with which they resumed this war; and so powerful was this thirst for dominion with them, that, regardless of every consideration, they sought to destroy a people to whom they were indebted for their greatness. The Emperor, however, gave no heed to their request. The Venetian Senate forbade the Florentine ambassadors from entering the territory of that republic, alleging that, being bound by alliance to the King of Naples, they could not listen to them without his participation. The Sienese received the ambassadors with kindly words, fearing lest they should be defeated before their allies could come to their defence. They preferred, therefore, to lull into inaction an enemy whom they would be unable to resist. The Venetians and the King of Naples, according to what was then conjectured, sent ambassadors to Florence to justify the war; but the Venetian ambassador was not permitted to enter the Florentine dominions, and the King's ambassador being unwilling to undertake the office by himself, that mission was left unaccomplished. And thus the Venetians learned that the Florentines showed them even less respect than they had shown the Florentines a few months before.

---

[15] July 1451. The creation of the alliance followed—and did not precede—the hostile initiatives adopted by Venice and Naples against Florence that are mentioned below.

27. [...] The Florentines [...] by way of increasing their reputation and intimidating the enemy, in conjunction with the Duke of Milan, formed a league with the King of France[16] for the mutual defence of their states, which treaty was published throughout Italy with great pomp and manifestations of gladness. With the opening of May 1452, the Venetians concluded no longer to defer open hostilities against the Duke, and attacked him with 16,000 horsemen and 6,000 infantry, in the direction of Lodi; and at the same time the Marquis of Monferrato, prompted either by his own ambition or by the Venetians, assailed him near Alessandria. The Duke, on the other hand, having collected 18,000 horsemen and 3,000 infantry, and having garrisoned Lodi and Alessandria, as well as the other places where the enemy might annoy him, attacked the territory of Brescia, where he damaged the Venetians very seriously. Both parties were thus ravaging the country and sacking the feebler villages. But the Duke, having defeated the Marquis of Monferrato at Alessandria, was enabled to move with greater force against the Venetians, and to invade their territory.

31. Besides the preparations made in Italy for repelling the forces of the hostile league, the Florentines had sent [...] their ambassador to the King of France, to induce him to empower King René of Anjou[17] to come into Italy to aid them and the Duke [...]; and that then, once being in Italy, he might attempt the conquest of the Kingdom of Naples; and to this effect they promised him assistance of men and money. Thus [...] the ambassador concluded an arrangement with King René to enter Italy in June [1453] with 24,000 horsemen; and upon his arrival at Alessandria the allies were to pay him 30,000 florins, and during the continuance of the war 10,000 florins per month [...]. René was most honourably received by Duke Francesco; and after uniting the French and Italian forces, they attacked the Venetians with such vehemence, that they recovered in a little while all the places which the Venetians had taken in the Cremonese territory. Not satisfied with this, they also occupied the whole of the territory of Brescia; so that the Venetian army, feeling no longer secure in the open field, retreated close under the walls of Brescia [...]. Thus the winter of 1453 was passed without any movement being attempted; but when the warm season returned, and the Duke thought the time fit to take the field and to attempt to take their inland possessions from the Venetians, King René notified the Duke that he was obliged to return to France. This unexpected decision surprised the Duke most unpleasantly; he went at once to dissuade King René from leaving, but neither entreaties nor promises could move him from his resolve, and all he obtained from King René was an agreement to leave a portion of his forces, and to send his son Jean to serve the league in his stead. The Florentines did not regret King René's

---

[16] Charles VII. The alliance was made in February 1452.

[17] René, Duke of Lorraine, kept the title of King of Naples even after being driven out of that kingdom by Alfonso in 1442 (cf. 4.3.4).

departure, for having recovered their own castles they no longer feared the King of Naples, and on the other hand they did not wish that the Duke should recover anything more than his places in Lombardy [...].

32. King René's departure caused Sforza readily to entertain the idea of peace; and the Venetians, King Alfonso, and the Florentines, being all tired of war, were equally desirous of peace. The Pope likewise had manifested and still expressed the greatest anxiety for it; for it was in that very year that Sultan Mehmed had taken Constantinople,[18] and had made himself master of all Greece. This conquest alarmed all Christendom, and more than all the rest the Venetians and the Pope, who both already seemed to see the Ottoman armies in Italy. The Pope, therefore, invited all the Italian states to send ambassadors to him with plenary powers to establish a universal peace. They all complied with this request; but when the ambassadors came to discuss the details of the settlement, they found great difficulty in the negotiations. The King of Naples wanted the Florentines to reimburse him the expenses of the war, whilst the Florentines made the same pretensions. The Venetians demanded Cremona from the Duke of Milan, whilst the Duke wanted Bergamo from them, as also Brescia and Crema; so that it really seemed impossible to solve these difficulties. And yet that which seemed so difficult to accomplish at Rome by so many was easily effected by two at Milan and Venice; for whilst the negotiations were being protracted at Rome, the Duke of Milan and the Venetians concluded the terms of an agreement on 9 April 1454,[19] according to which each resumed the places which they had before the war, and it was conceded to the Duke that he might retake the places which the Dukes of Monferrato and of Savoy had taken from him. The other Italian princes were allowed one month to ratify this treaty. The Pope and the Florentines, and with them the Sienese and the other smaller powers, ratified it quickly. Moreover, a peace for twenty-five years was concluded between the Florentines, the Duke of Milan, and the Venetians.[20] Of all the Italian princes, King Alfonso alone was dissatisfied with this peace: it seemed to him that the treaty had brought about little prestige for him, because he was being called be a party to it not as a promoter, but as an adherent. Thus he remained a long while undecided without letting his intentions be known. But as the Pope and the other princes sent many solemn embassies to him, he allowed himself finally to be persuaded, mainly by the Pope, and joined the league with his son for thirty years [...]. By way of preserving, however, the seeds of war in Italy, King Alfonso did not consent to make peace unless it was first conceded to him full liberty to wage war against the Genoese, Sigismondo [Pandolfo] Malatesta [lord of Rimini], and Astorre [II Manfredi], lord of Faenza, even if they did not injure him in any way [...].

---

[18] 29 May 1453.   [19] The Peace of Lodi.

[20] The Italic League. Born as a triple alliance in August 1454, it was extended to the Pope and Naples the following year. Such an arrangement was instrumental in preserving territorial and political stability in Italy until the French invasion of 1494.

5.2

Entrapping an Ally: France and Florence

Having relied mostly on the French army to defeat the Venetians in 1509, Pope Julius II soon realizes that Louis XII has grown too powerful in Italy. Accordingly, he changes policy—a shift that will lead to the Holy League of 1511. He thus makes peace with Venice (February 1510), invests Ferdinand II of Aragon as King of Naples, and secures to himself the remarkable Swiss infantry. Ferdinand makes no mystery of his sympathy for the Medici; as such, the Florentine republic needs the support of France more than ever. At the same time, Florence cannot risk breaking with the Pope. When Machiavelli is sent to Louis XII in June 1510, his mission is to prevent the French–papal conflict from escalating. As soon as he arrives, however, he is embarrassed by the peremptory French demand that Florence declares herself in favour of France—a perfect example of how a state tries to compromise an ally. When a possibility of mediation seems to materialize, Machiavelli looks at it as a great opportunity to reduce French pressure. At the same time, he begins to think of what Florence should do in case mediation fails (as it will). To him, Florence should resolutely side with France in return for some territorial gain (Lucca or Urbino); but the cautious Gonfalonier, Pier Soderini, will never take this idea seriously, and Florence will thus remain neutral. To make matters even worse, she will be forced to host in Pisa a council convoked by Louis XII against Julius II. As a result, when France is expelled from Italy by the Holy League in 1512, the republic will find itself at the mercy of an angry Pope and Spain—hence its collapse and the restoration of the Medici.

III MISSION TO FRANCE (1510)

Blois, 18 July 1510

[. . .] His Majesty received me most graciously, and said that he felt assured of your loyalty and affection towards his person, for you had received many benefits and great advantages at his hand, but that the time had come now to be more particularly assured of your feelings towards him; and then he said: 'Secretary, I have no enmity either with the Pope or anyone else; but as every day gives rise to new friendships as well as enmities, I desire that your government declare itself without delay as to what and how much it will do in my favour if it should happen that either the Pope or anyone else were to molest or attempt to molest my possessions in Italy [. . .]. I want to know who are my friends and who my enemies; and say to your lords, that in return I offer them for the safety of their state all the forces of my kingdom, and if need be I will come myself' [. . .]. After that I accompanied Robertet to his lodgings and remained some little time with him [. . .]. He told me [. . .] that as soon as matters became so hot as to cause any apprehensions, the King would come down into Italy as quickly as any private person, even if it were in midwinter, and that then he would make no terms with anyone that had shown himself hostile to him except at the point of the sword. These were times, therefore, when one ought to know how to take a resolution, particularly as experience had so often shown the King's readiness for war, the strength and resources of this kingdom, the fortunate success of his enterprises, and his friendly disposition towards our city and government. [. . . And he added]: 'I recommend you, therefore, once more to write to your government that these are times when much can be gained by making oneself agreeable' [. . .].

Blois, 3 August 1510

[. . .] Robertet one evening sent for Giovanni Girolami, who is engaged in some dealings here[1] [. . .]; and after having first talked with him about some of his private affairs, he suddenly turned the conversation upon these troubles that are brewing [. . .]. And going from one argument to another he concluded by saying that if the Pope were disposed to make peace, he would be met half-way by the King [. . .]; but that anyhow he did not see clearly how a peace could be brought about unless some third party intervened, inasmuch as the King would never be the first to yield, and as the Pope would probably take the same ground. And having therefore thought as to how such an agreement might possibly be brought about, he saw but one way, and that was that your lordships and the Cardinal of Volterra[2] should undertake the mediation [. . .]. This morning, whilst His Majesty had gone to breakfast, Monseigneur de la Trémoille, who for two weeks has assisted at every council together with Robertet and the chancellor,[3] called me, and, after some sharp words against the Pope, said to me that, notwithstanding all this, as Giovanni Girolami was going to Florence, he wished to tell me on the part of the King that His Majesty was satisfied and would have great pleasure in your lordships' intercession between the Pope and himself, and that you should send ambassadors to

---

[1] Girolami represented the Cardinal of Volterra at the court of France.
[2] Francesco Soderini, the Gonfalonier's brother.   [3] Jean de Ganay.

Rome for this purpose, and manage the whole affair as you thought best [...].
Your lordships will now with your habitual prudence take into consideration
what I have written, and what Giovanni will communicate to you, and will
then decide upon such measures as you may deem most proper; but in all this
business the greatest promptness is most necessary. I have not discouraged
these overtures, because I think that the enmity between these two sovereigns
would be one of the greatest misfortunes that could befall our city for reasons
that even the blind would see [...]. And I cannot but think that in becoming
mediators your lordships will gain great advantages, whether the negotiation
succeeds or not. If it succeeds, then it will bring about the peace we so much
hope for and desire, and we shall escape the dangers which the war would
bring to our very doors. And the more important the part which you take in
the matter, the greater will be the advantages which you will derive from it. For
you will have laid both the King and the Pope under obligations, having
laboured for their interests no less than for your own. And if it does not
succeed, His Majesty of France will remain equally obliged to you for having
done that which he approved of, and for having given him, in the face of the
whole world, more just grounds than ever for his contentions with the Pope.
Nor will the Pontiff be able to complain of you if, after your efforts to persuade
him to a peace, which he has rejected, you should take part against him in
the war [...].

Blois, 9–10 August 1510

[... The French] do not trust altogether, and will, in fact, never trust your
lordships until you declare yourselves openly in their favour and join them
with arms in hand. Their character is usually suspicious, and they suspect your
lordships the more, because they know you to be more cunning than ordinary,
and therefore not apt to expose your interests to great risks [...]. And you
may believe as you do the Gospels, that, if war breaks out between the Pope
and His Majesty of France, you will not be able to avoid declaring yourselves in
favour of one of the parties, wholly irrespective of the regard you may have for
the other [...]. And as in case of being obliged to do what I have just said,
your city will be exposed to some risk, it is the opinion of your friends here[4]
that it would be wise for you not to run that risk without receiving some
advantages by way of compensation. I have mentioned to you that the King

---

[4] That is, Machiavelli himself, as is often the case in much of his diplomatic correspondence.
Cf. his own suggestions to Raffaello Girolami: 'But to prevent such judgment on your part from
seeming presumptuous, it is well in your dispatches, after discussing the intrigues that are being
carried on, the men who are engaged in them and the states of mind that move them, to employ
phrases like this: "Considering now all I have written to you, the shrewd men here judge that it
will produce such or such an effect." This plan carefully followed has, in my day, done great
honour to many ambassadors' (*Instructions for Somebody Who Goes as Ambassador Somewhere*,
1522).

told me that he bore your interests in mind; and Robertet has on several occasions said to me, 'You never say anything to me about Lucca; it is time now to think of something'.[5] And even today [...] he came back to the same subject, and asked me whether the duchy of Urbino would suit us.[6] I turned the conversation, as I always do on similar occasions, and did not permit him to know my mind; for I make it a point to avoid entering upon a discussion of any subject respecting which I do not know your lordships' views. I notice, however, that my reserve increases their suspicions, and makes them the more pressing to have you declare yourselves for them. Nor do I believe that the strictest observation of the terms of the treaty will suffice them; they want more than that. For whilst the treaty stipulations refer only to the defensive, they want to force you to the offensive, so as to commit you the more effectually to them. Thus they believe that, if the war does take place, you will be obliged to declare yourselves in their favour, or become their enemy. But do not persuade yourselves that this would make them hesitate, or that they cannot do without you; for their pride and confidence in their power will never allow them to come down to that point [...]. And therefore those persons here who are really attached to you think that it will be necessary for your lordships, without waiting for time to press or necessity to oblige you, to attend to present events; to reflect well, and then take the direct course for the object you aim at; and that in any event you form definite resolutions. And when you think the time come for you to be obliged to declare yourselves out and out in favour of the King of France, then you ought at a suitable moment to think of your own interests; for when one thinks of the possible loss of your allies and your state, it is proper also that one should think of the advantages that may be gained. For if you come to the conclusion that it is well to risk your fortunes with those of France, the terms of the agreement would be that you can dispose of a good part of Tuscany as you may think proper, and [to that purpose, you are expected to] hire French troops with an annual subsidy for a length of time to be defined. And as opportunity is but short-lived, it behoves you to come to a prompt decision. As I am not a personage of sufficient consequence to begin negotiations of such importance, your lordships ought to charge the ambassador with it who is now on his way here, and as quickly as possible instruct him as to what arguments to advance in this negotiation; so that [...] he may be able promptly to say yes or no; for this business cannot wait. To have a clearer understanding of the state of things here, you must know that the French have their thoughts fixed upon two things. First, to make peace with the Pope, provided he will make the first advances; of this Robertet has again repeated to me his assurances. Second, if peace is not made, to win

---

[5] Lucca was a periodical target of Florentine expansionism: cf. 2.2.4, 4.2.2, and 4.3.2.

[6] The Duke of Urbino was allied with the Pope at the time.

over to their side the Emperor; for they do not see how they could succeed otherwise. I would believe in peace, were it not that those who say to desire it most themselves spoil the chance of it; for to bring the Pope to the point where they wanted him, they ought to have delayed sending assistance to Ferrara,[7] and should not have talked about changing the government of Bologna,[8] so as not to arouse the suspicions of the Pope and exasperate him the more. All this they promised at the time when Giovanni Girolami was sent, but they do not follow up their promises, and thus such projects fail. As to the Emperor, they will make him larger or smaller offers, according as they think they have greater or less need of him; and the King has repeatedly said to a person who is not given to tell lies: 'The Emperor has several times urged me to divide Italy with him, but I have always refused my consent; now, however, the Pope obliges me to do it'. Your lordships are thus exposed to two dangers in this war between the Pope and the King; the one that your ally may be defeated, and the other that the King of France makes terms with the Pope to your detriment [. . .]. Those of the Italians here who have anything to lose think that to avoid these dangers it is above all things necessary to see whether the Pope can be induced to make peace with the King of France, and if that cannot be done, then to convince the King that to hold the Pope in check it needs neither so many emperors nor so much noise; for those who in the past have made war upon the Pope have either overreached him, as was done by Philip the Fair,[9] or they caused him to be shut up in the Castel Sant'Angelo by his own barons; and these are not so entirely exhausted that no means can be found to stir them up again. Thus, in my ride yesterday with Robertet I talked of nothing else; I pointed out to him all the potential implications of the current situation, and told him, moreover, that in making war openly against the Pope they could not succeed without exposing themselves to danger. For if they attempted it by themselves, they could not but see that all the consequences would fall upon France alone; and on the other hand, if they attempted it in company, they would have to divide Italy with their ally, with whom they would afterwards have to have a new war,[10] that would prove much more dangerous than the one they had had to sustain against the Pope [. . .].

Blois, 13 August 1510

[. . .] His Majesty returned here today; and after dinner the chancellor, after a long exordium upon the services rendered by France to Florence, beginning from the time of Charlemagne and coming down to the present King Louis,

---

[7] Julius II was waging war against the Duke of Ferrara, who was, in turn, supported by the French.

[8] The Pope had taken Bologna back in 1506.

[9] In his feud with Boniface VIII in the late thirteenth century.

[10] Something like this had already happened between France and Spain over the Kingdom of Naples, in 1500–03: cf. 4.3.4.

said that His Majesty had understood that the Pope, moved by a diabolical spirit that had taken possession of his mind, wanted to renew his attempt against Genoa; in which case it might well be that Chaumont would have need of your men-at-arms to defend His Majesty's possessions. He therefore desired that your lordships should keep your troops in an operating condition, so that they might be ready for active service at any moment that Chaumont should call for them. And since His Majesty had understood that you had deployed a few thousand regular infantry on the frontier, he wished that those too were kept ready for service, so that in this way you would lay the King and the House of France under eternal obligations to you. I replied to all in accordance with what your lordships had written me [...] and that they ought to bear in mind that your dominion was almost entirely surrounded by the states of the Pope, who upon the least suspicion had threatened to have our merchants plundered, and would certainly do so upon the slightest demonstration on the part of your lordships, and that moreover he would leave every other war for the purpose of combating you. And that therefore, inasmuch as His Majesty could do without our being mixed up in the matter, he ought to have some consideration for your lordships. And as regards infantry, we had but very few on that frontier, and that these would have to be paid whenever ordered to be ready to march, and any expenditure in addition to the others they knew about would be actually insupportable by our city. They answered nearly all at the same moment to my remarks, saying that the troops would be wanted only for a few days to repel an attack, and that your lordships ought to remember that the King was as solicitous about your honour and interests as about his own; that His Majesty's preparations were on such a scale that he would make *caelum novum et terram novam*[11] in Italy, to the detriment of his enemies and the exaltation of his friends, showing me with long speeches and affectionate words how they cared for the primacy of Florence in Tuscany and how much they esteemed it, and that I ought to write to your lordships [...].

I see that things are going in the way I said they would; that is to say, these people here irretrievably want to involve you in this war. Thus, you should ponder even more carefully what I have written before, and not limit yourselves to fear a loss but think of some gain too [...].

Blois, 27 August 1510

[...] Robertet, as stated in my last letter, has been ill with this cough, and having called to see him a couple of days ago, and being alone with him, we had a long conversation [...]. The first thing to bear in mind, I said, was the fact that you were poor as a result of the long war in which you had been engaged[12] and the expenditures which you had been obliged to incur and from

---

[11] 'New sky and new earth', i.e. some radical change and transformation.
[12] The long-standing war to retake Pisa.

which you were not yet entirely liberated;[13] thus, you could not be called powerful nor well supplied as regards money. Next, the geographical position of our territory must be taken into consideration, being surrounded by the Pope and his allies, which made it easy for His Holiness, with but little expense to himself, to give you trouble from many quarters, and subject you to danger and enormous costs. The late modest demonstration of the Venetian fleet[14] had obliged you to send hundreds of troops to Pisa, which certainly could not have been done without costing you large sums of money. Therefore it was necessary to consider the matter carefully, and the King should have seen to it, when he claimed your assistance against the Pope, that your aid would do him good and not bad. For if this aid were not to be of great advantage to His Majesty, and only served to saddle you with another war, the King would be obliged not only to return to your lordships the aid lent him, but also to add some of his own troops, so that where His Majesty has now to provide for the defence of Ferrara, Genoa, the Friuli, and Savoy, he would then also have to provide for the safety of Florence and Tuscany. Such aid from you would therefore be more injurious than useful to His Majesty; and for that reason I begged him to be very careful and to weigh matters maturely; for if they wanted to act wisely they must regard this much as certain, that, if the war against the Pope went any further, the Florentines would be of greatest assistance to the King if they defended themselves with all the ability they possess, so as not to need any help from His Majesty [...]. It seemed to me that Robertet was pleased with my arguments, and he showed me that he had taken notice of them. Nevertheless, I cannot rid myself of the idea which I have stated in a previous letter, namely, that they desire anyhow to involve you openly in this war, in case it should be pushed on [...].

---

[13] The payments made by Florence to the kings of France and Spain.
[14] The Venetians had raided the coast of San Vincenzo a few weeks earlier.

5.3

What the Pope Should Do Now

Fallen into disgrace with the end of the republican regime, Machiavelli, between 1513 and 1515, entertains a lively correspondence with his friend—and Florentine ambassador to Rome—Francesco Vettori. At the beginning of December 1514, Vettori asks him a set of delicate questions, hinting that the Pope himself (Leon X) will read his answers. What is at stake, therefore, is no less than the Pope's benevolence; and the Pope being a Medici, the implications of his benevolence are obvious. The diplomatic situation Machiavelli is called to assess is the following: the King of France desires to take Milan back; he is supported by the Venetians and opposed by the Swiss, the Emperor, and Spain. What should the Pope do? What would be the advantages and disadvantages of an alliance with France, or with France's enemies, or of neutrality? Machiavelli's long letter consistently reflects many of the ideas and beliefs that recur over and over again in his writings. Events would show that his advice was sound indeed—even though the Pope did not follow it.

LETTER TO FRANCESCO VETTORI, 10 DECEMBER 1514

You ask me what plan His Holiness should adopt in order to keep the reputation of the Church such as he found it, if the King of France, with the aid of the King of England[1] and the Venetians, should decide at all costs to regain the duchy of Milan, and if on the other side the Swiss, the King of Spain, and the Emperor should unite to defend it [. . .]. I believe there has been no question more complex than this in the past twenty years, and I do not know any matter in the past so difficult to understand, so uncertain to estimate, and for which it is so risky to select and carry out a policy [. . .].

When a prince wishes to know what fortune will attend two states that engage in war, he must first measure the force and the cohesion of the two.

---

[1] Henry VIII.

The forces on the side of France and England are those preparations that these kings are said to be making for this conquest, namely to attack the Swiss in Burgundy with 20,000 men, to assail Milan with a greater number, and with a much greater number to attack Navarre in order to stir up the Spanish provinces and cause disorders in them; to put a great fleet on the sea and assail Genoa or the Kingdom of Naples, or any other place that seems to their advantage [...]. The Venetians [...] are of the same importance to the forces of these two kings as are the forces of Milan to the other alliance; I judge them few and weak, and to be restrained by half of the soldiers that are in Lombardy. Considering now the defenders of Milan, I see the Swiss fit to assemble two armies strong enough to fight with the French that come into Burgundy, and with those that come into Italy, because if in this matter all the Swiss unite, and the Grisons and the Vaudois unite with the Cantons,[2] they can bring together more than twenty thousand men on each front. As to the Emperor, because I never know what he will do, I do not wish to discuss what he may be able to do now. But if Spain, the Emperor, Milan, and Genoa join together, I do not believe they can exceed fifteen thousand soldiers, because the King of Spain is not able to furnish new forces, when he awaits war at home. As to the sea, I believe that the Genoese and Spain, if they do not lack money, can between them provide a fleet that can for some time balance in some way that of their adversaries. I think, therefore, that these are the forces of the two. Now when at present I try to see to which side victory is likely to incline, I say that the kings of France and England, because they have plenty of money, can keep their armies in the field a long time. The others,[3] because they are poor, cannot do so. Hence, considering the armies, the mode of proceeding, and the money of both parties [...],[4] I see for the alliance on this side [of the Alps] the sole hope of fighting a battle quickly—a battle which may be lost. On the part of the King of France, I see that he is also able to win the day, and if he protracts the war, he cannot lose [...].

If, then, His Holiness is forced to make a decision and joins the alliance on this side of the Alps, I think victory uncertain for the reasons given above, and because his accession will not make the alliance wholly secure. Even though his accession takes away opportunity and prestige from the French, it does not give the others the forces they need if they are to resist the French [...]. If His Holiness takes the side of the King of France, and does it so cautiously that he can without danger wait to come into the open, I think the victory certain. For

---

[2] The Grisons and the Vaudois were not members of the confederation of the cantons.

[3] Spain, the Swiss, the Emperor, Genoa, and Milan.

[4] In *Report on the Affairs of Germany* (1508), Machiavelli wrote: 'War has to be measured by the number and quality of the troops, by the amount of money, by conduct, and by fortune; and it is to be presumed that that party which has more of these advantages will be victorious'. But now, in his effort to be as rational as possible, he leaves fortune out.

then by means of the fleet he could throw a large army into Tuscany and unite it with his own, and by using the forces that the Venetians have in Lombardy he could at once make a great disturbance there. As a result, the Swiss and the Spaniards would not be able to resist two different armies coming from different sides, nor to defend themselves against the rebellion of the people that would immediately take place. Altogether, I do not see that in this case it would be possible to take the victory from the King.

You wish, in addition, to know whether the alliance of the King of France or of the Swiss would be less dangerous to the Pope, if either one of them should succeed because of his friendship. I answer that I believe that, just now, the faith pledged to the Pope by the Swiss and their allies and friends would be kept, and the promised states turned over to him. On the other hand, he would have to endure the demands of the conqueror. And because, so far as I can see, there would be no victor save the Swiss, he would have to endure injuries from them. These would soon appear to be of two kinds, namely taking away his money, and taking away his friends; because the money that the Swiss, now that they are making war, say they do not want, you may be sure they will by all means wish when the war is over. They will begin with this tribute, which will be heavy; and such a request looking honest, and for fear of irritating them in the very freshness of their victory, the Pope will not deny it to them. I believe, or rather I am certain, that the Duke of Ferrara, the Lucchese, and the like, will hasten to put themselves under the protection of the Swiss.[5] As soon as they have taken one of them, the liberty of Italy will be over, because every day with a thousand pretexts they will exact tribute and seize booty, they will change the government of states, and what they think they cannot do at present they will await the proper time for. Nor should anybody rely on their not thinking of this, because it is necessary that they think of it, and if they did not think of it, the natural course of things will compel them to think of it: one acquisition, one victory, gives an appetite for others [...].[6] You may say, 'There is a remedy for this, because we can unite against them'. But I answer that this would be a second error and a second delusion, because the union of many heads against one is difficult to make, and difficult to keep together when it is made.[7] As an example I give you the King of France, against whom everybody had united.[8] Then all of a sudden the King of Spain made a treaty with him, the Venetians became his friends, the Swiss attacked him without spirit, the Emperor was almost not to be seen, and finally the King of England joined with him. In fact, if the man against whom a coalition is made is of such enduring power that he does not immediately go up in smoke, as the

---

[5] Lesser powers bandwagon, as a general rule. Cf. the policy of the minor Italian states as Louis XII first descended into Italy in 4.3.4.

[6] Cf. 4.1.3. [7] Cf. 4.2.3. [8] The Holy League of 1511.

Venetians did,[9] he will always find a remedy in the variety of the reciprocal fears and suspicions of his enemies, as France has done, and as the Venetians apparently would have done if they had been able to continue two months the war they were engaged in [...].

If you wish, then, to know of me what the Pope must fear from the Swiss if they conquer, and he is their ally, I conclude that he should fear that they will demand tribute at once, and that in a short time they will bring about the servitude of the Pope and of all Italy, without hope of redemption. The Swiss can accomplish this because they are a republic, and so well armed that no prince or potentate can be compared with them. But if His Holiness were an ally of the King of France, and should conquer, I believe the King too would proceed to observe the conditions, provided they were suitable, and not such as they would be if too great eagerness had caused the Pope to ask too much or the King to grant too much. I believe he would not demand tribute from the Church, but from you Florentines, and he would consider the Church because of his connection with England, and because of the Swiss, who would not all be dead, and because of the King of Spain, for even if the latter were driven out of Naples, he would have to be taken into account, if he remained alive. Therefore it would appear reasonable that for his part the King of France would wish the Church on his side, with a high reputation and friendly to him, and would have the same feeling for the Venetians. In brief, whoever the victorious side may be, it seems to me that the Church will have to remain at the discretion of others. Therefore I judge it better for her to be at the discretion of those who will be most reasonable, and whom she has known before, rather than at the discretion of those whose intention she cannot know because she is not well acquainted with them.

If that alliance to which His Holiness unites himself should lose, I would fear to be brought to the utmost necessity, to be forced to flight, to face a council, and all that a pope can fear. However, he should remember that when one is obliged to choose one of two alternatives, he should, among other things, consider where an unfortunate outcome of either of them can put him, and should always, other things being equal, choose the alternative whose results would be less bitter, if it turned out badly. Without a doubt there would be less bitterness in losing with France as an ally than with the others as allies. If His Holiness has the friendship of France, and loses, he still holds his territories in France,[10] and that is enough to keep a Pope in the fullness of his dignity; he remains with a fortune which through the power of that kingdom can rise again in a thousand ways; he remains in his own territory, and in a place where many popes have had their seat. If he is on the other side

---

[9] In their war against the League of Cambrai in 1509.
[10] Avignon, the papal seat from 1309 to 1377, was still under ecclesiastical jurisdiction.

and loses, he will have to go into Switzerland to die of hunger, or into Germany to be derided, or into Spain to be swindled. Hence it seems there is no comparison between the ills that bad fortune in one policy or the other will entail.

I do not believe that remaining neutral was ever advantageous for anybody in the situation of the Pope: he is less powerful than any of those who are fighting, and possesses territories scattered among those of the combatants. You must understand first of all that nothing is more necessary to a prince than to conduct himself toward his subjects, his allies, and his neighbours in such a way that he does not become either hateful or contemptible, and if he has to let one of these go, he should not be troubled by hatred, but should preserve himself from contempt [...]. And I tell you that he who remains neutral will normally be hated by the loser and despised by the conqueror.[11] As soon as people begin to have no regard for you, esteeming you a useless friend and not a formidable enemy, you cannot but fear that every sort of injury will be done to you, and every kind of harm planned for you. And justifications for such conduct by the conqueror will not be lacking, when the territories of the neutral are mingled with those of the combatants, because the neutral will be forced to receive in his ports now this one, now that one, to take them into his country, and to provide them with lodging and with food. At the same time everybody will think he is being deceived, and countless things will happen that will cause countless complaints. And even if none of these things happen in the conduct of the war—and that is impossible—they will happen after the victory, because the lesser rulers, and those who are afraid of you, will immediately run to the protection of the conqueror, and give him opportunity to injure you. Somebody may say: 'It is true that some things may be taken from the neutral, but others can be kept'; to this I answer that it is better to lose all one's possessions valorously than part of them shamefully; and it is not possible to lose part of them without letting one's grip of the rest grow shaky. Let anybody consider carefully all the territories of His Holiness, and where they are situated, and who are the minor rulers included within them, and who, among those, is fighting in this war. He who does this will conclude that His Holiness is one of those whose conditions by no means permit him to remain neutral, and that if he does remain neutral he will always have to be regarded as enemy by the losing side and by the winning side, and that both will wish to damage him, the first to take revenge and the second to gain something.

Then you ask also if, after the Pope has come to an agreement with the Swiss, the Emperor, and the King of Spain, it would be possible for the King of

---

[11] Cf. 4.4.1; see also *Prince* XVI, XIX; *Discourses* I, 22 and the letter to Vettori of 20 December 1514.

Spain and the Emperor to deceive him and join themselves to France. I believe that an agreement between Spain and France is impossible, and that it cannot be made unless England joins in. England, however, is not able to make an alliance with Spain except against France. Hence France cannot think of such an alliance, because the King of England—a young man and eager for military glory—can turn his arms nowhere except against Spain or France; and just as peace with France would make him turn his arms against Spain, so peace with Spain would make him turn his arms against France. Therefore, in order not to lose the King of England and not to bring on himself a war with him, and because he has a thousand causes to hate the King of Spain, the King of France will not be inclined to peace [...]. As far as Spain is concerned, I believe that the Pope would have good reason for fearing everything; but as far as France is concerned, he would feel safe. As to the Emperor, since he is moody and unstable, any sort of change can be feared from him, whether or not it is to his advantage, for he is a man who has always lived in the midst of variations and fed upon them. If the Venetians should adhere to the party on this side of the Alps, that would be very important, not so much for the additional force they would bring, as that the alliance would be more evidently hostile to France; and if the Pope also joined in, the French would find innumerable difficulties in entering Italy and establishing themselves there. But I do not believe the Venetians will adopt this plan, because I believe they have made more advantageous agreements with France than they could do with the others; and after they have shared the fortune of France even when she was almost dead, it does not seem reasonable that they should abandon her when she is rising up again. So I fear they are as usual spreading rumours to their own advantage.

I conclude then [...] that there are more signs of victory on the French side than on the other, that the Pope by joining the French can make their victory certain but cannot do so for the others, that France is less formidable and more endurable as ally and victor than the others, that defeat would be more endurable if he were allied with the French than with the other party, and that he cannot securely remain neutral. For these reasons I think His Holiness should either join with the French, or should join the others if the Venetians also join them, but not otherwise.

5.4

Towards the Sack of Rome

After Francis I's defeat at the hands of Charles V at Pavia (February 1525), all the Italian states join forces with France in the anti-imperial League of Cognac (May 1526). Each ally, however, focuses primarily on his particular interest, thereby losing sight of the common goal of driving the imperial forces out of Italy: Pope Clement VII does not intend to give the Duke of Ferrara back the territories seized by his predecessors, and pushes him towards the imperial side; Florence is eager to take San Leo, thus alienating the Duke of Urbino who claims the same place; Venice is only waiting for the right opportunity to expand in the Romagna. As a result, the league wastes precious time: not only does it not exploit the weakness of the imperial army in Milan, but it does not even try to stop the lansquenets when they descend into Italy. In January 1527, the imperial forces and the lansquenets merge south of Piacenza and get ready to cross the Apennines. Machiavelli is sent on his last mission to Francesco Guicciardini, Lieutenant General of the Papal army, at the camp of the league to make sure that the preparations for defence are adequate. His dispatches reveal all his frustration: the enemies are disorganized, weak, seditious, tormented by bad weather. And yet, the league does not seem able to tackle them, plagued as it is with divisions and irresoluteness. In March, a truce is signed by Clement VII and the Viceroy of Naples, but it is not recognized by the Constable de Bourbon, the commander of the imperial army; in fact, he keeps asking for more and more money for his troops who, not being paid, are growing restless. The Pope, on the other hand, relies so thoroughly upon the truce that he will disband his forces, thus finding himself entirely unprepared when the constable and the lansquenets direct their march upon Rome.

MISSION TO FRANCESCO GUICCIARDINI AT THE CAMP OF THE LEAGUE OF COGNAC

Parma, 11 February 1527

[...] We hear various accounts of the enemy's movements. I wrote to you that the lansquenets who were at Milan had left the town to unite with those outside; today we hear that they have not yet gone out, but that they are to go. We are informed that they have secretly made provision of scaling ladders and spades.[1] Some say that they want to launch a surprise attack, others that they intend to prepare for taking with their spades those cities they cannot assail with their artillery [...]. And thus we hear at every moment different accounts of their movements, which are interpreted by some that they intend coming into Tuscany, whilst others think that they will attempt some enterprise on this side [...]. Thus, God only knows what they will now do, for perhaps they do not know it themselves. If they did, they would surely have effected it, so much time having passed during which they could have formed a union of their forces. It is believed that they are but little to be feared, if they are not aided by our own disorders; and all who have any experience in war judge that we ought to be victorious, unless either evil counsels or the lack of money cause our defeat. For our forces are so great that they should suffice to sustain the war; and we ought to be able to provide against those two issues, the first by taking good counsel, and the other that His Holiness does not give up [...].

Bologna, 18 March 1527

I wrote yesterday at length to your lordships, and informed you that the bad weather had prevented the enemy from getting started [...]. Thus the impediment which we could not, or did not know how to, give to the enemy has been, and is being, given by God [...]. If God had loved us completely, he would have deferred the storm until they had gone beyond Sasso[2] and entered those mountains. Perhaps this weather would have overtaken them there if they had started at the time they intended; but the mutinous movements of their infantry, which at the time seemed so dangerous, caused them to delay their starting, and thus saved them from the consequences of this storm. Nevertheless, we believe that they are badly off [...]. We have no further news of the illness of Georg Frundsberg,[3] owing to the above causes; but if fortune should change and favour us, he would die anyhow, and that would be the real beginning of our salvation and the enemy's ruin [...].[4]

I wrote to you yesterday evening that if one had wished to profit by this trouble of the enemy, it would have been necessary to make the most of the time which fortune was giving us; for if fair weather should return, and we find ourselves where we were before, the delay which the enemy experienced in going to Tuscany will have been injurious rather than advantageous to us. And if it be desired that we should be better prepared, then the Venetians ought to pay

---

[1] To climb city walls and dig up tunnels under them.
[2] Present-day Sasso Marconi, about 12 miles south of Bologna.
[3] The commander of the lansquenets.
[4] On the contrary, Frundsberg's illness proved deleterious: his lansquenets, no longer controlled, would find the rationale for their expedition in pillage and booty.

their troops and make their whole army join ours; otherwise, things will go badly [...]. The Lieutenant General[5] received letters this morning from Venice, from the nuncio and the [Florentine] ambassador,[6] which could not possibly be more full of good plans or greater hopes [...]. But the Lieutenant General, seeing how much these letters differ from the facts, has written them a letter of two sheets, in which he reviews all their former errors, points out how greatly their actions are different from the words spoken at Venice, and shows them exactly what they ought to do, if they intend to speak the truth with regard to their plans as well as with regard to the Duke [of Urbino]'s[7] hopes of victory. One does not know what the result of this letter will be; still we shall have the satisfaction of having brought the matter to their notice, and it will serve to show them that we are not easily fooled, and that fair words alone do not satisfy us [...].

Bologna, 29 March 1527

[...] Everybody regards the truce as good as broken, and that nothing remains except to think of war [...]. For it seems that in the new negotiations that are being carried on, it is agreed to expend what money you have in the payment of these troops; and then, if we wish the enemy to agree to a truce, you would need to have, besides this present payment to the troops, at least 100,000 florins disposable in your pocket. And as this cannot be, it is folly to waste time in making a bargain which we could not carry out afterwards for want of money. Let your lordships therefore prepare for war, win back the Venetians, and make sure of them, so that their troops that have left will return to our assistance. And bear in mind that inasmuch as this truce, if concluded, would have been our salvation, so it may in not being concluded and keeping us in suspense prove our ruin.

Imola, 2 April 1527

[...] Because our evil fortune has prevented this truce from being definitely concluded, then it will be better to try and bring it about by continuing the war than by showing that we desire it eagerly [...]. For what sort of an arrangement can you expect from an enemy, who, despite having the mountains between you and himself, and with the number of troops which you have on foot, still asks 100,000 florins of you within the space of three days, and 150,000 within ten days? When he gets to Florence the first thing he will ask of you will be all the money you possess [...]. The only inducement they have for advancing is the hope of pillaging your city. And there is no other way of

---

[5] Francesco Guicciardini.   [6] Altobello Averoldi and Alessandro de' Pazzi, respectively.
[7] Francesco Maria I della Rovere, at the service of Venice.

escaping these evils but to undeceive the enemy as to your ability to resist him; and if this is to be done, then it is better to do it before he crosses the mountains than before our city walls, and to employ here all the forces we have to keep him here. For if the enemy is detained in the mountains but a short time he will have to disband, as we learn from reliable quarters that if he does not succeed within the present month in taking some of the important places—in which he will not succeed unless one gives up—then he must of necessity succumb. And even if you should not succeed in defending your-selves on this side of the mountains, there will be nothing to prevent you from bringing the forces which you have here over to the other side. For I remember in the war with Pisa, that the Pisans, wearied by its long duration, began to discuss amongst themselves whether they ought not to make terms with you. Pandolfo Petrucci,[8] anticipating such an attempt, sent Antonio da Venafro to dissuade them from it. Antonio addressed them in a public meeting, and after many other things said to them that they had passed a very tempestuous sea, and wanted now to drown themselves in a well. I do not mention this because I think that Florence is about to abandon any idea of resistance, but to give you a certain hope of safety provided you are willing rather to spend ten florins to secure your liberty, than forty that would serve to enslave and destroy you.[9]

Forlì, 8 April 1527

[...] We are here at Forlì with the Swiss and the French troops, and we are fighting against a number of difficulties. These commanders, so soon as they are separated from the Lieutenant General, carry out the plans agreed upon either slowly or badly. These soldiers are insupportable, and the inhabitants of the country are so afraid of them that they receive them most unwillingly. The troops of the Swiss move very slowly, as they have no confidence in the truce, and the reported coming of the Viceroy [of Naples][10] would have disaffected them entirely if the Lieutenant General had not represented to them that it amounted to nothing. We also heard that the Duke of Urbino had urgently demanded to come here, but it is believed that his zeal would cool off if he should hear that the coming of the Viceroy has revived the subject of the truce. Nevertheless, seeing the enemy marching towards his home[11] ought to make him more solicitous than ever. The amount of all this is that the advantage we have of being masters of the strong places, of having a friendly country, money, and plenty of troops and experience—all these things amount to

---

[8] Lord of Siena, one of the hereditary enemies of Florence in Tuscany.

[9] Twenty-four years have gone by, but the Florentine attitude on military spending has not changed much: cf. 2.1.1.

[10] Jean de Lannoy, commander of the Spanish troops in Italy.

[11] That is, towards the duchy of Urbino.

nothing in consequence of our being divided into so many places and having so little confidence in each other. On the other hand, the disadvantages which the enemy suffers from being in a hostile country, where he is dying of hunger, and having no money—all this is overcome by their being united and acting together, and stubborn beyond all human belief [. . .].

Forlì, 11 April 1527

[. . .] The enemy passed the River Lamone today, and is going south towards the Marca [of Ancona]. They will make as little progress as usual, nor is it believed that they will lay siege to any other city whilst they are in the Romagna, for we are always before them in time to garrison the place. But it is believed that we shall not be in time to supply garrisons to any of the cities of the Marca. Indeed, it is not a good plan that does not permit us to advance with as many troops as to be able always to supply a sufficient garrison to the places we leave behind and take the remaining forces with us. For if one is wearied and has to withdraw one's troops from the cities left behind for the purpose of placing them as garrisons in those ahead, either one does not have the time to do it, or disorders and inconveniences arise that are apt to prove one's ruin. Following the orders given by the Duke of Urbino, we have commenced dividing our army in Parma, and we have come to consume it as far as here to Forlì, where not enough troops remain to us to permit our leaving any behind and advancing with the remainder to Cesena and Rimini; for Count Caiazzo[12] was sent to Ravenna, and the Swiss that were left here cannot be induced to separate, one part being unwilling to leave the other. If this could have been done, we should have left one part here, and would have gone with the other to Cesena; but as this was impossible, we found it necessary to begin to make use of the troops which we had left in detachments along the road. For it will not do to strip a place of its garrison, unless the enemy is so far off that he cannot return to attack it before a sufficient force is sent back in turn for its defence. It would be necessary to make the right provisions all the time, and to do everything very carefully, if we wish to avoid the occurrence of disorders in front or in the rear. As our provisions cannot always be right, it is impossible that such disorders do not occur. Thence the contradictory orders, according to which at one moment the troops were coming from Tuscany, and the next moment they were not coming. Thence came the untimely evacuation of Imola, and the apprehensions for that city and therefore for Bologna. It results from this that with such a system and such embarrassments it will be impossible for us to defend the Marca; to which it must be added that the cities there are much less strong than those of the Romagna [. . .]. If we have to carry on the war, and the league does not unite

---

[12] Roberto da San Severino.

its whole army, everything will go to ruin, unless, indeed, some of the necessities on which we have several times based our hopes should force the enemy to disband; but the obstinacy which the enemy manifests deprives us of all hope that this will happen. Matters have come to that point that we must either revamp war or conclude a peace, which, some having[13] chosen the worst allies, we should not decline, provided the conditions are endurable. For if we continue the war, and all our forces are not united, and if the commanders are not satisfied, and the King of France and the Venetians do not prove themselves better allies, and the Pope does not show himself more liberal with his money, then we shall be exposed to the most evident dangers of utter ruin.

---

[13] Unclear: probably the Pope (or the Duke of Ferrara).

Index of Names

Index

.